Sir Roy Strong is well known as an historian and garden writer, lecturer, critic, columnist and regular contributor to both radio and television. He was Director of the National Portrait Gallery from 1967 to 1973 and of the V & A from 1974 to 1987. In 1980 he was awarded the prestigious Shakespeare Prize by the FVS Foundation of Hamburg in recognition of his contribution to the arts in the UK. He has published a number of highly acclaimed books and his recent publications include *The Story of Britain, The Spirit of Britain, A Country Life, Feast: A History of Grand Eating* and his own diaries.

Sir Roy lives in Herefordshire. Sadly his wife, the film, television and theatre designer, Julia Trevelyan Oman, died in 2003.

ROY STRONG
THE LASKETT

THE STORY OF A GARDEN

BANTAM BOOKS

LONDON • TORONTO • SYDNEY • AUCKLAND • JOHANNESBURG

THE LASKETT
A BANTAM BOOK: 0 553 81519 9

Originally published in Great Britain by Bantam Press,
a division of Transworld Publishers

PRINTING HISTORY
Bantam Press edition published 2003
Bantam edition published 2005

1 3 5 7 9 10 8 6 4 2

Set in 11/13 pt Sabon MT by
Falcon Oast Graphic Art Ltd.

Bantam Books are published by Transworld Publishers,
61–63 Uxbridge Road, London W5 5SA,
a division of The Random House Group Ltd,
in Australia by Random House Australia (Pty) Ltd,
20 Alfred Street, Milsons Point, Sydney, NSW 2061, Australia,
in New Zealand by Random House New Zealand Ltd,
18 Poland Road, Glenfield, Auckland 10, New Zealand
and in South Africa by Random House (Pty) Ltd, Isle of Houghton,
Corner Boundary Road & Carse O'Gowrie, Houghton 2198, South Africa.

Printed and bound in Great Britain by
Cox & Wyman Ltd, Reading, Berkshire.

Papers used by Transworld Publishers are natural, recyclable products made
from wood grown in sustainable forests. The manufacturing processes
conform to the environmental regulations of the country of origin.

Now thank we all our God

CONTENTS

THE LASKETT

PREFACE

I AM NOT SURE HOW TO INTRODUCE THIS BOOK. IT IS ONE which had to be written, or rather which I felt within myself that I had to write, even if it was to remain unpublished. I have read a number of books by people who have made gardens, but somehow what you will read here doesn't quite fit into that category. Indeed, I can't think where it fits. I suppose if I had to place it within the orbit of my own writing I would site it somewhere between the *Diaries* and *A Country Life*. It is in a sense a horticultural autobiography, the life of a man who, suddenly at thirty-eight, was entranced by gardens. And not only for the horticultural delight they offered him but perhaps even more for the deeper resonance they could express about human relationships and aspirations and life. One person in a sense lives many lives. In my own case there has been the life of scholarship, amply charted in the steady stream of books over four decades; another is one's public life, recorded in the diaries of my years as director of two of our greatest art institutions. The latter catch something of the mask and the face, for the making of The Laskett garden always figures in them as an inner joy, one of the deepest and most creative expressions of the private man. *The Laskett* is, in a sense, a fuller exploration of that territory. Those familiar with the verses of the hymn of which the first line only is etched onto the dedication page will know precisely what this book is about.

ROY STRONG, THE LASKETT

Prologue

THE ELOPEMENT

ON 10 SEPTEMBER 1971 I ELOPED AND MARRIED JULIA Trevelyan Oman in the church of Wilmcote, Shakespeare's mother Mary Arden's village, just outside Stratford-upon-Avon. Why elope? I was thirty-five and Julia was forty. Both of us felt passionately that marriage was a deeply personal and private affair, a sacrament, not to be sullied by the hurly burly of a public wedding. Neither of us would have done it in any other way. Thirty years on, the romance of that elopement is as vivid to me as on the day.

This may seem a strange point of departure for a book about the creation of a garden, except, but for that event, there would have been none. Not that the making of a great garden together had even flickered across my mind at that juncture, although I was even then acutely conscious that the world of plants meant much to Julia. I knew that somehow our wedding breakfast table had to have at its centre at the very least some sprays of rosemary (she had already given me one) and, above all, honeysuckle. Why rosemary and why honeysuckle, you may ask. Both are old-fashioned English plants, one a herb, the other a flower; both had flourished in the gardens of Shakespeare's England. They also shared the beguiling attribute of scent. It was, indeed, working together on a little book on my heroine, Elizabeth I, which had been the prelude to my proposal. Honeysuckle stood for great Gloriana, for in her portraits her dresses could be embroidered with its spiralling leaves and flowers, and in one she actually holds a sprig of it in her hand. This was a marriage brought about by the Virgin Queen.

And what of the rosemary? A branch of rosemary was

always to have resonance for Julia and this is the reason. Her mother, Joan, one of the eight children of Sir Ernest Trevelyan, had lost her mother when she was just one. Although Sir Ernest was quickly to marry again, in a sense the children remained tragic souls, orphans, but for one person, a nanny whose nickname was Dooks. She gave her whole life and love to raising the Trevelyan children in a rambling late Victorian house in north Oxford. That giving is summed up in the fact that at some stage she had married, but neither Sir Ernest, nor their stepmother, nor they, ever knew, until one day by accident Dooks forgot to take off her wedding ring, and then it could no longer be concealed. They loved and cherished Dooks to the day she died, and it was from her that the great bushy, coarse *Rosmarinus officinalis* at Putney, Julia's parents' home, came. Understandably its status was iconic, caught supremely on the day of my mother-in-law's funeral, when Julia went into the garden, pulled off a huge billowing branch and laid it as the solitary floral tribute on her mother's coffin. Its descendants were to thrive and multiply in the garden that I did not guess then we were to create together.

It was one thing to know that the presence of these plants was to mean so much to Julia. It was quite another to get them. In this I had the good fortune to have as my best man David Hutt, a keen gardener, now a canon of Westminster Abbey but then a curate attached to the priest who married us, the eccentric and lovable Gerard Irvine. It was David who secured a branch of rosemary and who searched the hedgerows for a last lingering sprig of wild honeysuckle and saw that the required flowers were in the middle of the table at our wedding breakfast.

That I proposed to Julia at all had a plant context. On the day before I did, I happened to be talking at a party to Lindy Dufferin – the painter Lindy Guinness – saying how I adored Julia, and Lindy, in her role as matchmaker, said, 'Grab her, whatever happens, she is there as happiness and home, loving and caring for each other, watching the plants grow together.' The next day, 20 July, I popped the question, appropriately in St James's Park. Almost three decades later I found myself sitting next to Lindy at a lunch given in the grounds of Croome Park, the great landscape masterpiece by 'Capability' Brown. The gathering was in memory of someone else who will figure in this narrative, the late George Clive, whose memorial is a contribution to this garden's restoration by the National Trust. Sitting at a trestle table in a dilapidated farm shed, I reminded Lindy of her perceptive matchmaking all those years ago, which she had quite forgotten. Looking back, it was her description of marriage being about planting a flower together – nurturing it, watching it grow and then blossom – which stuck in my mind, and still does today.

Everything was in place for the wedding to happen on the morning after the first night of Julia's production of *Othello* for the Royal Shakespeare Company at Stratford. Julia's profession is that of a designer, by that date a distinguished one with credits such as Jonathan Miller's *Alice* and Tony Richardson's *The Charge of the Light Brigade* to her name. I was still the young and somewhat dashing director of the National Portrait Gallery. One small detail of our marriage service was also a presage of what was to come. It opened with an exchange of gifts, which Gerard wished to bless by sprinkling them with holy water. But, alas, the tiny dog-kennel of a church was bereft of stoop and sprinkler, so a branch of dark green yew was plucked from one of the ancient trees in the churchyard. Little did I know then that so much of the coming decades was to be taken up with the nurturing, training and clipping of that most magisterially English of all garden plants.

Although I was wholly unconscious of it, much was already in place indicating that a garden of some kind was to be part of the scheme of things. But a garden calls for space and when

I married all I could offer was the tiny paved courtyard garden of a small Gothick town house in Brighton. Moreover, marriage calls for making a home together. And so it was that in the spring of 1972 we began the search that was eventually to lead us to The Laskett.

One

THE INHERITANCE

WHY DID WE WISH TO LIVE IN THE COUNTRY, THE READER
might ask. After all, I had been born a Londoner and
my work was London-based. Julia had been born and had
lived in London also, and her work, too, was London-based.
I think I can best answer by quoting from a letter I wrote to
my Dutch friend Jan van Dorsten, shortly after we moved in
May 1973: 'London is such HELL these days – the gas is on
strike, the hospitals, the Civil Service, the railways. It's a bad
period for people in these islands, full of deep unrest.' We had
made up our minds already, after marrying, that we would
buy the house where we would ultimately end our days, but
the decision that that should be sited away from London was
sharpened by the climate of the times. I recall that we sat one
weekend in my pretty house in Brighton devoid of heating
and unable to cook as the electric companies were on strike.
Even the traffic lights didn't work. An urban environment we
saw as vulnerable. The seventies was one prolonged period of
dislocation and turbulence. At least, we thought, with a
house in the country we could grow our own food and
burn our own wood. In addition, we longed for privacy, for a
space away from the perpetual glitz and glitter of what in
retrospect one can see as the dying throes of the swinging
sixties extravaganza.

The early seventies was an unpropitious time for house-
hunting and we had little money, but we began by drawing up
some kind of specification of what we sought, a document
which now reads as appallingly naive and optimistic: 'Type:
small manor house, rectory or gentleman's house', ending
with the sentence: 'We are not interested in land basically but
want a maintainable garden.' Not much sign of *furor hortensis*

there as yet. This specification was then distributed hopefully to various estate agents.

Our initial foray was in the Oxfordshire area, for Julia had spent much of her war-time childhood in Oxford in Frewin Hall, a rambling old house with extensive grounds surprisingly tucked away in the middle of the city. It had been leased to her grandfather, Sir Charles Oman, Chichele Professor of Modern History and Fellow of All Souls, from Brasenose College. So Oxford it was to be, and though in the end that was not to happen, both Oxford and the Omans were to become etched into the garden story.

The idea of a house in that area of the country was to linger in the background throughout the search, and we saw many, but we were outpriced. Ludicrous price tags were attached to what were little more than decrepit cottages. Failure to purchase half of a splendid seventeenth-century house in Northamptonshire left a tearful Julia and me determined to take some kind of immediate action. It so chanced that I mentioned our woes to a friend who promptly said that there was a rectory listed for sale that day in the property section of *The Times* at Bishop's Frome in Herefordshire. It was to go to auction on 20 September and was billed in *Country Life* as follows: 'A substantial village residence offering considerable scope for improvement.' A photograph showed an extensive brick-built Victorian house with commodious windows overlooking an expanse of lawn.

So it was that we left London early the next morning for Herefordshire. It was not a county I knew, apart from a brief visit with a friend when I was an undergraduate, perched on the back of his motorcycle, visiting remote churches. It was, however, far more familiar to Julia. Her parents had had friends, the Gardners, who had inherited the estate attached to Yatton Court in the north of the county, a beautiful Georgian house bordered on one side by the waters of the River Lugg, with a yew walk whose mysterious beauty had cast its spell on her when, as a teenager, she had stayed there. But, as we were to learn, north and south Herefordshire are two different worlds, cut asunder by the hill topped by Queenswood north of Hereford itself. Those in the north look northwards to Shropshire and Cheshire, those in the south to Gloucester, Cheltenham and the Malverns. Our destiny was to be in the south, and Bishop's Frome lay close to Worcestershire.

I'll never forget that first drive west. There's an extraordinary moment after Gloucester when the land suddenly rises just past Highnam (seat of Thomas Gambier Parry, the great art collector, and later, I was to find, gardener) and winds and twists its way up and over, by way of Weston-under-Penyard, to the hilltop town of Ross-on-Wye. Suddenly I was aware that I was entering the landscape of the Picturesque, that part of the country celebrated at the close of the eighteenth century by the likes of William Sawrey Gilpin and Sir Uvedale Price. Its beauty resides in its asymmetry, its dramatic changes of level and rich afforestation, its ruined abbeys and castles, as well as the modest, huddled houses and farms scattered along its sinuous silvery waters, above all the River Wye. Each twist and turn of the road brought another vista, another view whose beauty was framed by the branches of ancient trees. Later I was to discover that Downton Castle, Richard Payne Knight's legendary garden, fount of the Picturesque, was in Herefordshire, and, not so far away from where we were to live, was the Repton landscape of Garnons, at that time being restored by the peppery Sir Richard Cotterell.

We made the drive on one of those golden autumn days effulgent with Keatsian mellow fruitfulness, which, in Herefordshire's case, was expressed in the cider apple orchards that stretched on either side of us as we travelled through the lowland areas. It made everything before that ascent and descent seem like the suburbs. Here, it seemed, was the golden land, remote, beckoning, a place in which to hide and be hidden. But, alas, much to our disappointment, we failed in our bid for Bishop's Frome, in retrospect a blessing for it carried only an acre of land and the cost of restoring the crumbling house would have financially crippled us. Retreating dispirited, we took up an invitation made through the Gardners to the firm of local estate agents, Russell, Baldwin & Bright, for we had reached the decision that it was to Herefordshire that we would come. David Wells, their cheerful representative, faced with the two downhearted newlyweds, said, 'Don't worry. I'll find you a house, if it's the last thing I do.' And he was to be true to his word, sooner than was ever anticipated.

Not long after, the telephone rang and it was David Wells. 'I think I have a house for you,' he said to Julia. 'It belongs to a lady recently widowed who wants to sell it privately. But you must come quickly.' Little did we know that David was in fact choosing his neighbours, for he and his wife still live opposite, a little along the lane.

It was already late October and the leaves had fallen when we first set eyes on what was to be the site of our future garden, the house called The Laskett. It lay midway between Ross-on-Wye and Hereford, two fields off the A49 along a lane called Laskett Lane. Looking three decades on at the photographs taken during that winter, I am struck above all by the emptiness, almost bleakness, of it all, the house and its surroundings seeming little more than a blank canvas awaiting the artist to wield his brush. But the house was pleasing, reminiscent of a small rectory out of a novel by Jane Austen, rectangular, built of pink sandstone with a steeply pitched tiled roof and tall chimney stacks, at the front three sash windows above, and below two later bay windows, flanking a wooden entrance porch. As Julia remarked it was building, not architecture, rural Regency of an undistinguished kind, but the proportions were good. There were later accretions, a small wing to one side and additions at the back. Behind there 'was a stable coach house across a narrow yard with a mount-ing block. And that, apart from the garage and some nondescript sheds, was it.

The garden was tidy but unexceptional. A wide, high thuja hedge lined the drive to one side, obscuring a clear view of the facade of the house, around which stretched lawn at the front and to one side. There was an herbaceous border before it that led on to a gravel path flanked by a rose bed. A mock wellhead was a solitary indication that perhaps once the garden had been more interesting, but now everything had been reduced to an expanse of easy-to-maintain greensward backed by a new shrubbery screening out a view of the farm, Penny Pitt, behind. On the drive side of the house there was a Judas tree planted on an island, around which cars could turn, backed by a larch screen with rambler roses. That led on to the vegetable garden, then a decayed greenhouse and, finally, the garage.

We hardly took in the adjacent two-acre field, still called by us the Field, which, we were told, was let out to a local farmer for his cattle. But, adding that to what we had taken in, the area overall was a fan-shaped tract of land in which the house and garden proper were tucked into the easternmost point. What we did fall in love with on first sight was the mighty cedar of Lebanon that stood proudly at the base of the front lawn. I see it now as I write, its branches bearing fronds of evergreen needles reaching out towards me. To have such a tree is a wonderful bonus for any garden, for it becomes a ref-erence point from every part of the domain. To that could be added a line of Spanish chestnuts up the drive, a magnificent beech to one side of the house and a Turkey oak and ancient yew on its other side, plus a scattering of elms. One more tree had significance, a tall pine at the top of the drive on the left. My father-in-law, Charles Oman, the distinguished authority on silver and former Keeper of Metalwork at the Victoria & Albert Museum, on first seeing it remarked, 'Ah, a Charlie tree,' meaning that The Laskett was a safe house for Jacobites, for tradition has it that such trees were planted as covert signals to the Young Pretender that here he would find welcome and shelter.

The house itself was south-facing, sited on a gentle gradient. Westwards the view was to the Black Mountains, gaunt barren hills seemingly either holding the Welsh in or keeping the English out, certainly firmly reminding us, as the place names did, that this was oft-fought-over border country. Soon we were to learn to dread the west wind pounding both house and garden. Looking south-west from the front of the house the view was of rolling farmland with fields full of the prize Herefordshire cattle of our neighbours, the Symonds of Llandinabo Court. In the distance was May Hill, topped by a circle of pine trees. For years when we drove down we would spot May Hill from afar signalling that home was on its other side.

I need hardly add that the decision to purchase was immediate. The house was to be ours on May Day 1973. Millie Bryant, the vendor, wrote to us on 24 October saying, 'I do so hope you will find happiness and peace here,' ending, 'That's Rosemary for remembrance,' enclosing a sprig from The Laskett garden. Today that sprig is mounted in our scrapbooks alongside the photographs of the house as we found it. From Millie we learnt a little of its history, in particular that Sir Edward Elgar had visited The Laskett, apparently pinching the maids. Be that as it may, Elgar's presence only served to make everything seem even righter, for one of Julia's greatest triumphs had been the ballet *Enigma Variations* danced to his haunting music, her concept but choreographed by Sir Frederick Ashton for the Royal Ballet in 1968. Everything was in place for the great day when we would move in, which was fixed for 3 May 1973.

WHAT DOES THE WORD 'LASKETT' MEAN? APPARENTLY IT IS Herefordshire dialect for a strip of land 'without' the parish, as the historic term goes. That accords with the dictionary definition: 'lasket (or latchet), one of the loops or rings of cord by which a bonnet is attached to the foot of a sail; alternately, latchet, a loop; *a narrow strip of anything*, a thong.' The Laskett is literally a strip of land outside the main confines of the parish of Llanwarne. Another explanation is that it derives from 'glas-coed' or greensward, but even that is uncertain. Early Ordnance Survey maps record a Laskett Wood or Grove further along the lane on the south side.

The three acres in which the house stands were once part of the Blewhenstone estate and were sold by Sir Edwyn Francis Scudamore to one Joseph Ashbarry on 12 November 1839, when they were in the tenure or occupancy of Charles Meadmore. No mention is made of a house, but barely six weeks later Ashbarry sold them on to William Matthews. In this document the house for the first time appears: 'all that messuage or dwellinghouse and all other Erections and Buildings lately erected and built and standing. . .' The vital word is 'lately', indicating that the house must be late 1830s, that is, early Victorian in date. The earliest Ordnance Survey maps from the 1830s show no sign of the house, which first appears on the 1840 Tithe Award Map. Mention should also be made at this point of the very narrow strip of land along Laskett Lane also recorded on that map, on which stood what was then called Cross Collar Cottage. That, by the time we arrived, had become Laskett Cottage, and was eventually to be incorporated into our garden as The Folly. The map also provides field names; in the case of our field, it was called 'The Two Acres'.

The Matthews family were timber merchants who owned what was to become Whitewells House opposite, close to Cross Collar. The land in that area must then have been wooded, for what fortune they made came from supplying timber for ships during the Napoleonic Wars. The Laskett passed from William Matthews (1804–1863) to his third son,

Thomas (1848–1929), a chemist and JP of Ross-on-Wye. None of the Matthews family seems ever to have lived here. The house began quite humbly as Laskett Cottage but, by 1900, was known as The Laskett and was let out to a succession of tenants. The earliest was a cleric, the Rev. Rowland Hill, who was in residence in 1840. From 1900 onwards the occupancy is clear and a contract of 1905 letting it to Henry Hogarth Bracewell contains the earliest references to a greenhouse, a conservatory, a stable coach house, the three acres of meadow or pasture and 'the lawn garden'.

In 1922 Thomas Matthews sold it to George William Wilkes, described as 'gentleman', and in that deed we learn further about the grounds in the phrase 'with the Gardens Pleasure Grounds and Lands and appurtenances . . . Together with the Greenhouse Stable Coachhouse and other buildings and meadow or pastureland'. Poor greenhouse! It was still standing when we arrived, albeit decrepit. We asked the builders for an estimate to repair it but by the time that was produced it had blown down. From Wilkes The Laskett passed, in 1934, to a hunting widow, Edith Wreford Brown. She modestly extended the domain by purchasing a rectangle of land, now our kitchen garden, from the Paines of Penny Pitt, for kennels for the hounds.

Mrs Wreford Brown appeared to live here in a degree of style and I only wish we knew more about her. Laskett Lodge, as it is now called but then was Withy Brae, erected directly opposite what became The Folly, was built by her for her chauffeur and general handyman, Jack Bevan, who lived there with his wife long after we arrived. They were rubicund, kindly people (it was whispered that she had once been in royal service), who kept an eye on The Laskett and fed our cats during all those years when we had to be in London. To extract any information about the house in its Wreford Brown days was agony. Jack would begin only to be halted in his tracks by his wife who would say, 'Now, Jack . . .' He did, however, produce photographs showing that once the windows had been shuttered, and he did also, more tantalizingly, describe the garden on the far side of the house, where the well was sited, as being 'like the pages in a book'. What this exactly meant I have never discovered, but something substantial must once have been there, judging by the barrowloads of rock carried away from that site whenever one dug deeper than a foot. It was Jack Bevan who 'designed' the extension to one side of the house to accommodate the cook-housekeeper, and at the same period it was extended at the rear to incorporate a bathroom, scullery, back stairs and stable maid's bedroom. To Mrs Wreford Brown we owe the garage with its observation pit, the thuja hedge up the drive and a rectangular pond which, we were told, was constructed on the outbreak of war in 1939 to house water to be used in case the house was bombed!

Mrs Wreford Brown died in 1946 and the house passed to Colonel and Mrs Jenny. Its great days were over and one senses a steady downhill descent in the new servantless age. From the Jennys it fell into the hands of developers and from them it passed to Colonel and Mrs Bryant and thence to us. From the moment the transaction was made I was enchanted by the place, although Julia pointed out its lack of a large room and how, ever since marrying me, she had come to live in smaller and smaller houses. In my case the reverse was true. But in the years to come all of that was to be remedied. So the scene is set, but what were our gardening credentials?

Mine could never be described as other than thin. Anything to do with the garden and gardening during my childhood was overshadowed by the figure of my father. The garden, to use my mother's words, was 'your father's', a domain untouchable by any other member of the family. George Edward Clement Strong, to give him his full name, was one of life's failures. He should never have married, much less have had children, for he treated my mother like a servant and took no interest whatever in the three boys whom he had sired. But he was, I have to admit, a gardener, in retrospect a saving grace. I have often puzzled as to where this feeling for the earth came from and I would hazard that this redeeming gift came from his mother. Rachel Peake was a strong-willed countrywoman born at South Elmham, near Bungay in Suffolk, in 1864, and one of those countless thousands who drifted to the metropolis in the late Victorian period. She was always to maintain her links with her country origins. It is easy to forget how much that vigorous tradition of modest urban gardening, which was to last until just after the Second World War, owed to that generation. The cottage garden, with its emphasis on self-sufficiency, had not yet become a distant memory. To them it was still a living reality to be transported into the city. So, whenever she visited my parents' house, she always demanded to see the garden. There she would stand and pronounce on the fruiting potential of this or that tree for the year.

Colne Road in Winchmore Hill in North London was part of one of those developments that mushroomed between the wars, adding yet another belt to the ever-widening conurbation of London. It was newly built on what had been orchard land in 1928, the year my parents married, a terrace house with bay windows, a wooden gate opening onto a crazy-paving path flanked by lawn leading to the front door. The front garden itself was held in by the kind of privet hedge that was so fashionable at that period, part of which was trained to form steps and domes and swags. In my teens I was allowed to cut it and it gave me huge pleasure to re-establish its architectural shape. It was my earliest essay in what was to become a passion, topiary.

At the rear the garden was the usual long rectangle of London clay with fencing either side topped by trellis, and a wooden garage at the far end. Faded photographs tell me that garden was not devoid of delights. The large rectangle of lawn, necessary with young children, was framed by flower borders rich in herbaceous plants, above all Russell Lupins and feathery cosmos. The straight crazy-paving garden path, which led to the back gate, was straddled by four larchwood arches luxuriantly festooned with climbing roses, and before the garage stood another larchwood screen for climbers. Close to the house there was a Victoria plum tree, along one of the fences two espaliered William's pear trees, and, next to the back gate, a rowan that sported bright orange berries each autumn. Everything was kept in immaculate order.

I don't remember that pre-war garden, for I was just four when war broke out in 1939. My earliest memories are of what replaced it. 'Dig for victory' meant that both front and back gardens were given over to the cultivation of produce. Beneath the bay windows at the front stood rows of neatly staked tomatoes, their fruit-bearing branches trained and tied for support. To hasten their ripening they would sometimes be picked green or on the turn, brought into the house and left to ripen on a warm windowsill. In the back garden the lawn, the rose arches and screen all vanished, giving way to rows of vegetables. I recall potatoes, runner beans, marrows, turnips, spring onions, radishes, cucumbers and lettuce. At the bottom of the garden a chicken run was built, which provided us with eggs through the year and, at Christmas, a roast bird to mark the festival. When the Victoria plum fruited, my mother went into overdrive making jam, and the inevitable glut of green tomatoes was made into chutney. The William's pears would be harvested hard by my father and carefully wrapped, each one in newspaper, and stored in a dark dry place until such time as they ripened. Strangely enough he never planted an apple tree, at times, it seemed, almost deliberately just to annoy my mother. But during these war-time years a heavy crop of produce in any neighbour's garden brought generous gifts. Looking back, I am grateful to have experienced this degree of self-sufficiency. I was to rediscover it again at The Laskett.

Was I never given a packet of Rainbow Mix, the fate of every child? Of course I was. The packet carried a storybook image of a thatched cottage arising from an explosion of sweet-scented stocks, hollyhocks, cornflowers and larkspur. I scattered it on a small patch of earth with impatience. Nothing as far as I can remember germinated. Once I was given a tiny area to cultivate and into it I moved plants such as marigolds in full flower only to find them dead the next day. After the war the garden never regained its pre-1939 glory. A lawn and borders of sorts came back and my father constructed a small pond for goldfish backed by a rockery by which he would sit on warm summer evenings. In summer the front garden was planted up with antirrhinums grown from seed, the borders edged with the blue and white of alyssum and lobelia typical of the Victorian age. Each summer two hanging baskets were suspended from the projecting front porch, filled with pelargoniums. Their watering every evening was a daily ritual of recrimination as my mother complained of the debris that fell onto the doorstep. Sadly the overall memory left by that thirties suburban garden was that it was part of the division that rent the house in two throughout my childhood. It was never at any time a shared joy.

The reality of gardening was not to impinge on my consciousness again until, in 1969, I purchased a Regency Gothick terrace in Brighton, my first house. This brought with it an apology for a garden, a small walled enclosure that I decided to pave but attempted to enliven with a *bocca* of a dolphin's head spouting water in the midst of the far wall. Near to the house there was a rudimentary trellis screen of three Gothick arches and a scattering of small beds accommodating climbers to smother both it and the surrounding walls. But it always remained essentially a garden of containers and this is what Julia married into, a world of pots, one of which already contained a descendant of Dooks's precious rosemary. Under her aegis the pots multiplied. Soon there was a wide range of culinary herbs, sage, rue, thyme and marjoram, as well as geraniums grown from cuttings that were set against the silvery-grey foliage of *Senecio cineraria* (syn. *Cineria maritima*), as a foil to their pink and scarlet flowerheads. Over thirty years on, much of this garden is still with us, for the containers left with the furniture on the final removal day. Brighton also marked my first encounter with box, for among those pots were two containing handsome glossy-green cones under a metre in height. These I planted here where we can still see them each day from our breakfast-room window, significant sentinels, now more than two metres high, silhouetted against a beech hedge flanking the entrance to the Small Orchard.

If my horticultural credentials were minimal, Julia's were far more robust. The Oman house at Putney was one of those substantial residences built for the professional classes not long after 1900 and set into a quarter of an acre of land. At the back a broad raised terrace afforded a panorama of lawn with a lion from Barry's Houses of Parliament (whose particular history I will later retail) as its focal point, flanked by a quince tree to the left and a plum to the right. This tableau was surrounded by borders filled with a spring and summer display of flowers with a shrubbery backing. There were other fruit trees – a Cox's and 'Devonshire Quarrenden' apple and an 'Oullins Gage' – and a greenhouse and vegetable garden. My mother-in-law Joan Oman was trained as a teacher at the Froebel Institute. There much stress was laid on the value of building on a child's natural curiosity about the world around him. So it was that my wife and her brother were brought up to understand the nature of plants. Each had a little garden of their own and the vegetables they cultivated as children would be carefully harvested and cooked to be eaten. Self-sufficiency and a sense that the garden was a part of domestic economy was a given. My father-in-law tended the vegetables, keeping the kitchen supplied with spinach in particular. A 'Brown Turkey' fig, given to him by the composer Gerald Finzi, with whom he shared war work, was trained across the back of the house and, as the fruit ripened, it would be picked and displayed temptingly on a dish on the dining-room table.

Julia's love affair with the garden, therefore, began young. Not long ago, riffling through papers kept by her mother, she came across the 'magazine' she had compiled at seven and a half. Page three has the heading 'my garden' and a short essay of sorts follows: 'I do love my garden it really is fun I have got soum seedes and I have got soum sun flowrs in it to and I have got soum red roses to.'

The orthography belongs to the world of Daisy Ashford, but the sentiments are clear. On the bottom half of the page there is what I take to be a stalk with a solitary bloom at its summit and, at its side, Julia's earliest self-portrait.

Memory is a sacred attribute in any garden and our first herbaceous plants came from Putney, bright scarlet poppies and brilliant orange daylilies among them. Although the colours may jangle I would not be without them for all the world. Each year when they spring again to life and flower I think of that Putney garden, now long gone, and of the graciousness of my in-laws to the man who ran off with their daughter. Four plants in particular speak of a special continuity, for cuttings or suckers from them now flourish in The Laskett garden. One is the 'Albertine' rose with its nearly double coppery-pink blooms. That was trained over arches across pathways, and a cutting from it now clambers up the facade of The Laskett, encircling my writing-room window. In summer some of its blooms impinge on the window glass itself, much to my delight. This is a real between-the-wars rose, 1921 to be exact. The other three plants all go back to Oxford and Frewin Hall. The white jasmine now engulfs a tiny summerhouse close to the house. The tender agapanthus winter in the conservatory and make their annual debut only when we are free of the threat of frosts. These succulent plants with their spiky leaves and blue flowers are now entering their third century, for they were certainly at Frewin in the late Victorian period. Their blue is of the intensity one associates only with hyacinths. Finally, and most important of all, there is the quince.

Let my wife tell that story in her own words, for in 2001 in *Country Life* she wrote its history:

My paternal grandfather, the historian Sir Charles Oman, lived in Frewin Hall, Oxford, a Brasenose College property, for some forty years from the turn of the century. Only two fruit trees grew and flourished in that unloved city garden: a mulberry, planted when my father, as a child, kept silkworms; and a quince, formidably occupying the end of the lawn, facing the house. The tree's origins I know not, but I surmise it could have been a century old, as the girth of leaf-spread was so considerable.

I still find it fascinating to attempt to conjure the origins of this extraordinary tree, whose progeny grows in our garden today. Before my grandfather died at the end of the Second World War, my father, who had an affection for it, dug up from under its skirts a sucker which he planted in our Putney garden sited, as at Frewin Hall, facing the house. Later, during the bleak days of food rationing in the late 1940s, autumnal guests would leave with the gift of a quince to add to their stewed apple.

I could not live in a garden where no quince tree grew. My father knew this and on the announcement of our discovery of a house with a garden in Herefordshire, he immediately earmarked two suitable quince suckers, which arrived at The Laskett with the furniture, much to the astonishment of the removal men. The trees are now 28 years old and this season were weighed down with fruit.

As our Frewin quinces, the name by which we still know them, started to grow and flourish, I became aware that they were not the same shape, nor did the trees grow in the same manner, as those I purchased as named varieties to place through the garden. With care I packaged three fruits and a sprig of leaves, together with a payment, to the fruit identification department of the Royal Horticultural Society at Wisley. A letter came back which left me no more certain as to our quince's variety. 'Possibly Lescovatz, a Serbian quince from Lescovata.' So to this day the tree remains firmly designated 'the Frewin quince', and we speculate as to its origins.

So it was that at last, at the end of the first week of May 1973, we came to rest at The Laskett.

THAT SUMMER WAS A KIND OF IDYLL, IN SPITE OF THE FACT THAT the removal van carrying our furniture had crashed, reducing much of it to splinters. The sun seemed only to shine. Anyone moving into a new house in spring will share that feeling of elation, for a new life begins simultaneously with the reawakening of the world of nature. The house martins arrived the day we did and the front of the house was hung thickly with the pale violet panicles of an old wisteria. Soon the roses burst into bloom and the vegetable garden produced its cornucopia, first purple sprouting broccoli and then raspberries followed by strawberries in abundance. Everything that happened during those first summer months took on the quality of a dream, upon which the practicalities of owning and running a house and garden began only slowly to impinge. Apart from holidays that Arcadian idyll was a weekend one, for most of our time was spent in London in our rented Westminster flat.

'We have settled into Hereford very happily,' I wrote to my Dutch friend Jan early in July. 'One sits in the sun and watches the landscape unfolding in every direction for miles untouched, or contemplates the great 1812 cedar on the front lawn [so we were told, but it must have been planted twenty years later], or one gardens.' And then follows the significant sentence: 'I have really become a passionate gardener.' Somehow within those opening weeks some kind of Pauline conversion had taken place, for I have to admit that I did say to Julia, when we bought the house, 'Don't talk to me about that garden.' With her accustomed taciturn wisdom she said nothing and wasn't in the least fazed when, within a couple of weeks, I donned wellington boots and was to be seen marching into the vegetable garden spade in hand.

That was necessary, for Millie Bryant's ancient jobbing gardener, Mr Gommery, had decided against continuing to garden. Suddenly we were faced with an ocean of lawn that demanded cutting. We found the solution to that in contract gardeners and it was they who saw us through this first summer when there were no dramatic changes to the existing garden. Julia created a small but necessary bed of culinary herbs close to the garage and also a flowerbed near to the house. I laboured to keep the existing vegetable garden in order and tended the rose beds. The truth of the matter was that our minds were firmly elsewhere, not only on the building works which had to be done to the house, but, in Julia's case, on the designs for her production of *La Bohème* at the Royal Opera House, and in mine, on the fact that I had set my sights on the directorship of the Victoria & Albert Museum which, by chance, had fallen vacant. My appointment as its new director was announced in September and I was to take up the post on 1 January 1974. Also in the autumn my mother-in-law tragically died too young of cancer. To her we owe our earliest present of gardening tools, and I recall when she presented me with a spade that she had covered the handle with a bag on which she had doodled my moustachioed face.

This was a year of change on every side, both public and

private. The effect of the oil crisis was just beginning to bite, precipitating inflation and what was to become an increasingly turbulent decade. In the light of the appalling problems I had to cope with in my new post the creation of a garden seemed positively peripheral, although in fact it was to become a kind of salvation, seeing me through some of the darkest and most difficult years of my entire career.

I wish that I could write that both of us had a blinding vision in 1973 of the garden as it is now, but we didn't. That vision took time to formulate, although I can write with truth that it was fully there by 1975, the consequence of a sharp learning curve, in its turn prompted by the decision of the farmer who rented the Field that he didn't want it any more. Suddenly we were confronted with a two-acre expanse of pastureland that had to be husbanded in some way. By then we were acutely aware of the exposure of the house and the need for windbreaks. Our initial response was to turn for advice to the firm that supplied our contract gardeners, Severn & Wyevale Landscapes. On 11 November I wrote to Jan of our gardening activities, in a manner that will at least set the scene:

> In the country we are gardening furiously. I pruned a hundred [untrue!] rose-bushes last week and we have cut into our field two grand walks, one called Elizabeth Tudor and the other Mary Stuart, both to be poplar avenues backed by leylandii and yew. We love all our fancy names after our books ... We planted hundreds of bulbs in the wilderness [beneath the cedar at the front of the house] last weekend so we shall see them carpeting the grass in the springtime. Eight elm trees had to be felled which had the dreaded Dutch elm disease. This leaves gaps which will never quite be filled in our lifetime. . .

That letter now makes strange reading for within a couple of years we were to realize the folly of those poplars, all of which had to be moved and planted elsewhere as windbreaks on the Field's boundaries. At this stage I had no idea that a black poplar, *Populus nigra*, threw up suckers so strong they could pierce a tarmac drive. The suckers shot up everywhere and to add to the problem we were mistakenly told that the poplars' lifespan was short and that we would have to fell them in our own lifetime. But the poplars do shed light on the way we were thinking in garden terms. One was a concern with avenues. Those great walks are still two of the grandest features of the garden, one, which ultimately became of pleached limes, running east–west, and the other running north–south, ascending the slope of the garden, ultimately up to the Victoria & Albert Museum Temple. Even with all the changes and additions of the next three decades, they were already there in 1973. The second fact that emerges was a decision to name parts of the garden in commemoration of events in our lives, in this instance marking two tiny books we did together in 1971 and 1972, *Elizabeth R* and *Mary Queen of Scots*.

We owed those fatal poplar avenues to the advice given by a representative of the firm that provided our gardeners. Their invoice fills out the picture. Eighty-two *Populus nigra* were planted at twelve-foot, and thirty-six *Cupressocyparis leylandii* at six-foot intervals. The latter was to create a hedge high enough to eliminate the view to Laskett Cottage. The invoice also includes forty-five *Taxus baccata*, 'arranged in rows in the field adjacent to the house as discussed'. These in fact were used to form a yew circus punctuating the north–south avenue, my first real essay in garden design, creating what would, when fully grown, be the circular room now known as the Hilliard Garden, after a little book I wrote on the Elizabethan miniaturist Nicholas Hilliard. At the same time the contractors took out the rose-bed walk near the house and planted instead thirty yards of beech hedging. The bill overall, including the labour, was £491. 31.

That there was some kind of overall scheme at the back of my mind emerges from the first interview I ever gave on the garden, which appeared in the February 1974 issue of *Harpers & Queen*. It was by the formidable and knowledgeable wife of Osbert Lancaster, Anne Scott-James, and must go down as one of my more asinine public appearances. But it does reveal certain impulses that were to condition the concept of the garden. One was a search for privacy, and the second a strong desire to enclose:

'Thinking ahead again – what will be the view from the house ten years from now? I don't know. Perhaps there'll be a bungalow development in pea-green plastic just beyond my land and, if so, I don't want to know about it. So all the garden is being enclosed . . . private . . . secret.'

That impulse we've certainly lived up to, but on others nothing could be further from where we are now, a real instance of out of the mouths of gardening babes. 'Nothing is sadder,' I went on to say, 'than to see something in retreat and I don't want to take on more than we can keep up. We have about three-and-a-half acres of land of which one acre will be cultivated and the rest left rough and wild.' In fact we have colonized every inch of our territory with garden. But some things still ring true even now. Anne Scott-James wrote, for example: 'They want the garden to remind them of their friends and every cutting and seedling from a friend is treasured carefully. "Looking at things which remind one of people gives a sense of continuity. I want a garden of sentiment."' And the article ends with one delicious blow beneath the belt: 'He has his desk by the window so that he can look at the garden as he writes, "I love watching the squirrels running up and down the cedar tree." In this, it must be admitted, Dr Strong betrays his inexperience, for squirrels are almost as destructive as rabbits. A more seasoned gardener would want to shoot them.' Clearly I had much to learn. I was in fact already immersed in that extraordinary process so wisely designated by the great garden designer Russell Page as 'the Education of a Gardener'. And it is a consideration of that to which I must now turn the reader's attention.

Two

INSPIRATIONS AND INFLUENCES

THE FIRST PERSON EVER TO WALK ME AROUND A GARDEN OF their own creation was Sir Cecil Beaton, the photographer, designer and diarist. He entered my life in the summer of 1967, shortly after I became Director of the National Portrait Gallery, when he agreed to a retrospective exhibition of his portrait photographs at the gallery, which was to be landmark. Through him I was introduced to another world, that of houses in the country with marvellous gardens. Reddish House, a delectable small late-seventeenth-century red-brick house, stood in John Aubrey's village of Broadchalke, not far from Salisbury. Cecil had purchased it in 1947 and the garden was a showpiece. John Morris Smallpiece, his gardener, said of him: 'He had a good instinct for gardens.' I would concur with that observation, battling as he did with terrain which had, in some places, only a few inches of topsoil. Whenever Cecil wished, for instance, to plant roses, the ground had to be excavated and soil brought in as a base. Twice a year the garden was open to the public and every effort was made to see that on those occasions it was immaculate, boasting what the Suttons' representative from Reading said was 'the best lawn in the West Country'.

In the last weekend of May 1968 I was asked for the first of several weekends that I spent with him before I married. The centrality of the garden to Cecil's life was something quite new to me and I recorded it:

> Cecil always opened up as he strode around the garden. There
> were the palest pink roses swagged on to garlands, long ropes
> worthy of a Gaiety Girl, climbers all over the house, a terrace
> which led on to a broad swathe of lawn and further gardens,

the whole held in by rising land on which grew a concealing curtain of mature trees. There was an orchard, a wild garden with spring flowers, a broad walk to a seat flanked with wide herbaceous borders, a kitchen garden and a new little abstract lavender garden round an old sundial.

That dial now stands as the focal point of the garden we made in commemoration of the Queen's Silver Jubilee, a monument to the precious friendship I had with him. It will reappear later in this narrative. Not far from it still grows the unusual, if invasive, white willowherb Cecil obtained from a gardener in Regent's Park. 'Flowers,' I wrote in that diary entry, 'were the key to this house. No room was without them, nor dining table devoid of a bouquet.'

Anyone who has made a garden from scratch will share with me the impact that such an experience can have. It opened my mind to the possibility of something I had never even thought about, not that at that stage it was a possibility, but the seed was firmly sown that gardens, quite large ones, could be made. But I was also acutely aware that they called for labour, for Cecil had his splendid gardener, Smallpiece, plus one or two assistants. Cecil would have been wholly unconscious of the effect of that walk on me, although I know that thirty years on it would have given him pleasure to know that someone cherished his memory not so much for his photography or his designs but for his talent as a gardener.

It was his habit in the country to don a coat and a fedora hat, pick up a trug, complete with secateurs, and set off on a garden tour. Roses were his great passion and in that drawling dandified voice of his he would give a running commentary on their names and how they had flowered that year. Some, as I've already said, were trained on ropes, others clambered up fruit trees in the orchard, some he trained horizontally over wooden frames. The house was smothered in roses and, because he loved them as cut flowers in the house, there was a whole bed of 'Iceberg' with its green tinged with pink-white blossoms. Cecil certainly accounted for the early old-rose phase in the history of The Laskett garden, for his preference was always for these with their soft mutant colours, salmon-pink to white 'Penelope', apricot-pink 'Gloire de Dijon', carmine-pink 'Zéphirine Drouhin', blush-pink 'Fantin-Latour' or the vivid carmine-pink 'Königin von Dänemark'. Scent also meant much to him, so there was rose-mary, lavender and lilac in abundance. Indeed I returned from that weekend laden with sprays of lilac. Spring flowers, nar-cissi naturalized in huge drifts, were another major feature of Reddish, and he had strong views as to how these should be placed in huge bunches into glass vases so that their stalks could clearly be seen.

An inspiration, yes, but Reddish was never to be the kind of garden I wanted. To me it lacked mystery and surprise. Virtually everything was seen at a glance. Nor was it archi-tectural, although there were ancient yews clipped into amorphous shapes and paths bordered by neat box hedges. But they were not the essence of the garden. If I had to char-acterize it I would say that it was a miniature landscape garden, one vast beguiling tableau of Englishness which spread its skirts outwards to one side of the house, enticing the visitor on through what was essentially an asymmetrical, painterly vision. The garden was held in by the land that formed the bowl in which it sat, onto whose natural undula-tions were embroidered plantings in the Jekyllesque manner with a careful consideration of colour combinations and a love of old cottage flowers, like hollyhocks and *Lilium candidum*. Later, after marriage and after Cecil's ghastly stroke, it was sad to see that garden cut back as the labour to main-tain it could no longer be afforded. On one visit we saw the wide herbaceous borders being turfed over and came away with a box of herbaceous plants. Our last visit to him was in October 1979. He died two and a half months later. For me it was the end of an era. To him I owe my first horticultural stirrings.

Although I was aware of the kitchen garden at Reddish it somehow never figured much in Cecil's garden vision. He belonged to that vanished world in which people were seemingly unable even to make a cup of instant coffee. John and Myfanwy Piper offered the sharpest of contrasts for they were practical, hands-on people used to catering for themselves. I had worshipped John Piper's paintings since childhood. They offered the pastoral vision of England, bred of the Second World War, which I have always cherished, whose essence was the manor house, the parish church, the village and the embracing landscape. It was patriotic, picturesque, deeply romantic and fiercely insular. I still have in a folder one of my youthful essays in the Piperesque style, using watercolour and crayon in an attempt to depict the tomb of Sir Henry Norris in Westminster Abbey. That was when my career was firmly pointed in the direction of the practising arts, a path which family impoverishment was to deny me. Myfanwy, his wife, was new to me but I quickly learnt that I was in the presence of a Betjeman heroine and one of Benjamin Britten's most distinguished librettists.

My earliest memory of them was of walking up to the flint and brick farmhouse at Fawley Bottom one golden evening and seeing John sitting like an Old Testament prophet on a bench with Myfanwy at his side, shelling peas from the garden into the capacious kitchen bowl on the table before him. Thirty years on I'm still mesmerized by that simple image. Few people's living style have I wished to emulate more, for its innate modesty and lack of pretension, its belief in honest work and for the focus of any artist's house to be the facilitation of creativity.

Julia had known them both from childhood, for her mother and her sisters had purchased a nearby farm for Dooks, their beloved nanny. Sometimes, when Julia was there, young Mr

Piper would drive by and give her a lift into nearby Henley. Fawley Bottom they had moved into the year that I was born and I first glimpsed it not long after marriage. It was a magic place and I remember coming away thinking that that was how I wished us to live at The Laskett. But what kind of influence did their garden exert on me? This was after all far from formal; on the contrary, it was rambling and relaxed, crammed with herbs and cottage garden flowers and unashamed about the weeds springing up. Its real heart was the kitchen garden, with its rectangular beds filled with neat lines of cabbages, potatoes, onions, leeks and runner beans bordered by an explosive tapestry of species roses and flowering shrubs set against the verdant landscape beyond. One was overwhelmed by its sheer profusion. But everything was held together in the way only an artist can by the exertion through his hands of his aesthetic eye, much like Monet at Giverny. This was an artist's garden.

That evening I remember John's pride in the line of giant sunflowers he had sown and brought to their full glory. They were almost incandescent in the evening sunlight. But the prime lesson here was of the interconnection of garden and kitchen, for the peas were not the only home-grown ingredient that was consumed at dinner that evening. Myfanwy was an inspired cook and it was John's kitchen garden that stays in my memory. It was to be one of the major inspirations behind what I regard as my wife's kitchen garden, and perhaps the effect was more potent on her aspirations for our garden, for I have always been the cook.

THOSE VISITS TO THE PIPERS OCCURRED AT PRECISELY THE PERIOD when we had to reach decisions about what kind of garden The Laskett would be. That was in fact determined by a group of gardens I came to know in the first few years after marriage. The first was King John's Hunting Lodge at Odiham, near Basingstoke, the creation of the great decorator John

Fowler. Later, when I came to know David Hicks, the stylish interior decorator and passionate gardener, he too saluted this garden as his prime inspiration. Julia had known John from her filming days, when the Lodge had been used as a location for Tony Richardson's film *The Charge of the Light Brigade*. Julia had the task of redecorating its interior back to the 1850s. John was someone new in my life, a benign and tetchy figure, but someone who had created the style which in the eighties was to be disseminated around the globe as the English country-house style. John's decoration of his own tiny house was a distillation of the essence of his taste, fresh, restrained, with an abundant use of glazed chintz and dragged paint together with a superb deployment of drapery. There was nothing flashy about the Fowler look. Nor was there about the man, who was a mine of information on interior decoration and a monument to understatement of a kind his many imitators never quite achieved. He pioneered the whole topic of the restoration of historic interiors in such a way that in his last years he was brought in to advise the National Trust.

We stayed there in December in 1971, just three months after our wedding. The time of year is important, for my first experience of the Hunting Lodge was in winter. Once more I was moved to put pen to paper:

> But the garden is the thing. An avenue of pleached hornbeam leads to the brick facade. There are little lead statues of shepherds flanking it, pretty flower-beds with wire obelisks, and in the middle of the garden there are two Gothic gazebos of trellis which face each other. And there's John's latest addition, a large garden-room, both beautiful and comfortable, with windows looking onto a lake and a box-hedge garden.

John had planted that aerial hedge of hornbeam in 1947, just two years after the Second World War, at precisely the period when formality, training and topiary were about to go out of fashion because they were seen to be so labour-intensive. Those stilt hedges were not the only clipped elements. There were elegant glossy green cones of box in tubs that acted as movable vertical accents, two large domes of Portugal laurel terminated the hornbeam vista, and the Hunting Lodge was my first serious introduction to box-edging. The rose beds were memorable, edged with low box hedges, the roses underplanted with lime-green lady's mantle (*Alchemilla mollis*), a delectable combination I copied in the Rose Garden here.

King John's Hunting Lodge, which John left to the National Trust, remains the most perfect small formal garden I have ever seen. It was also created by a man who never had much money, but certainly had great style. The Hunting Lodge garden demonstrated what could be achieved, provided one had the patience, with very little. For the first time I knew that if I ever had a garden it would be of this kind, strongly architectural, a paradise of different greens trained and clipped to form walls, entrances and a multiplicity of other shapes superimposing onto an empty space delight, definition and surprise. John lives on at The Laskett also in another way. Although he gave us lessons in how to induce mistletoe to grow in a fruit tree, the results have always been a failure. What he did successfully teach us was how invaluable house leeks were to attain a low-maintenance effect in containers. In the long years before we actually lived full-time at The Laskett, urns had soil mounded up in them and were planted with sempervivums. These multiplied and provided a handsome, carefree and stylish trophy. In our scrapbooks we have a picture of John prising some off a gate pier to give to us. Their descendants still flourish here.

It is difficult not to think that much of the inspiration for the Hunting Lodge garden must have come from Lawrence Johnston's Hidcote Manor, whose most famous feature is a parallel hornbeam stilt hedge. Hidcote we first visited on 16 February 1974, by which time the dread poplar avenues had already been planted. My mind was awash with *furor hortensis* and we owe that visit to the indomitable Lady Pamela Berry, by that date Lady Hartwell. She had entered my life earlier and was the person instrumental to opening up a covert dialogue as to what my chances would be of becoming the next Director of the Victoria & Albert Museum. I am sure that she always believed that I owed my appointment partly to her intriguing skills. Be that as it may she was a remarkable force in the social life of London at that date, the last of the great political hostesses. Her election fêtes, luncheon parties and late-evening soirées drew into one room the world of politics, smart society and, in her latest phase, the arts. Not that I think Pam ever knew anything much about the arts, but, rather, here was a new and fashionable field for her to conquer. Her knowledge of any subject was in truth incidental to the quality of the woman. What was so striking about Pam was her astounding energy, appetite for all kinds of information and gossip and also genuine generosity. The cut and thrust of high political and social life were meat and drink to her. However, whatever Pam was interested in, it certainly wasn't gardening.

There's a twist to this relationship, for the gardener was her husband, the taciturn, hesitant but hugely intelligent and kindly Michael Hartwell, proprietor of the *Telegraph*. Any weekend at Oving House, their country home not far from Aylesbury, was punctuated by the arrival of Michael, exhausted, after dinner, having put the paper to bed. Guests generally left on Sunday evening and Michael's day off was Monday, and that he spent in his arboretum. His daughter Harriet used to recount how once he never appeared for dinner so they mounted a search for him, discovering his recumbent form beneath a tree under which he'd fallen asleep while pruning. Much to Pamela's amazement we loved being walked around the arboretum, for Michael was hugely knowledgeable about trees and we knew little. More, the arboretum at Oving was structured in architectural terms with avenues, walks, vistas and junctions punctuated by tableaux of Vicenza statuary in the classical mode. I was entranced.

Pam and Michael drove over to The Laskett to see us early in the August of the following year. Michael wrote to me after, I now realize, an extremely significant letter. Its significance can be registered by the fact that my earliest ground plans for the entire Field garden were drawn after that letter was received and are vivid evidence that I was working out on paper the implications of what he wrote. These are the key paragraphs:

> Now for 'the forest'. Everything seemed to be growing like one o'clock in its first season so you obviously have green fingers, and there were many species which I admired. I would really like to have gone round again to have got the layout into my head. I like your broad avenues which people usually make too narrow. What I wondered later was whether there is enough mystery. The field is roughly square and the three main avenues I spotted were parallel to the field boundaries and at right angles to each other [they in fact aren't]. This means your vistas will also be the same length and there will be no surprises. One at least of them should be impeded and this will coax you into introducing some curves. I would also drive towards the centre.

He then went on with an even more pertinent suggestion:

> One further point on mystery. A small wood will seem much bigger if you can't see through it. So where your avenues are not built of evergreens you might in due course think of underplanting with evergreen shade-bearing bushes.

The letter ends with a quite unnecessary apology: 'I hope some of this may be helpful; as a non-artist addressing not one but two artists I feel a bit of a fool.' Far from it, for what Michael's letter establishes is that he had a genuine eye for garden composition and that his contribution to this garden was signal.

Pamela died, alas, too young, of cancer in 1982. She was a great loss and after her death we never went to Oving again. Michael became virtually a recluse, especially after his loss of the newspaper. Years later, when I first wrote about the making of this garden for the magazine *Hortus*, I recorded my debt to him and sent him a copy of the article. I'm only sorry that he never came again to see what his 'pupils' had achieved thanks to his advice and inspiration.

But let us return to Hidcote. That garden was in the care of the National Trust and was, of course, closed as it was winter the weekend we were staying at Oving. However, if Pam decided that she was going to get into something she would bring all kinds of pressure to bear on any of the officials who held the keys. So it was that on one of those rare, frosty, crisp but bright February days we swept through its gates.

Lawrence Johnston was an American who lived partly in England and partly in the south of France, where he laid out another equally famous garden, La Serre de Madone, at Menton, which is now being restored. He had a great deal of money and an astounding talent for garden design and planting. Hidcote was laid out by him in the years immediately preceding the First World War and the garden is recognized, along with Sissinghurst, as the prime prototype of a garden disposed as a series of contrasting 'rooms', that is, the division of space into compartments, corridors and circuses. Hidcote looked stunning without a flower to be seen, except perhaps a few fugitive winter ones. The lesson already appreciated from the Hunting Lodge was here writ large, that the key to any successful garden is structure. At Hidcote the visitor is 'controlled' by Johnston's avenues and hedges which lead him on towards a beckoning statue, to contemplate borrowed landscape or head for a comfortable garden seat. Hidcote taught me that the test of a good garden was if it was as interesting to visit on the coldest January day as it would be on a day in floriferous balmy June.

One other garden left its imprint and that we visited slightly later, on 5 April 1976, after having lunched with Cecil Beaton at Reddish. Cranborne Lodge is one of those dream houses, a rose brick and stone hunting box built for Robert Cecil, 1st Earl of Salisbury in the Jacobean period. Its original garden had been the work of the great plantsman John Tradescant, but it had been transformed by its present chatelaine Lady Salisbury, the great pioneer of organic gardening and the person who was to help Prince Charles with the initial layout of Highgrove, where I was later to design and cut the hedges she had planted into swags and pilasters. She had been a great beauty in her day, one of the three Wyndham Quinn sisters whom Cecil Beaton had once photographed in a composition based on a group by John Singer Sargent. With a deliberately cultivated pallor of complexion and an idiosyncratic way of dressing, in a manner I'd characterize as aristocratic Bohemian, she exuded a certain style, above all in her gardens. Once again the visit left its mark:

> We went on to see the Salisburys' garden at Cranborne. What a paradise. Perhaps the most perfect small-scale country-house garden I have ever seen [along with the Hunting Lodge, I hasten now to add!], delicate, sensitive, English, wholly resistant of conifers and quick-growing effects. The setting of the house is idyllic, in a valley, with a pretty walled courtyard and red-brick gatehouse. There was an all-white garden at the back with dianthus and pinks used as ground cover beneath a walk of espaliered old apple trees, on one of which mistletoe

had swagged itself to the ground. Beyond, gates led on to a noble avenue of elm leading the eye into the distance. There was an orchard with a tapestry hedge of beech, box and yew, planted with nothing but flowering crabs and carpeted with daffodils, which had walks cut through it. At the bottom ran a little stream, just created, with a walk on its further bank through trees, shrubs, primulas, etc. She [Lady Salisbury] had recently made a box garden into which she had planted all the flowers mentioned by John Tradescant. There's a formal garden with a mount, indeed a whole series of gardens away from the house including a marvellous herb garden and an apple tunnel. Perfect, personal, intimate, secret. And full of old-fashioned flowers: double primroses, Elizabethan primulas and old roses I'd never even heard of. We left plant-loaded, including the rose 'Cranborne', which I shall grow around the obelisk in the Yew garden.

Alas, it died and the obelisk was moved, but that should not detract from the romance I felt about that garden. For me, as an historian of the Elizabethan and Jacobean age, it had huge resonance, for in essence what Mollie Salisbury was creating was a garden in spirit with the house. Unlike Hidcote, its scale was akin to the land available to plant at The Laskett; it was a garden of rooms, smaller in size than the Hidcote ones, and it was filled with what I can only describe as telling embroidered detail, such as standard honeysuckles and much intricate clipped box-work.

If I had to analyse the Salisbury style in terms of garden design I would categorize it as close-focus, gardens whose essence was detail rather than bold structure and architectural effect, most of which at Cranborne had been inherited. And perhaps here one might suggest, mischievously, that women in the garden are generally the ones for detail. Vita Sackville-West and Harold Nicolson at Sissinghurst are prime examples of this generality. It was Harold who conceived the layout (not, in my opinion, that good) and it was Vita who enlivened it with her plantsmanship. This was to some extent to be true of The Laskett garden. Julia has always been the better plants person. From the outset I have been concerned with the overall concept of its design and the allocation and orchestration of space. That is not to say that Julia made no contribution to the design of The Laskett garden, because she did, but only to indicate at the outset the balance between us.

What I did not record in my diary entry on Cranborne, which was an important source of inspiration, was anything about practicalities, for much of this garden was new. I could see yew hedges that were thriving and for the first time I realized that they grew quite quickly if you fed them. The importance of farmyard manure and compost as essential to any garden's success also dawned on me. Then there was the great avenue carpeted with primroses by the thousand. How was that enchanting, unbelievable vision achieved? The answer was a simple one: do not cut the grass until quite late in July, by which time the seed will have fallen and propagated. It is a rule we keep at The Laskett to this day. But I came away with a deep desire to plant parterres and patterns in box and to explore the old garden books of Elizabethan England. What I now regret I failed to come away with at that stage was a decision to be from the outset organic.

IF GARDENS THEMSELVES ARE A SOURCE OF INSPIRATION, SO ARE those seen in the pages of books. In creating The Laskett I was following an historicist impulse, the desire to go back, first to the gardens of late Victorian and Edwardian England, and then, reaching even further back, to those of the age of Gloriana or, rather, those that masqueraded as re-creations of them. Simultaneously with garden visiting I began to put together a garden library, searching, in particular, for any books which would tell me about the old formal tradition. Among my very earliest purchases were four books that were profoundly to influence the nature of The Laskett garden. The first and most mesmeric was *Gardens Old and New: The Country House Garden and its Environment*, edited by H. Avray Tipping and illustrated with photographs by Charles Latham. This ran to three handsome, large volumes issued by *Country Life* about 1910, but incorporating what was in fact an anthology of garden articles by its first garden editor, Tipping, stretching back to the year of the magazine's appearance, 1897. Tipping, an aesthete and an encyclopedic authority on country houses, was a brilliant creator of gardens himself, and over twenty years later we visited the gardens he had made – though one of them, Mounton, which lies not far from The Laskett in Monmouthshire, was now a ruin. Today he is known more through the garden he designed for Chequers, the country house given to the nation by Lord Lee for the use of the prime minister.

Within the covers of *Gardens Old and New* are gathered not only all the gardens of the great historic houses, ones like Chatsworth or Melbourne, but also a number of far more recent gardens which had been laid out in the Old English style towards the close of Victoria's reign, ones like Blickling in Norfolk and Montacute in Somerset. All of them embodied that vision of a timeless England whose values and roots lay in the soil of the countryside as opposed to the squalor, grime and commercialism of the industrial city. This was arcadia. I can't claim that I've ever read these volumes cover to cover, but, and much more to the point, I endlessly went for walks in the enticing photographs during the planning stages of our garden.

Why were these volumes so hypnotic? First because they conjured up a security and a plenitude that had gone. I'd always had a romance about the years before 1914, prompted, when I was a schoolboy, by the world of Edwardian opulence and style conjured up by Cecil Beaton on stage in those revivals of plays by Oscar Wilde just after the war. Nothing could have presented a greater contrast to the drear austerities and lack of high glamour of post-war Britain. Later all my memories of visiting country houses as a young curator at the National Portrait Gallery in the early 1960s had been of cutbacks, of owners struggling on with little or no help, watching the place disintegrate around them. The gardens were always the first to go. Most of those in the book had had to be simplified, and many had simply vanished, sunk without trace due to the tide of social change, the lack of labour and of the money needed to maintain them.

Charles Latham was the first great garden photographer and we are fortunate that he recorded these aristocratic paradises and endowed them with a seeming timelessness. This is the garden vision which drew me, one of mellow crumbling stone walls and stairways, ancient clipped yews, espaliered fruit trees, immaculately kept parterres, swathes of velvet lawn and sheets of still water like mirror glass. Occasionally the loss would be made more poignant by the intrusion of a solitary figure, a lady in a straw hat caught on a garden seat or lingering for a moment, parasol in hand, on a terrace. How wonderful, I thought, to attempt to create, even on a modest scale, something of the atmosphere evoked here. It would, of course, have to be on a far smaller scale and also be achieved with little labour and money. But it would be worth the challenge.

That mood of heady nostalgia for the illusory secure world before 1914 was fuelled after marriage also by something else, which I saw only later: my wife's ballet *Enigma Variations*, choreographed in 1968 by Sir Frederick Ashton. A garden is about creating a certain mood or atmosphere, one perhaps that never outlives its creators, and certainly *Gardens Old and New* is redolent with the haunting ethos of another era. In a similar way in the ballet the same period lived again, through Julia's quite miraculous scenery and costumes, evoking the interior of the composer Sir Edward Elgar's Worcestershire house, its garden and the elm-filled landscape beyond. At the opening a gauze dissolves to reveal a quite magical tableau of late Victorian country life caught in a golden autumn early evening light. The mood is melancholy, Chekhovian. A lady lies in a hammock to one side with a young man in a straw boater leaning over her. At one moment a few stray autumn leaves flutter to the ground. Children bowl hoops and a gentleman arrives on a period bicycle. Each of Elgar's friends pictured within, as he subtitled the composition, danced their variation. I recall Dame Ninette de Valois saying at Ashton's memorial service in Westminster Abbey that this ballet and the other Julia was to do with him, *A Month in the Country* (to which I will return), were his greatest delineations of human psychology and relationships in terms of the dance. This is a poignant, moving ballet, which portrays one man's quest in his art, which ends happily with the arrival of a telegram telling of the acceptance of his score. I have never been able to see it danced without the tears welling in my eyes. Gardens are the fruits of security and I wanted The Laskett garden to conjure up its own golden age, resonating with the one we had lost.

Gardens Old and New embodied, therefore, atmosphere. It wasn't practical, for there were no ground or planting plans nor any attempt to tackle practicalities. For those I turned to another book, again one which has since been reissued, *Gardens for Small Country Houses* by Gertrude Jekyll and Lawrence Weaver. First published in 1912 and firmly a child of that era, my edition was the fourth, dated 1920. This not only dealt with the different, component, parts of a garden – steps and stairways, water, walls, paving, pergolas and so on – but also gave the ground plans and planting details of a series of what were then thought of as small gardens. Today they would be classified as large but, in fact, they were roughly the size of the domain we had available to develop. Their style inevitably is Jekyllesque, that is, with strong geometry at ground level and equally strong vertical built and evergreen architecture. Both were softened by the rich planting typical of the Jekyll style and went through her classic progression, working from formality around the house gradually outwards to wild woodland planting. These gardens too were visions, but ones I could see were of a hands-on practical variety, with enough information provided for me to crib ideas here and there, which I did.

Two other books were important to me. One was Reginald Blomfield's *The Formal Garden in England*, published in 1892. At the time I was wholly ignorant of the furore that this publication unleashed in the late Victorian gardening world, causing the venerable William Robinson, Jekyll's mentor and author of one of the great garden classics, *The English Flower Garden*, to fire off rockets in rage. In Blomfield's view the landscape style had deprived buildings of their proper settings and this now demanded reformation by the reassertion of the architect's role in the garden. At this juncture all of that passed me by. All I knew was that this was one of the two books in print on the making of formal gardens. The other, to which I'll come shortly, appeared in 1902. It is extraordinary to think that no new book on the subject was to appear until the modest one I wrote in 1989, *Creating Small Formal Gardens*. Blomfield's book argued for the land around any house to be divided up architecturally into rooms and corridors and compartments. It was a call to reinstate the old gardens of Tudor and Stuart England with their mounts and knots, arbours and palisades, galleries and pleached avenues, statues and topiary. Unlike *Gardens for Small Country Houses* this book was illustrated not by photographs but by a beguiling series of line drawings, many in fact re-drawings from old engravings, by F. Inigo Thomas. They were, however, deeply evocative. Many were reinterpretations of the bird's eye views of the great gardens of late Stuart England, as recorded in Jan Kip's *Britannia Illustrata* (1707). Soon I began to buy odd original prints as they turned up, ones which I eventually framed and which now hang in my bathroom as perpetual sources of inspiration.

For me a line-drawing aerial view beats both a photograph and a ground plan when it comes to suggesting the eventual reality of a garden composition. The pictures in Blomfield's book presented large-scale gardens which seemed to me to be perfectly manageable in terms of very limited labour. They consisted of grass, paved and gravel paths, built architectural elements, avenues of trees and plants, such as evergreens, cut into hedges or repeat shapes, like cones or drums. Using such a repertory I thought order and visual excitement could be conjured out of a large piece of land, but of a kind that would only demand mowing through the growing season and giving a once-a-year cut and prune to the trained elements. Moreover, such a garden could be planted and slowly grow, and only as and when they could be afforded need the statuary and built parts be added. Whereas most people's reaction on seeing these illustrations would have been one of horror at the sheer scale of it all, my reaction was exactly the opposite. Here was a way to tame The Laskett. There was no need for that most demanding of horticultural phenomena, elaborate flower borders. Indeed, anyone who has read the indomitable Celia Fiennes's travel diaries inspecting the great gardens of late-seventeenth-century England will recall that she hardly ever refers to flowers at all. This was the direction in which we would initially travel. Like so many of the other books that were to be seminal to me in the mid-seventies, Blomfield's was to be reissued in facsimile in 1985, by which time formal gardening was coming sharply back into fashion.

The final book was H. Inigo Triggs's *Formal Gardens in England and Scotland*, a costly folio issued in the year of the coronation of Edward VII, 1902, and capturing the full effulgence of the decade to come. Triggs, like Blomfield, was an architect, and his hero was André Le Nôtre, who had created the gardens of Versailles for Louis XIV. Le Nôtre was the greatest of all the French garden designers, the man who epitomized and defined the French formal style with its swirling baroque parterres of box and its use of axes to create formal vistas that seemed to stretch away towards infinity. Once again the photographs were by that genius Charles Latham, but this time printed in sepia, thus endowing them with a textural subtlety of tone that makes each one a collector's item. Most of the gardens had already appeared in *Gardens Old and New*, but one thing set this book apart. Here there were not just pictures but garden plans and elevations drawn to scale, which was useful, a veritable practical mine of information on every ingredient of the formal repertory.

No books since have given me the same excitement and sense of discovery as these did during the planning stages of The Laskett garden. I particularly treasured any photograph of a garden with a young yew hedge, for this was an image of hope, telling me that hedges didn't just arrive overnight but took time to grow and that one should not despair. Although I was thirty-eight and Julia forty-two when we began the garden, we had time on our side, although I was keenly aware that we must get on with it if we were to see it in our lifetime.

THE FOUNT OF THE FORMAL TRADITION IS ITALY. THE PROCESS OF planning such a garden inevitably led me in that direction. I had first fallen in love with Italy in 1955 when, as an impoverished student, I had set eyes on the Lombard plain after passing the night on a hard banquette crossing over from France. But the Italy I then fell in love with and pined for was that of Botticelli and Piero della Francesca, the temple of art and beauty as dreamed about by generations of Englishmen before embarking on the Grand Tour. I knew nothing about Italian gardens, nor was I interested until the advent of The Laskett. And then came a revelatory moment. Like huge numbers of other people my eyes were opened by a pioneer book by Georgina Masson, whom we visited at Impruneta in 1973. She was then in her early sixties and I described her as looking 'as though she had been transported hither from a rectory and a long-suffering rector'. Impoverished, she would have written on anything that would have helped pay the bills. *Italian Gardens* appeared in 1961 and was the only accessible book available in English which covered the origins and development of the great renaissance and baroque gardens of the Italian peninsula. Julia had a copy, which I borrowed and devoured. Later a larger, handsomely illustrated edition came my way in the bequest to me of half of the library of Julia's aunt, Carola Oman, the historical biographer.

It was not to be until the eighties that I began regularly to visit these great masterpieces of formal design, but they had already left their imprint on my imagination through Georgina Masson's book. Over the last twenty years and more I have returned again and again from these unforgettable seminal creations, such as the Villa Lante at Bagnaia or the Villa Farnese at Caprarola, always fired by their extraordinary beauty, their masterly way of orchestrating a terrain, their architectural majesty of concept. Of course we could aspire to nothing of such splendour, but here were endless lessons to be learnt about the disposition of space, above all the handling of ascent and descent, for that was the great architect Bramante's invention when he first terraced the garden of the papal Villa Belvedere, now part of the Vatican in Rome, at the very opening of the sixteenth century. It was the sheer unashamed theatricality of these gardens that appealed to me, their fantasy and their concern with meaning as well as design. There was nothing tame about them. What was more, they re-emphasized the importance of firm structure, for however decayed and badly maintained an Italian garden, it was still beautiful because its geometry always remained intact.

There are three to which we still often return. The first is the Villa Lante, an extravaganza constructed for the Cardinal Gambara in the 1560s, an allegory of the loss and search for the restoration of the Golden Age as described in Ovid's *Metamorphoses*, spilling down a hillside not far from Viterbo. I have never been much interested in the classic English progression of the dissolution of garden into woodland and then into the landscape around. Bearing in mind what farmers could do, I knew that The Laskett garden had to be wholly self-contained and inward-looking, a segment carved out of the landscape. The Villa Lante is exactly that, a walled rectangle, its interior an essay in symmetry with those classic ingredients of the Italian garden, a firm central axis and a number of cross axes linked by steps and terraces and by the deployment of water splashing downwards through fountains and rills towards a spectacular parterre at the bottom. Alas, I knew that we would never be able to afford water on this scale, nor did the sharp frosts of England allow it.

The second is the Villa Farnese at Caprarola for the *palazzina*, a banqueting house away from the two main winter and summer gardens, reached by means of a rising woodland walk. I cannot imagine anything more breathtaking in garden design than the approach to this ensemble: a monumental staircase, flanked by grottoes, down the centre of which a rill falls from two recumbent river gods. At the top this leads on to a box garden around the small palazzo lined with incredible herms rearing up and piercing the blue sky and, on the other side, reached by yet another ascent, a garden of fountains. The element of surprise in garden-making is all-important here. Can anything cap what you have just seen? And here, of course, it does, for the sightlines are perfectly controlled so as never to spoil the sense of constant revelation as you climb upwards. Our earliest visits were to a garden all but abandoned. Since then it has been restored and the innumerable fountains, jets and rills of water once more sparkle in the sunshine.

Finally there is Bomarzo, the famous *Sacro Bosco* or sacred wood, created by Vicino Orsini in the 1550s. This is quite unlike anything else, a kind of mad counter-statement to the order of the renaissance garden, for here everything is asymmetrical and the visitor meanders through a wood encountering dragons and monsters, huge giants and vast recumbent figures – not to mention an elephant, an ork, a vast tortoise together with a threatening hellmouth, and a serenely classical church in an allegory which has so far defied interpretation. Many of these ghostly apparitions are sculpted from the rock that arises from the terrain. What was the lesson learnt from this astounding creation? Still it speaks across the centuries of the need for madness in the garden, for fantasy. As I get older I see its value more and more, for it embodies a release from convention, telling the gardener to defy it and let his imagination run riot. During the initial phases of The Laskett garden it was the order and calm of the renaissance garden that remained the prime inspiration. In its later phases, Bomarzo has been a spur to invent and stand the world on its head.

Other gardens, of course, contributed to the making of The Laskett, but not in its initial planning. Two in particular spring to mind. One is Het Loo, that miraculous restoration and recreation of the great late-seventeenth-century baroque garden of William III at Apeldoorn in the Netherlands. We were there in 1979 when they were excavating the terrain, peeling off the layers added to transform it into a *jardin anglais* at the beginning of the nineteenth century and revealing the fountain basins, paths and terraces of the original garden. That restoration was not to be completed until 1984, since when we have returned many times in admiration. But it did not affect our planning phase. Later, in the eighties, I was to shrink down one of its parterre designs for The Laskett.

The second was the painter Monet's Giverny, which we visited even later, in the early nineties. This, like John Piper's, is an artist's garden and its prime lesson is colour, strong colour of a kind that was wholly out of fashion when we started our garden. Then pale colours, the acme of restrained good taste, were all the rage. The result of Giverny was to pack the borders with virulent yellows, among them clumps of heleniums, helianthus, ligularia and rudbeckia. Their joy resided not only in their colour, but the fact that they came late in the season, triumphantly trumpeting when so much else had gone over. And who could resist planting nasturtiums once that pathway across which they intrude so miraculously at Giverny has been seen? No year has passed since that Julia has not arranged for them to spill artfully somewhere in the garden. But I am anticipating part of the saga to come.

GARDENS ARE NOT CREATED IN LIMBO. HOW FEW IF ANY BOOKS I have read on particular gardens have ever spelt out the social, political and economic climate against which they were conceived. Only when the dust and decay of centuries has accrued do historians appear and set this or that garden into context. I was fully conscious from the outset that The Laskett garden was a child of its time, the middle of the seventies. When I talk to groups I am about to escort around the garden I always evoke those years as the backcloth to the making of The Laskett garden. In front of me I often see nothing but a sea of bewildered faces, as though gardening was a world apart from reality. I remind them how in January 1974 I went to the Victoria & Albert Museum and began my directorship in the midst of the three-day week, with the miners on strike and the imminent collapse of the Heath government. My secretary and I sat and worked by candlelight, for government had decreed that the lights be turned off. This was the prelude to over five years of social turmoil until, after the so-called Winter of Discontent in 1979, a Conservative government under Margaret Thatcher came to power. Even then it was not until the middle of the eighties that anything remotely resembling stability and economic prosperity returned.

Our lives were radically affected by these events. The museum, as part of the Civil Service, had to shed over a hundred staff in one year and there was a union bloodbath along with the worst row in the arts for years. Money became appallingly tight. In spite of all this we soldiered on through the misery and planted a huge garden. Why? That, I think, can be answered in one word: hope. To plant a garden is a pledge to that virtue, a belief that one day you will see it reach maturity and flourish. But in the midst of the turmoil of the late seventies there were times when I wondered. That gesture was linked to another motive, this time connected with one of the most celebrated of all the exhibitions staged at the museum during my fourteen-year directorship, *The Destruction of the Country House*.

Not long after my appointment was announced, I was approached by the distinguished architectural historian John Harris, who urged upon me the need for a polemical exhibition on the plight of our country houses. Their parlous state had come to the top of the agenda thanks to a brilliant report by the architectural writer and *Country Life* contributor John Cornforth, but the contents of that needed to be got over to a far wider public, especially in view of the threatened introduction of a wealth tax by any incoming Socialist government, then in the mode of Denis Healey's famous remark that he intended to squeeze the rich until the pips squeaked. In this case it was not pips but a great swathe of our architectural heritage that would suffocate and collapse. This was the genesis of *The Destruction of the Country House*, which opened to the public in the October of 1974. By then a Socialist government was in power and to stage such a show was an act of defiance and bravery by a museum that was part of government. At the time it created a sensation.

One telling tableau in the exhibition said it all. As the visitor turned a corner he was confronted with the massive columns and facade of a country house collapsing on him. That was followed by the realization that on each block of masonry there was a photograph of a house that was no more. A tape recited a litany of the thousand lost houses against the sound of crashing masonry and smouldering timbers. I recall time and again going into the exhibition and witnessing its impact on those who came. Some turned back, unable to go on, they were so overwhelmed. Others stood with the tears streaming down their faces.

The exhibition also covered, of course, country-house gardens and it was Miles Hadfield, a pioneer historian of gardens, who wrote a short piece when such a subject had barely been invented. Photographs told the story far more vividly. The great gardens of the Duke of Newcastle at Clumber were no more, nor were those at Easton Lodge in Essex or those of Hewell Grange in Worcestershire, to name but a handful. In fact, in 1974 no one knew how many gardens had gone, for the topic as such hardly existed. Over a quarter of a century on, much of that research has been accomplished and the realization of the losses is even more devastating. At the same time many have been restored to life, Easton Lodge and Hewell Grange among them.

What I do know is that that exhibition had an enormous effect upon me. It came as a challenge. Englishmen throughout the centuries had planted great gardens in the country. Was this tradition to end? Not if we had our way. In defiance of the times and of the ideology of the age we would plant, in what in terms of times past was a modest domain, just such a garden. It would be idiosyncratic and English. It would be filled with stately avenues and massive yew hedges, topiary peacocks and waterfalls of old roses. It would be carpeted with drifts of flowers in spring and the branches of the trees in the orchard would bend low beneath the weight of the rosy fruit each autumn. It would be a garden of vista and surprise, private and mysterious but also celebratory, a garden of memory about two people, their lives and their friends. The seventies was for me, as it was for so many, a period of public misery and private happiness. It was the creation of The Laskett garden that saw me through.

Three

PLANNING PARADISE

IT WAS THAT GREAT GARDENER AND FRIEND ROSEMARY VEREY who taught me the criteria for judging a garden. Of course she took into account the maker's aesthetic vision, design abilities and plantsmanship, but there were two other aspects, generally never referred to, which also had to be put into the balance before judgement was finally given. First, the financial resources available to the creator, and second, the labour at his disposal. That seemingly elementary lesson has stood me in good stead and many a time caused me to pause before utterance. Too often I have seen what I call cheque-book gardens, instant bought taste of a kind that is soulless, gardens devoid of atmosphere and that elusive quality known as power of place. That quality is hard to define, but perhaps the key attribute is identity, those things that set a garden apart and make it memorable as a powerful reflection of its creators. Everyone who visits gardens, as we do, knows that moment when you are transfixed and suddenly taken into another world. Endowed with power of place any garden will continue to haunt the memory for a lifetime. I have seen gardens with that quality achieved with only the slenderest of financial resources, the result of the makers' own physical exertion, their plants cuttings from friends and their ornaments devised from the contents of skips.

Money and labour are crucial resources for garden-making, particularly on a large scale. It is not my intention, therefore, to shy away from the topic, for the increase and decrease of both elements certainly account for the ebb and flow of the development of The Laskett garden over three decades. My salary as Director of the Victoria & Albert Museum was £9,000 p.a. in 1974 when I took up the post, and three times that when I resigned it at the close of 1987. I was the first director devoid of a private income, which used to be taken as a given by holders of such public positions. Indeed, one of the reasons for my resignation was an acute awareness that I had to make a second career in the private sector to provide for our future. That is not to say that Julia did not contribute towards the making of the garden in financial terms. Whole sections of it, such as the Orchard or the Kitchen Garden, were part of her domain, while, for instance, each year it was she who ordered and paid for the large numbers of spring bulbs. On any major structural project the split was generally fifty-fifty. But I need hardly point out that theatre design, for all its seeming high glamour, is a poorly paid profession, not that museum work is much better. Indeed, in the late seventies my salary was frozen, so that the heads of department within the museum were earning more than its director. As my second career took off, first as a consultant to Olimpia & York on the public spaces in the Canary Wharf development in the Docklands, and latterly as a professional writer, the built structure, envisioned from the outset, began, piecemeal, to be put in place. The success of first *The Story of Britain* in 1996 and then the *Diaries* the following year facilitated major changes and the addition of significant sculptural ornament. Nonetheless, it has to be said at the outset that the financial resources behind the creation of this garden have never been other than modest. Each addition and innovation has had to be carefully phased and tightly budgeted. Ingenuity with seemingly disparate materials has been one of the keys to some of the garden's most spectacular effects.

Although the second half of the seventies was marked by roaring inflation, we were fortunate in one major fact, that plants remained relatively cheap. A random invoice for trees lies before me. It is from the forester who was attached to the Lucas-Scudamore estate at Kentchurch (the Scudamores are one of the oldest families in the county) and lists twenty-five *Thuja plicata*, six *Robinia pseudoacacia*, along with eight specimen trees, including conifers, a *Ginkgo biloba*, a Swedish whitebeam and a *Koelreuteria*, all for the princely sum of £17.

Labour is as pertinent as financial resources. When we arrived we began with David and Glyn, gardeners who came one day once a fortnight from a firm of contractors, a service offered by a local garden centre. Their task above all was to mow during the growing season. Soon one of them, David, decided to set up his own little business with a colleague, Terry, who was eventually succeeded by Wilf. If we were lucky, Wilf would come on his own for a day in between their joint visits. In the winter, the mowing over, they went on to what we called projects. These could vary from digging new beds to laying paving. Anyone who has relied on a labour force of this kind will know how elusive those who give it can be. So desperate do you become to retain their services that you will put up with almost anything. Their most irritating habit was miraculously to avoid ever coming in summer on a day when we would be here. On the whole, looking back, we must be grateful to them for keeping us going during the years when the garden was in its infancy.

David was a beaming rubicund countryman, one of those people in whose hair one would expect still to find the brush, a mobile bundle of grubby working clothes with the buttons, often as not, fastened in the wrong places. He wore the same clothes the whole year round, for I was always struck how in summer he looked fit for the Antarctic. A number of his teeth were artificial but it was entirely arbitrary as to whether he would remember to put them in or not. David combined a love of Wagner with an attractive haziness, which from time to time could result in such disasters as digging in a bed of newly planted fruit bushes which Julia had just shown him with the injunction to respect them. Nor was she to forget the cherry trees, given her by her father, which he cheerfully mowed over, although, when this was pointed out, he arrived on his next visit with a gift of plants. He had a permanent expression of puzzled surprise and amazement.

Wilf, who was a builder and not a gardener, was endowed with a genuine sweetness of nature. Small of body, hesitant, shy and thoughtful, it was he who carried out our first modest ventures in hard landscaping. I can see him still with his knitted pixie hood, which I don't recollect as ever being washed, and his T-shirt with a woodpecker blazoned on it (the logo of the greatest local industry, Bulmer's Cider), which was worn beneath a jacket several sizes too big for him. But he always gave a degree of careful consideration to everything he did.

Well intentioned they certainly were, but any idea of the exact measurement of anything was wholly alien to their way of thinking. Although given specific instructions as to the proportions, for instance, of the trench for the Rose Garden hedge, the result was not the rectangle I had asked for but a rhomboid, just enough out of true for me to be preoccupied ever since with working out how to deflect the eye from the fact. In the same way they would be told to plant trees at an exact distance apart. But, oh no, that was not how they thought. Wilf, in his role as number two, would stand silently by as David would pace out the distances with his large feet encased in wellington boots. The result, of course, was that no two of the lengths were ever the same. Some would be eight, others nine and some even ten or eleven feet apart. No matter; gardening, as I've learnt through bitter experience, is the art of fudging it. David's most recurring chant still rings in my ear: 'Yes, Dr Strong,' signalling that sometimes he had taken in what I'd said and sometimes he had not.

But over the years what they charged gradually escalated until, in 1992, we reached the decision that, if we could provide the accommodation for such a person, it would be far more economical to go over to a gardener who would be more or less full-time. By that we asked for four days a week. So it was that Robin Stephens arrived. He is summed up in a note I made in my Garden Diary at the close of that year: 'Robin is a slow worker, but he has a far greater attention to detail in every way.' He was not a trained gardener, but having had a miscellaneous career from hairdresser to general factotum in another country house, he did have an eye and was dedicated to tidiness. That was reflected above all in his appearance. He was always immaculately turned out for the job, his thin frame in addition giving his every movement an elegance. His timekeeping was beyond reproach. We could have set our watches by his appearance in the morning as much as by his exit in the evening.

With someone four days a week we were able to make rapid advances during the five years he was with us. Then, when we had to search for a successor, we discovered that we could actually afford a properly trained gardener – and that was when Shaun Cadman arrived. The advent of someone knowledgeable and fascinated by plants was just what a maturing garden needed, for the infrastructure was fully grown and it was time to enrich the planting. Nonetheless, bearing in mind that the garden now extends to four acres and that it depends on Shaun and ourselves, it is no mean achievement.

What this constant struggle over resources taught us was to be relaxed. Gardening on the grand scale, as this inevitably became, is not that close-focus, and I soon learnt that no one is going to notice the weeds if the overall *coup de théâtre* is dramatic enough. Their eyes will simply be deflected from the shortcomings. Also, it is pointless getting agitated over when and if things get done. Early on I began resolutely to ignore those gardening columnists who were forever telling me the jobs in the garden for each week. If I had acted on their injunctions I would have abandoned the pursuit years ago. In the early stages I would carefully note what had to be done. So, give or take a bit, things were done as and when the labour came and also when we were there for any length of time beyond two or three days, which was generally for periods over Christmas, Easter and especially August. A trained horticulturalist would, I am sure, be horrified by what I cheerfully pruned in August, but it had to be, or at least it had to be until 1987, after which date we lived here. Before then both of us were at the peak of our careers in highly demanding professions. In my case gardening was the antidote to ploughing through mountains of paper. I never cease to give thanks for discovering its healing qualities. With my hands happily in the soil every trauma would be quickly soothed or slip away.

August above all was the magic month when we were here for four whole weeks, apart from a brief trip to London to clear the desk. That was the period each year during which I cut the yew hedges and the topiary and often embarked on heavy work on a new project. Each day was the same. I worked in my writing room in the morning on a book or a pile of museum papers, and in the afternoon, straw hat on head and equipped with a pair of secateurs, shears and a radio, I snipped away. My garden diaries record again and again what became a litany of recurring gardening chores: fertilizing the roses, putting bonemeal on the yew and box in springtime, digging up brambles, pleaching the limes, and forever weeding in rotation what we called the garden's state apartments: the Yew Garden, the Rose Garden and Jubilee Garden. But even to mention these is to anticipate, for I have not yet described their creation. All three belong to the heady years running from the autumn of 1974 to the summer of 1977, which saw the making of The Laskett garden. It is therefore now time to return to my narrative.

WE LEFT THE GARDEN LAST WITH THE AVENUES IN THE FIELD planted in the late winter of 1973. By May 1974 I was becoming obsessed, and that is caught in a letter to Jan. Jan van

Dorsten was an academic in the University of Leiden, a renaissance scholar, tall with blond hair and blue eyes, which made him irresistible to women, a fact of which he was aware. He was the man with the longest list of wives and mistresses I'd known. But, like all Netherlanders, he had an instinctive feeling for plants and flowers. Everywhere he lived – and as a consequence of his love life he was in a constant state of migration – there were pot plants on the windowsills and, in spring, the ritual of tulips, arriving either singly or in bunches as a gift from a guest, to be greeted with delight and given pride of place in the room. My letters to him, until his premature death in 1985, along with my diaries, chart the story of the garden. His gift to us was always one of tulip bulbs, so that he was one of the earliest of our friends to be as it were pictured in the garden, in his case in 'Dillenburg' tulips.

The letters, as a series running from the middle of the fifties, are autobiographical, but what they capture in the case of the garden is a sense of excitement and immediacy that would be entirely lacking from any retrospective account. I usually wrote long letters to him about three times a year, which updated him on what had passed during the intervening period. They covered what was happening in my public life, exchanges of academic information about this or that book, how Julia and our life at The Laskett was faring, and always but always the garden. That appears as a beacon of hope in each missive, whether it is celebrating the appearance of spring flowers, describing new projects, lamenting the loss of treasured trees and plants or recounting the harvesting of produce.

No great schemes are mentioned in that letter of late May 1974, but one can note a considerable advance from the horticultural ignorance of the previous year:

> Our greatest joy and love is The Laskett, looking each time more beautiful as we create our great garden and the plants

thrive and spread, burgeon and blossom. It is indescribable happiness to be there together. . .I have seriously got interested in plants and trees. We mark up great reference books with what we have got, rush off to Royal Horticultural Society shows, the Chelsea Flower Show and stop on the way down or do detours to nursery gardens to order plants. Somehow the garden has R areas and J areas which is lovely.

I have become fascinated by old roses. There is my *Rosa hemisphaerica*, first recorded in 1625, sprouting and promising flower. There are the old roses of Provence, of York and Lancaster, the Bourbon roses, engraved by Redouté and created for the Empress Josephine at Malmaison. Somehow they are history and they have such marvellous names: *Rosa* x *centifolia* 'Cristata', *Rosa gallica* 'Versicolor', 'Variegata di Bologna', 'Reine des Violettes', 'Louise Odier'.

The herb nursery has progressed so well that we can now propagate bits into other areas of the garden and one aches for great old sagging rosemary bushes, marjoram borders, huge clumps of lavender (we have about ten varieties so far), in fact the whole feeling of an old English country house garden. The hedges we have planted are growing and the orchard grass is now fit to tread upon.

Already I had the beginnings of what was to become over the years a formidable garden library. It started to grow, like so many, with the acquisition of plant dictionaries. What excited me initially about plants was their history. Habit, form, colour and texture of course fascinated me, but the dimension of time added an unforgettable richness. A rose that grew in the Duchess of Portland's famous garden at Bulstrode Park in Buckinghamshire in the eighteenth century, or a flower that made its debut in the awful Miss Willmott's garden at Warley Place in Essex in the Edwardian age, will always, as far as I am concerned, have an extra horticultural frisson.

When we came to The Laskett I hadn't a clue how to propagate plants. It was Julia who stood over me as, with almost trembling hands, I was told how carefully to prise apart the roots of, say, a hardy geranium, and then replant the several sections. I learnt how, in order to take cuttings, the stem that was pulled off a plant must have a heel, and I was introduced to hormone rooting powder. Into that I dipped the cutting and then carefully secured it in the earth. The fact that something promptly rooted and later threw forth new shoots came as a revelation to me.

On the subject of learning about cuttings, my most memorable encounter was with the late Dowager Lady Radnor. As a consequence of the exhibition *The Destruction of the Country House*, I made a film on the topic entitled *Going, Going, Gone* . . . It involved a lot of work on location and one of the interviews I did was with Isabel Radnor, who was a great gardener. In her time she had been the formidable chatelaine of Longford Castle in Dorset, but now in her widowhood she was busy making a second garden. Between shots I explained how we were beginning ours and the excitement of it and then, to her horror, I talked about the plants we had purchased. 'Remember,' she said, 'it is a very vulgar thing to buy plants.' I was suitably chastened, but she, with that generosity that endears all gardeners to me, proceeded to pull off cuttings from plants in her own garden, carefully putting them in plastic bags to keep them moist until I plunged them into the soil of The Laskett. Something similar happened in 1975 when I was filming at Montacute for an episode in the architectural series *Spirit of the Age*. From that I came back with cuttings of *Brachyglottis* (Dunedin Group) 'Sunshine', a beautiful grey foliage shrub with a disagreeable brilliant-yellow daisy-like flower, from the forecourt garden whose borders I was told had been planted by Gertrude Jekyll. (I was later to learn that they weren't; they were in fact the work of Phyllis Reiss.) The descendants of those cuttings are still going strong here today. It is in this way that plants in The Laskett garden take on the potent role of living memory.

ALL MY READING ON FORMAL GARDEN DESIGN DURING THOSE early months had worked from a number of premises, which I was quickly to discover clashed with the reality of our site. Formal gardens start with a house at the centre of an area of land with an avenue leading to the facade. Around the house should be arranged, in symmetrical fashion, a series of emanating alleys, usually one broad central one interpenetrated by a number of cross axes. The result would be a grid of squares and rectangles that could contain a parterre, a fountain, a pond, a hedged shrubbery or indeed any other garden feature. At the garden's periphery there was generally a gradual dissolution into the surrounding landscape. If I had known that our garden was to become such a fixation we would never have opted for The Laskett in the first place, for here was a house sited in one corner of an irregular triangle of land. There was no way that the house could ever be the focal point of the entire composition. It was, therefore, with a sense of bitter frustration that I set about seeing what could be done with what we had got.

The only site in proximity to the house which was flat and which could architecturally be related to viewpoints from the windows was to the east, where the windows opened on to what we deemed a cottage-garden area, with a bed around the inherited artificial wellhead which then led on to a large flat expanse of lawn. And it was there in August 1974 that I pegged out a large rectangle of what was to be our first yew room, and dug the hedging beds for what was to become the Yew Garden. Once fully grown, it would afford two vistas from the house, and once within it, a central vista out of the enclosure. The first two vistas were to finials or urns of an early-eighteenth-century design, while the final vista was to be to an obelisk flanked by symmetrically planted fastigiate

Irish yew and specimen conifers, set against a hedge of the thuja we had purchased from Kentchurch and which, when fully grown, would screen a crumbling pond that was to be used as a dump.

That reproductions of old garden ornaments could be had from firms manufacturing them in reconstituted stone was a major discovery. I'd seen them at the Chelsea Flower Show. My delight at discovering this fact was unbridled, for the resources to buy originals were way beyond my purse and these reproductions fully fulfilled my belief that garden ornament was one of stage scenery and props. As long as a thing looked right it really didn't matter much what it was. And, as I was soon to discover, giving them a coating of sour milk or yogurt would hasten the ageing process, encouraging the moss and lichen to grow, bestowing on them a phoney antiquity.

Next came the Rose Garden. It was Julia who observed, standing looking at the Field one day, that part of its surface formed a raised, rectangular plateau which must once have been a lawn tennis court in days gone by. She was right, for later excavations in the area were forever throwing up sections of drainage pipe. Here, suddenly, in the midst of what had seemed a daunting expanse of meadowland, was a ready-made garden room. If we had had to pay for it to be landscaped ourselves, the cost would have been prohibitive. Indeed I spent much time at that period lamenting the fact that the Field was on a slope and not flat. I had yet to discover that we were lucky, for changes of level form some of the most exciting elements in garden design. So it was that we had the grass cut back and on about two-thirds of it I was to lay out the Rose Garden. Its full name is the Pierpont Morgan Rose Garden, for I paid for its planting with the fee I received for delivering the Walls Lectures at Morgan Library in New York in the autumn of that year on the subject of *The Victorian Vision of the British Past*.

Let my letter of 21 October 1974 to Jan, written shortly before we left for the States, take up the story:

I planted another thirty trees a few weeks back. The Wren finials shaped like urns and an eight-foot-high obelisk have been placed in position in the Yew Garden. When I get back from the States I have to plant the hedging, which will be very seventeenth century when it grows up in eight years or so. The Garden is about fifty by sixty feet in size and will, when complete, be full of tantalizing mystery and vistas.

In the Field the grass tennis court which we have reclaimed needs trenching for more yew hedging (is the man mad?) and old-fashioned nineteenth-century and earlier roses will arrive to create a secret Rose Garden there. Le Nôtre Strong is in full flight. I thought it might amuse you to see a plan, which I send. It [gardening] really does interest me more than anything. Julia can hardly drive past a nursery without me wanting to get another tree. It's a whole area of creativity I just didn't know about and it is amazing how fast things grow. Even in a year with our feeble efforts the garden is already unrecognizable. In ten years' time it will be arcadia. And there's so much to plan, more and more little areas and surprises, because I love old gardens where you can't see round the corner and everything is planned to give one a vista and a surprise. It will take absolutely years to exhaust the possibilities of this rather large patch.

Yew hedging, I realized, was the essential ingredient of any really significant garden. That had to be planted as soon as possible and I anxiously inquired of anyone I thought would know how long it would take to grow. The very mention of the fact that we were busy planting yew produced in most people a horrified reaction, best summed up in the sentence: 'You'll never live to see it.' One person who came our way who certainly did know about yew was Lanning Roper.

Lanning was American but had come to England and, during the post-war period, become one of the leading garden designers of the day. He always insisted, however, on billing himself as 'garden consultant'. We met him around on the London social scene and he was hugely encouraging to us. I asked him about yew hedging, its rate of growth and how to treat it. 'It'll be there sooner than you think,' he enthused, 'but be sure to feed it with soot.' In fact, it was fed with bone-meal and steadily rose at the rate of a foot a year. Innumerable visitors were trudged around the garden looking at what were no more than eighteen-inch sprigs arising from the soil, while I would dilate on how and why they were standing in this or that room. Horticultural Huns who visited our garden in its early stages had disbelief writ large on their faces.

On 2 December the roses arrived from Mattocks the nurserymen and were planted. Within the Rose Garden the scheme was a simple one. There were were four L-shaped spandrel beds around a central square one, later to be made circular, in which, for the time being, I piled up rocks found on site to form any kind of rudimentary focal point. At that moment I was too impoverished to afford one more reconstituted-stone ornament. I say the roses were planted, but looking at the planting plan it would have been better to say overplanted, for it is the typical failing of all beginners to overplant. Into the space I ludicrously crammed thirty-four old roses. The next year they were dramatically thinned out, and instead we added pillar roses like 'Mme Isaac Pereire' and 'Grüss an Teplitz' in small separate beds to give much-needed height to a rather flat composition. Later, in 1976, four *Amelanchier lamarckii*, delightful small flowering trees, were planted around the central bed with the same objective. In spring these had pretty frothy pink blossom and in autumn their leaves turned brilliant scarlet. There was lavender edging to the beds and a further underplanting of pinks.

That garden was to stay more or less the same for over ten years, its mainstays being the four large roses in the corners of the spandrel beds: bright-pink 'Complicata', paper-white 'Blanc Double de Coubert', cerise-pink *Rosa glauca* (syn. *R. rubrifolia*) with its beautiful blue-grey foliage, and creamy-white 'Mme Hardy'. The garden was not without problems, for on one side the soil was only a foot deep with rock beneath. In the end that was to spell the demise of the amelanchiers, but all of that lay ahead in the winter of 1974/5 and, as is always the case in gardening, you win some, you lose some.

The rudimentary sketch plan I sent to Jan is the earliest I have, but it gives vivid expression to the compartmentalization of the space that was already under way by the close of 1974. It shows that we had also made some attempt at formalizing the area in front of the house, with a hedge to one side leading to what is labelled a wild garden, and by planting a mini-avenue of what were six *Juniper communis* 'Hibernica', slow-growing evergreen stately columns leading away from the front entrance towards the glade presided over by the cedar. That summer too I had crenellated the existing old thuja hedge up the drive to enhance the formality. Re-cutting existing hedges, where it can be done, provides immediate effect. Stepping back I glowed with pride at the sight of my instant baronial topiary.

To the west of the house, I can see on the sketch that the island with the Judas tree was planted with conifers in the same year, although, behind it, the larch pergola we inherited was still in place. Beyond that what had been the kitchen garden had been grassed over to form an orchard enclosed by beech hedging. In it we planted piecemeal a walnut tree, a Cox's apple, an 'Alfred' apricot, an 'Oullins Gage' and a morello cherry. To it we added, in March 1976, a mulberry tree, which was planted by Hugh and Reta Casson. (Sir Hugh Casson, the architect, had been Julia's professor at the Royal

College of Art in the early fifties.) Shortly after, through the post, came one of Hugh's typical whimsical drawings of the planting ceremony, ending 'Long may it flourish in your garden'. Julia always maintains that contemporary architects are enemies of horticulture, preferring to cement over everything in sight. The fact that that tree died shortly after perhaps says it all. Of more importance was the creation of a new kitchen garden that winter in the area that had once housed kennels for the hounds, on the other side of the garage.

The Field on the plan makes an interesting study. It reveals that when it was drawn I had not even finalized the design of the Rose Garden or the shape of the beds within it. There are crescents indicated at either end of the poplar avenue we had christened Elizabeth Tudor, and to the west of the Rose Garden there is written 'Arboretum – specimen trees' (which never happened) and 'More Orchard'. So far this was a garden of isolated incidents, but with no overall coordinating scheme. The terse reference to 'More Orchard' is important, for one of Julia's great contributions to the garden has been her interest in fruit trees, in particular apples, for Herefordshire is cider country, ever since cider apple trees were brought to the county from Normandy by the great Lord Scudamore in the first half of the seventeenth century.

Julia's interest in fruit trees had been first aroused by her visit to one of the Royal Horticultural Society's annual shows at their exhibition hall in Vincent Square, close to where we had our London flat in Westminster. Here the fruit is elegantly piled in pyramids in baskets, a tableau to incite even the most philistine to want to plant a fruit tree. On that occasion the information stand was manned by the society's expert, Harry Baker, who was immensely encouraging to a beginner. When Julia asked him what nursery she should approach for stock, he suggested F.P. Matthews, who were within striking distance of The Laskett in north Herefordshire. Julia rang them and elicited a somewhat grumpy response until the number of trees, some thirty or so in all, was mentioned. At that point there was a change of tune and so began what has been a happy thirty-year relationship with that nursery. On 23 December 1974 Julia returned from it with the back of the car resembling Burnham Wood in winter. On Christmas Eve what became known as the Christmas Orchard was planted.

This marked the opening salvo of Julia's old-apple collection, for besides much-needed fruit trees such as pear, cherry, damson and plum, she planted intriguing old varieties of apple like 'Egremont Russet' (1872), 'Blenheim Orange' (c.1740), 'Warner's King' (c.1790), 'James Grieve' (1890) and the 'Devonshire Quarrenden' (1676). These were all on dwarf rooting stock, giving us trees about three metres high and six in circumference, an ideal size for both pruning and harvesting the fruit. A broad central walk divided the orchard area into two but a yew hedge to enclose it was not to be added until 1980. Julia then began to compile her book on the orchard, noting exactly what had been planted and seeking out the history of each tree and photocopying it. This was the beginning of what was to become a formidable garden archive.

On the very day that the trees went in I sat and wrote to my Dutch friend:

We have retreated down here for Christmas. Massive new plantings. The Pierpont Morgan Rose Garden with thirty-four roses planted, each bed edged with lavender and the whole of it enclosed by a yew hedge. The Christmas Orchard went in today, thirty-five fruit trees; more self-sufficiency in action. In three years we will buy no more apples, pears, cherries, plums or damsons. After Christmas the new raspberries, gooseberries, etc. go in. Our spring cabbages and spinach are already in. Life must be simplified and made more economical against the horrors of inflation hitting this tottering country.

A further report on our progress followed early in the April of the next year:

The garden stands poised and about to sprout, shortly to be coerced by Dr S's hand laying fertilizer on thick. Plagues of rabbits threaten the future of the Pierpont Morgan Rose Garden, squadrons of fat, beastly pigeons rip up plants for fun and the rabbits have even learnt to eat huge holes in our plastic netting and go through and gobble up our cabbages and then retreat. At any rate the new Vegetable Garden is well begun and the soil is so much better. The old one we are now busy grassing over to finish off the Small Orchard (as against the large Christmas one). I have gone mad in the Yew Garden and dug more beds with box hedging and pyramids and grey santolina – Le Nôtre would be thrilled.

We were beginning to live out the rural idyll as an escape from the uncertainties of urban life. In the country we knew that there would be fruit and vegetables. There would be wood to burn if the electricity went on strike. We even bought bicycles to fall back on if petrol became unavailable. The store cupboards were filled with tinned food, dried fruit, beans and pasta. Candles were bought in bulk and candlesticks with matches placed in every room. There was a Calor gas stove so that we could cook if there was a power failure. The creation of the garden must be set in this context as not only the deliberate making of a self-contained arcadia but also born of the practicalities of living in Britain in the late seventies.

THIS IS THE GARDEN THAT MICHAEL HARTWELL SAW IN THE summer of 1975 and which prompted his letter pointing out both its shortcomings and the possibilities. That was to result in the rest of August being spent making what in effect was the first overall plan for the entire Field, taking into consideration everything he said about mystery and surprise, the importance of underplanting and the need for curves. In that ground plan, done on the reverse of a proof sheet of the latest book, we begin to witness The Laskett garden assuming the guise in which we know it today. Even though it has since been infinitely elaborated in terms of built structure, planting and ornament, beneath it all lie the decisions made in the summer of 1975.

In that plan the disparate elements are pulled together far more systematically. The new beech hedges in the area of what had been the old kitchen garden have been formalized into two rectangular areas with a central alley labelled 'Tatiana's Walk', a reference to the opera *Eugene Onegin* which my wife had designed for the Royal Opera House. This led to a flight of steps and a vista straight through the Rose Garden. From one corner of the latter a descent leads to a winding walk which bends and twists its way all over the place through a thick shrubbery beneath trees, and in the middle of which there is a clearing with a 'Lime Tree Avenue' and a seat at either end. Off the upper end of the avenue, here called 'Mary Stewart', there is a yew bay close to a 'Nut Grove'. The bay looks towards an entrance to the winding pathway. Studying the plan I feel sure that its inspiration was not directly Michael Hartwell's injunctions for improvement but that these proposed innovations also owed something to my having seen aerial views of English rococo gardens at the opening of the eighteenth century. That was the period when the rigid formality of the age of Henry Wise and George London began to dissolve with the introduction of wilderness areas filled with what can only be described as squiggly walks of exactly this kind.

The result was the Serpentine, a winding walk that descended (not by way of steps, which I couldn't afford, but a simple gradient) from one corner of the Rose Garden, leading the visitor to the yew circus on the far side of the Field which was to become the Hilliard Garden. I plotted that walk with a pot of white paint and a brush directly onto the field grass late in August and our gardeners rotavated two long beds which gave the impression of winding into the distance. It was to be a rose walk, evidence that my fervour for filling the garden with the old varieties was as yet unabated. In fact this was a far more truncated squiggly walk than the one I originally envisaged. As nothing was drawn to scale, when it came to practical execution my initial concept proved far too ambitious for the space.

A second plan, dated autumn 1975, records what was actually done and also indicates that my mind was beginning to move towards hedging the Christmas Orchard. In the middle of Hartwell Grove, at the meeting of the great two avenues, there is a large circle, recording my desire for something important there as an eye-catcher. For the first time, too, Julia's little triangular garden immediately behind the Rose Garden vista is articulated as the Scandinavian Grove. This was a planting of silver birch trees which, as they grew, provided a stunning skyline with their sinuous branches and fluttering leaves, green in summer but, in the autumn, pale gold. The yew bay off what is called here 'Mary Queen of Scots' has a major vista through into the Christmas Orchard with four symmetrically planted yews framing it. That bay is unlabelled, but my wife during that autumn was busy working with Sir Frederick Ashton on his ballet based on Turgenev's *A Month in the Country*, which had its triumphant first night on 12 February 1976. This was to be the Ashton Arbour, a memorial to Julia's association with Fred in two of his greatest ballets. Ashton was touched and would always ask me how his arbour was coming on and, in response, I would indicate, with a gesture of my hand, what level the yew had reached.

That autumn there was a massive planting of conifers and shrubs of all kinds, eventually to hide the view of Elizabeth

Tudor from the Serpentine. Set against what was to be a tapestry of tall evergreens in contrasting shades and textures, which included *Thuja plicata*, *Chamaecyparis lawsoniana* 'Columnaris Glauca' and *C. l.* 'Triomf van Boskoop', there were evergreen shrubs, various viburnums, skimmias, Portugal laurel, elaeagnus, cotoneasters and the occasional single specimen, like the *Cornus mas*, beautiful in winter and which has grown to a quite astonishing size. In December the roses were thinned out from the Rose Garden and were replanted along this new walk together with a tremendous influx of new ones, totalling nearly sixty and epitomizing a kind of rose madness on my part. My penchant for roses as a kind of horticultural *Almanach de Gotha* is here all too apparent! On 8 December I wrote to Jan:

> We have been busy digging a vast rose walk serpentining through the Field, and shrubbing the Field through so that mystery and surprise will be created in ten years. It is now dotted with dwarf shrubs which will be huge in time.

That mood of creation and optimism continued through the winter and into the spring of 1976:

> The country is looking ever more marvellous. It is full of the promise of spring. Snowdrops and crocuses along the drive and your tulips are pushing their heads up in the Yew Garden in formal patterns. The Elizabeth Tudor walk is bursting with the five hundred daffodils which I planted flanking it.

In my diary late in February I recorded further activity:

> The gardeners came and the other half of the old kitchen garden was cleared . . . Beds were dug around the yew in the Ashton Arbour [by then named]. Bulbs pushing up along Elizabeth Tudor. Ordered an obelisk for the termination of

the Mary Queen of Scots walk. Decide to plant the edge of the field with specimen trees [the arboretum which never quite was].

That report of late February was followed by another enthusiastic communication to Jan in late April:

Quickly to write and say that your glorious red tulips [the 'Dillenburg' ones] gladdened our Easter holiday. They were planted in patterns in the little beds of box in the Yew Garden near the house and look quite marvellous . . . The break was glorious. I made another garden [the Hilliard] on the far side of the Field by moving about eight hundred old bricks and two or three tons of stone chippings. . .

In this way I recorded the making of the Hilliard Garden within the yew circus I had planted on the far side of the Field three years before. The turf was skimmed off and a circular bed was made in which I was to plant a *Rosa* 'Cantabrigiensis'. This was to form one of the garden's glories for many years. A vigorous and free-flowering shrub rose, it quickly rocketed up to three metres in height and as much in diameter. It burst into bloom in late May, a spectacle of myriad pale primrose single flowers, and was worth every penny of the sixty I paid for it that April. The beds surrounding it were filled with herbs, for it was to be a herb garden, and all of them were edged with up-ended old bricks and the whole area gravelled. Looking at the photographs now, I can be sure of one thing: I would never gain employment as a construction worker. But for me it was the creation of another little paradise distant from the house, and that indeed was one of the features that was to make The Laskett garden out of the ordinary. The Serpentine Walk was designed to lull the visitor into believing that he was about to undergo a traditional garden experience: the progression from the formal and architectural around the house to the looser plantings and then informal shrub and wild plantings. The shock of suddenly finding himself in a strictly formal garden again would be a satisfying jolt to the system. Today it still comes as a surprise, even to me. The bricks and gravel for the Hilliard Garden were paid for out of the fee I had received for my tiny book on Nicholas Hilliard, the Elizabethan miniaturist whose work I had fallen in love with as a schoolboy. When I was allowed for an hour or two to be a scholar in the Victoria & Albert Museum I spent my time cataloguing the collection of Elizabethan miniatures.

At the close of the same letter to Jan I went on to throw up a sinister flare as to what we were already into that year:

> At the moment we are in the grip of drought, the worst since 1821, no water anywhere and no rain. It is extraordinary and we may end up trudging with pails to get water from a central pump so dire is the situation.

The drought was simply terrible, a withering hand on our young trees and shrubs, for we were not there to water, and nor were we allowed to, for there was a ban on hosepipes. Instead we had to watch the plants die. The most spectacular loss was a vast handsome beech tree at the top of the drive, at least a century old. It never recovered from the shock of that summer. Down it came two years later. Of all of the losses the one I regretted most was a catalpa tree, a housewarming present from Patrick Plunket. He had a rule to give all his friends who set up a new house this tree. Lord Plunket was Deputy Master of the Household and the nearest thing that the Queen ever had to a brother. He was a delight and wickedly funny, but died tragically young of cancer. I had met him through the young Dufferins. He and Martin Charteris, the Queen's Secretary, were the two people who saw that the monarchy moved on to embrace the social revolution of the late sixties. Valiantly we ordered another catalpa, planted it and called it the Second Lord Plunket. It flourishes to this day. He would be amused.

The drought was not the only woe that year, for I embarked on a long series of public horrors imposed by government's savage cuts to the museum, the result of the necessity to cut public spending in the aftermath of the oil crisis. There were ghastly rows and unending union trouble. The garden seemed almost an emblem of where we had got, as I told Jan of our miserable summer during which 'we looked out on a parched garden, pale yellow with dying trees and shrubs' and how we 'had to bail out our bathwater in buckets and cart them down to save a few precious things. I cannot,' I wrote, 'tot up the plant obituary notices until next spring, but it looks dire...' 1976 was what is known as a bad year, saved only by a tortoiseshell cat adopting us, the Lady Torte de Shell, whom I greatly loved. The following year, 1977, was to be worse, but not, thankfully, for the garden.

ON THE AUTUMN 1975 PLAN A FLIGHT OF STEPS, WHICH DIDN'T yet exist, was sketched in. It led down to an open area of grass surrounded by trees which acted as a forecourt to the Rose Garden. The surrounding evergreens were planted in February 1975 and included various kinds of thuja such as *T. occidentalis* and *T. o.* 'Rheingold', as well as *Cryptomeria japonica* and an extensive list of cypresses: *Chamaecyparis lawsoniana* 'Pottenii', *C. l.* 'Ellwoodii', *C. l.* 'Burkwood Blue', *C. l.* 'Erecta Viridis' and *C. pisifera* 'Squarrosa'. Early in May 1977, in a diary entry recounting progress, I recorded my decision to create a garden there:

This year for the first time the Rose Garden actually looks like a Rose Garden. I cut the central bed into a circle and filled it with senecio and lavender and other grey foliage plants. The four amelanchiers in the spandrels have flowered for the first time this spring and the yew hedge is now four feet high and sprouting to take it even higher. The great project this year is a flight of steps down into a new garden before the Rose Garden.

The planting with grey foliage plants owed its inspiration to a great plantswoman, Mrs Desmond Underwood, whose nursery stand at the various Royal Horticultural Society shows was always a sophisticated source of wonder to me. On 1 September I wrote to Jan:

Very busy creating a new garden in honour of the Silver Jubilee. It is in the first part of the old tennis court before you reach the Rose Garden. It will be reached by a flight of steps, not yet built, but I did lay quite a nice little brick path across it and in the middle there is a circle of stone and an urn and, at the entrance to the Rose Garden, there are two reproduction statues of children in Roman kit, copies of late-seventeenth-century ones. The garden will have all white flowers against a backing of evergreens.

This was navvying for me on the grand scale, although builders were to add the simple flight of steps down, quite beyond my competence. The path is still there and Julia loyally always tells me that it is her favourite. The bricks were old ones. But what was the source of the garden? The fact that the planting was to be all white spells only one influence, the White Garden at Sissinghurst, which we had visited with Pam Hartwell in July two years before. It was one of Vita Sackville-West's most famous creations, planted in the main between 1949 and 1954, a phantasmagoria of fluttering white and silvery bloom held in by glossy green box hedges and silhouetted against dark green clipped yew. To that, I suppose, I would add Cecil Beaton's diktat that white flowers were the only chic ones. What a vision ours could be, I thought, as dusk fell on a summer's evening seemingly lit by its incandescent blooms.

A huge order was sent off that month to Carlisle's Loddon Nurseries for practically any white herbaceous flower they had – campanulas, delphiniums, asters and phlox head a gloriously long list. From Mattocks came the foundation stones of that garden, the 'Iceberg' roses, those which I had first seen grown in quantity in Beaton's garden at Reddish. They are still going strong after three decades and offer wonderful floral value with their second late flowering in early autumn. Even in its first year this garden was a resounding success.

This was the year of the Queen's Silver Jubilee, a celebration that went off remarkably successfully amid the economic gloom and general depression. I was among the crowds that stood outside Buckingham Palace and cheered on the great day in June when the Queen went to St Paul's Cathedral to give thanks. Soon after that I went to the palace for a reception for the Civil Service to mark the occasion. I recall attempting to tell the Queen that I was going to plant a garden in her honour, but she probably thought that I was completely dotty. But there it is to this day, a loyal tribute to the crown and not to be the last one.

Initially the garden's focal point was to be a sundial, a phoney one of course, which was delivered along with the boy warriors. Once placed in position it proved to be rather out of scale and remains the most itinerant of all our garden ornaments, never quite finding a home. It is generally true that an ornament will have to be moved at least once until it finds its last resting place as part of a perfect composition. Since the sundial proved redundant, an urn from my Brighton garden discharged that role until, on Cecil Beaton's death in 1980, I purchased at the Reddish House sale the sundial that had been at the centre of his lavender garden. It was Christopher Gibbs, a man of great taste who was later to advise the young Paul Getty but who was also a great gardener, who bid for it for me in the sale. With its sinuous rococo stem supporting an armillary sphere, it draws the composition together elegantly, a happy marriage in a garden graced with the 'Iceberg' roses and the white willowherb he loved. Cecil lives on not only in my memory but in this garden. That, I know, would have meant much to him.

THAT YEAR, 1977, WAS REMARKABLE FOR SOMETHING ELSE: MY serious incursion into writing garden history. That is caught in an outburst to Jan in a letter late in July of that year:

> Oh, I'm so fed up with publishers. . . I have no intention of writing to order [Thames & Hudson were trying to persuade me to write a cultural history of Britain in 50,000 words]. I shall be forty-two in August and life is too short for writing what they want. So, at last, I am right into my new subject and I've struck gold, the history of the theory and practice of gardening and actual gardens in England from 1500 to 1700, that is from Henry VIII's Privy Garden at Hampton Court to the advent of rococo Gardens of Delight. There has been a mass of literature on the eighteenth century over the last ten years, but nothing on the formal garden. There is so much material that I can hardly move and it is all virtually virgin. I'm stunned and feel as exhilarated by it as in my earliest research days at the Warburg Institute twenty years ago [from 1956 to 1959]. Here is a whole big new subject untouched and so many angles to it. The State Papers haven't been looked at for a start. . .

It was the making of The Laskett garden which had led me to garden history. I had joined the Garden History Society in 1974 but even in 1977 their journal still remained in stapled typescript, reflecting that this was a pioneer organization and a pioneer subject. Naturally, as an historian of the English renaissance, I had a curiosity about the gardens of the era fed by Georgina Masson's account of Italian renaissance gardens. That had already affected The Laskett garden with its quotations from the letters of Pliny the Younger describing his country and seaside villas. In the gardens, box had been planted and clipped into the initials of the owner. It can't be a coincidence that it was precisely then that I planted the Yew Garden with its first proper parterre, a quatrefoil superimposed onto a lozenge and two beds with R and J in box.

The books that did touch on the Tudor and early Stuart period were never more than nostalgic, though useful, explorations of the old gardening books like the Elizabethan John Gerard's *Herbal* (1597) or the Jacobean William Lawson's *A New Orchard and Garden* (1618). Most of the accounts I could find were those still suffused with the late Victorian quest for the gardens of Olde Englande. The palace and country-house garden was a new phenomenon in the sixteenth century. Where did it come from and what did it represent, not only in terms of its design and planting, but in those of ideas about the natural world and society? This was a tremendous inter-disciplinary subject which would stretch my mind in every direction, through history, art, literature and the world of ideas, not to forget those of practicality. The result was *The Renaissance Garden in England*, which was published simultaneously with the first exhibition ever mounted on the history of gardening in this country, staged at the Victoria & Albert Museum in 1979.

The Garden, like *The Destruction of the Country House*, is recognized to have been a landmark. It not only triggered the first listing of gardens under government aegis but lit the torch of garden history and restoration. Since then we have seen a steady procession of major publications on every aspect of British garden history, the advent of garden archaeology and the taking up of the subject in all its myriad aspects by academe. It was also through *The Garden* that I came to know Rosemary Verey.

All of this was taking place against a backcloth of appalling turbulence in my public career as I struggled, in the aftermath of the cuts, to get the museum free of government. In late December of Jubilee year I wrote to Jan: 'I hope 1978 will be less horrid than 1976 or 1977. I really couldn't endure it.' This was a cry of anguish from the heart, mollified only by the comfort that in spite of the ghastliness of everything there was still The Laskett, still the garden and, above all, still Julia to cling to: 'How lucky I am to have Julia and our blissful working loving professional existence, and this glorious house and garden which I love more than any other patch of earth in the world and which yearly becomes more us. Count your blessings. . .'

And I did.

Four

BRAVE SPIRIT AND THE
BRINGER OF RAIN

A T THIS JUNCTURE I WANT TO PAUSE IN MY NARRATIVE AND let the garden grow in the reader's imagination while I follow a different tack. Gardens are about friendships, none more so than ours, and many are embedded in the soil of The Laskett, in the form not only of plants but also of artifacts enshrining a memory of this or that person or this or that network of friends. But for anyone who creates a garden there gradually emerges as it were an inner circle, a group, soulmates in a way, with whom there is regular horticultural interchange and a mutual delight in each other's achievement. In the case of The Laskett garden during the years of its making our closest links were with two other gardens. One was in Gloucestershire, Barnsley House, near Cirencester, and the other in Herefordshire, at Whitfield, about ten miles west from us at Allensmore, but like us firmly south of Hereford itself. The people concerned are Rosemary Verey and George Clive.

Both knew The Laskett garden from quite early on, George Clive almost from its inception and Rosemary Verey from about 1980. We, in our turn, had the pleasure of following the progress they made in their gardens, very different in style and aspiration from our own creation. But each spurred the other on. Both of them span the length of this narrative and in the case of both I mourn their passing. George Clive died tragically young at fifty-eight in 1999 and Rosemary Verey two years later in her eighty-third year. To be without either is for us the removal of two points of reference, two anchors, who had watched and wondered as The Laskett garden burgeoned and changed almost beyond recognition. One of them was a quiet, unassuming English country gentleman, the epitome of a continuity and stability that is the essence of England. The other was again in her way an English woman of the shires but, by the time I got to know her, already attaining almost cult status as the representative of a certain phase in garden style, one which was to be exported across the globe. Before I resume my narrative I wish to plant them firmly at the heart of the garden story.

I FIRST MET ROSEMARY ON THE OCCASION OF *THE GARDEN* exhibition at the Victoria & Albert Museum, but it was not until the middle of the 1980s, after her husband David had died, that it became an active friendship, with constant toing and froing between Barnsley and The Laskett. Looking back, I can understand why we were drawn to each other. My approach to gardening had been through history. So, in its way, had been hers, for her first major book, *Classic Garden Design*, which appeared in 1984, has for its subtitle *How to Adapt and Recreate Garden Features of the Past*. In her preface she explained her aim:

> Numerous books have been written on the history of gardens, but they are often both too scholarly and too unspecific for practical gardeners wishing to reconstruct or adapt features that impress them. My intention in writing this book has been to provide an introduction to garden history by bringing the subject alive to gardeners, and to look at the history and design of different parts of the garden in order to show how these can be rich sources of ideas.

This remains still by far her most important book, for it opened up the possibility for everyone to adapt those elements of what was essentially the old formal country-house garden style into gardens whose compass was of a modest late-twentieth-century kind, where labour resources were limited. There were chapters, for example, on topiary, on training hedges into interesting shapes and on laying out a knot garden or a potager. At that date only those with access to rare books would have found a way into such mysteries. To her the past was a way of moving forward, although the Barnsley style could never have taken off without the twin factors of the heritage country-house cult and the advent of serious garden history and restoration, both eighties phenomena.

That way of going back in order to go forward is summed up in an early encounter I had with her at the Chelsea Flower Show. I had been struggling with how to do yew topiary. I couldn't find out anything about it from the books then in print. Bumping into Rosemary I opined on that fact, to which she immediately replied: 'Nathaniel Lloyd, *Garden Craftsmanship in Yew and Box*.' I went at once to one of the antiquarian bookstands nearby and was lucky. They had a copy. The book was published in 1925 and cost me what I considered the large sum of £25. But it is evidence that subjects such as topiary, which she dealt with in *Classic Garden Design*, had had nothing written about them for sixty years. It is not surprising, therefore, that in 1989, when I produced the first book on formal gardens since 1892, *Creating Small Formal Gardens*, the dedication read: 'For Rosemary Verey, my Garden Muse.' The tribute was truly meant.

That I was to write about garden design at all I owe to Rosemary. In 1985 Alison Cathie, the publishing director of Conran Octopus, came to see me with a proposal that I should write a book on small garden design. I was attracted to the idea but naturally tremulous, bearing in mind that I had had no formal horticultural training. I rang Rosemary and asked her opinion. 'Write it,' she said. 'If you get stuck I'll help you.' But I didn't get stuck, and *Creating Small Gardens*, which appeared in 1986, remains in print to this day in more languages than I care to remember, and it was to be the first of a succession of design books I wrote through the late eighties into the early nineties. But the initial impulse goes back to Rosemary. She was the great encourager, and not only to me but to many others whose careers in the sphere of gardening were made possible by a kindly word from her.

Although she cultivated a lady-of-the-manor presence with silk dress and strings of pearls, she was in fact quite a bluestocking, having been educated at University College, London, where she went to read Mathematics and Economics. As her fame grew and America adopted her she rather revelled in her celebrity. There was a spiky side to her, but I never came up against that. But then her preference was always for men rather than women. On arrival at The Laskett the ritual would always be a fond kiss on the lips and embrace between us and then a glance over my shoulder towards my wife and, 'Hallo, Julia.' But that was the nature of the beast.

Barnsley House came to her from her husband's family in 1951, and gardening came even later, when her hunting career reached its end and her several children had grown up. It was only then that she seriously turned her attention to transforming the four acres around the stone three-storey William and Mary house. What we saw when we first went to Barnsley in the early eighties was a garden that was essentially a creation from the sixties onwards. Through her own writings and the endless photographs that appeared, this became one of the most famous and influential gardens of the eighties. Thousands visited it each year, making pilgrimage to what had become a horticultural shrine, over which Rosemary benignly presided.

I was entranced by it. It had so much that I aspired to at The Laskett: the neat clipped box beds delineating architectural enclosures for plants; the Knot Garden based on an Elizabethan pattern with its four great topiary holly 'Golden King' sentinels; the stately vistas to the Temple viewed across

The Luskett garden as we found it, winter 1972-73

23 Colne Road

The Lady Torte de Shell, February 1977

With John Piper at Fawley
Bottom, June 1976

John Fowler's box
garden in winter

With Cecil Beaton,
after his stroke

The Serpentine Walk is cut, 1975

The Yew Garden in winter, 1977

With Robert and Mollie Salisbury at Cranborne, April 1976

Planting my first tiny box parterre in the Yew Garden, spring 1977

The Tradescant Garden

My first topiary initial
R in the Yew Garden

The Hilliard Garden as
I first laid it out, 1976

The Rose Garden,
August 1975

Beloved Muff

Joan Henderson

A gardening legend:
Mien Ruys

With Rosemary at Barnsley, summer 1983

*Carola Oman and Patch before Frewin Hall, Oxford,
with the All Souls pinnacle behind, 1911*

*Nymph and shepherd: Cecil Beaton's
photograph a few days after the wedding*

Thirty years on

a pond, and the Laburnum Tunnel closed by a splashing fountain. I suppose what I most admired was her plantsmanship, her ever-changing colour combinations and her incredible ability to fill borders throughout the flowering season with such a dazzling array of contrasting yet harmonious plants. That ability I knew I could never rival. Nor her attention to detail which, as I've already written, seems to me to be an especially female garden attribute.

Yet, if pressed, Barnsley lacked what I coveted most, mystery and surprise. Virtually everything was seen at a glance. That surprised me on my first visit, because photographs in books inevitably depicted this or that section of the garden and gave no idea that they were in fact in such close proximity to each other. The potager, which had to be reached by passing through a garden gate and crossing a track, alone had that quality of romantic discovery as some hidden jewel. And, although it was a miracle of beauty, it was hardly practical. It was not the kitchen garden of someone who cooks, which must be far more robust. No one can really give thought to harvesting the vegetables and at the same time be concerned with preserving the patterns, colours and textures of their design. Nonetheless, Barnsley was full of things recently done which I wanted to know about and introduce to The Laskett.

I never wrote a proper account of any of those visits in my diary, except one in August 1987, which we made in the aftermath of lunching with Princess Michael of Kent at Nether Lypiatt, to which Rosemary had also been invited. It was a beautiful summer's day. I print it for what it is worth:

> By the time that we got to the garden at Barnsley to collect the box hedging we were really knocked out. Never mind, Rosemary Verey is one of life's enhancers, the garden of unbelievable loveliness and joy. It is always wonderful to tour it and suggest ideas and alterations, this time resiting a statue of her by Simon Verity, fast disappearing through the lush growth of

shrubbery. And then we had dramas because we were shown what *Homes and Gardens* intended to use for the article on our garden, and it was very upsetting. This, in the end, resolved itself when mercifully the close-up of a bust in a yew hedge was dropped and Jerry Harpur's [the garden photographer] wonderful vista of the Jubilee into the Rose Garden was put in. Rosemary is moving out of the great house and the cottage joined to it is being transformed for her, including a conservatory with Ionic pillars which will be very splendid.

That was the day we collected the box to add low containing hedges to the beds in the Rose Garden. It was always known to us as Verey Box. Rosemary was on the brink of moving into what was called The Close, a small separate house, yet attached to the main one. Its most signal feature was to be its conservatory with a grotto by the sculptor Simon Verity. The article referred to was the first one ever to appear on our garden. We were naturally tremulous, well aware that it did not as yet match up to the marvels of Barnsley.

That article appeared fifteen years ago in November 1987. When Rosemary toured The Laskett garden in order to write it, I was terribly nervous and aware of its shortcomings and rather thrown by her when, on sitting down on a bench, she exclaimed, 'It's just like the Victoria & Albert Museum.' Slightly horrified, I said, 'What do you mean?' 'Oh,' came the reply, 'it's all corridors with things at the end of them.' To a degree she was right, but on re-reading the article a decade and a half on, and after enormous changes to the garden since it was written, I am struck by her perception of our intent. As this was our debut in print it is perhaps worth quoting some of her words:

Sir Roy Strong, art historian and writer, admits that he is a theatre designer *manqué*. It is, of course, the profession for which his wife, Julia Trevelyan Oman, is distinguished. At their home in Herefordshire they have combined their talents to create a remarkable garden, carved from a 3-acre field. . .

I know of no other husband and wife since the war who have attempted such an ambitious garden, so firmly based on structure, architecture and geometry. To enrich the Elizabethan formality, Roy has a wonderful eye for perspective, a sense of scale and the ability to place sculpture to its best advantage. . .

Roy's approach to his garden is very individual, even in his methods of planning. The formal gardens he drew out to conventional practice, on paper. But the pattern of the Serpentine Walk was outlined in white paint on to the rough field itself by Roy.

As you end your journey, you realise that everything in the garden records an event in Roy's and Julia's life. The stories will accumulate and the garden will develop but, true to Elizabethan style, it will remain essentially a garden whose vistas are contained within its boundaries . . . This remarkable garden unites the strengths of both the sixteenth and twentieth centuries.

It was to be through Rosemary that in 1989 I was asked to design and train the hedges and topiary at Highgrove for the Prince of Wales. Later still she brought me in to design an Italian garden for Sir Elton John. In that case, I could only achieve it if one of the gardens she had designed for the pop star was demolished. It was indeed an embarrassing conclusion, but Rosemary took it in good heart, forwarding to me the ground plans in her possession and wishing me luck.

But I like to think of her most of all in terms of the dialogue between the two gardens. I would go round Barnsley suggesting this and that. Once she was concerned that her holly cake-stand was such a failure. I pointed out to her that all she had to do was chop out every other 'shelf', which would then give it the boldness of silhouette it lacked. 'I'll do that later this afternoon,' and she did. On looking at the sixty-yard-long clipped leylandii hedge at The Laskett, which had a straight top, she said, 'You love pompoms. Why don't you train it into something?' And I did. She took one look at the field hedge up the drive and said, 'Why on earth don't you cut it into a shape?' And, once again, I did. On hearing me groaning that a copper beech had self-seeded where I didn't want it, she said, 'Why don't you topiarize it?' Of course, I did. On her last visit here she looked at the *Juniper communis* 'Hibernica', which I had planted over twenty years before at the front of the house, and said: 'They only last twenty-five years. If I were you I'd buy some in now to replace them when the time comes.' And I always remember her advice, when I had been cornered by her into appearing in a gardening quiz in aid of charity. I said that I was hopeless over plants and their diseases and some person was bound to ask something awkward concerning some ghastly affliction that had seized their aspidistra. 'Don't worry,' she said. 'Say what I always say. "Dig it up, throw it away and buy a new one."'

She very much took in the originality of The Laskett. I remember her, for instance, looking at one of our beech hedges which had 'windows' cut into it. It was something Lanning Roper had told her to do to the ones at Barnsley. As she stared at them she suddenly realized what Lanning had meant, because to make a window, trunks, acting as glazing bars, had of course to be left in situ to support the hedge higher up. That caught her eye for detail, but I think what amazed her the most was the vast scale of it all and its unashamed theatricality.

Rosemary would always arrive at The Laskett with a gift of plants, and we would never leave Barnsley without some treasure in the back of the car. Often they were more than generous ones, like four-foot-high, ready-trained, golden box cones, which would have cost a small fortune from any nursery. She instinctively knew that whatever it was it was going to an appreciative home. My Garden Diary occasionally records the advent of such gifts. In 1987 in April I noted: Planted Rosemary Verey's plants. . . *Thymus vulgaris* 'Silver Posie', *Salvia argentea* and *Lychnis coronaria* 'Alba'. Two months later again: Planted Rosemary Verey's plants: *Salvia sclarea* var. *turkestanica, Aster novae-angliae* 'Andenken an Elma Pötschke' and *Lychnis flos-jovis*. She was always 'discovering' plants. One year it would be bidens, another a ground-cover salvia with the prettiest blue flowers, and yet another attempting to restore golden privet to favour. All of these enthusiasms left their mark permanently or temporarily on our garden. But the most refreshing quality she had, as far as I was concerned, was that she was someone with whom I could walk around the garden and have a serious constructive conversation.

In 1998 she was eighty and the occasion was marked by a series of fêtes; we went to all three. One was a dinner at the Tate Gallery on Millbank, the second another dinner, this time at the Garrick Club, and the third, a surprise, to which the Prince of Wales came, was on a private aerodrome in Gloucestershire. At the time I wrote:

This is 'Rosemary Verey is eighty' week. Although that doesn't actually happen until 21st December no less than three parties are being held in her honour. Two were London-based, one at the Tate Gallery given by its chairman, David Verey, a remote connexion, and the other by Arthur Reynolds [an American friend of Rosemary's] at the Garrick Club, courtesy of me. The first was for *tous les grands*, or as *tous* as could be garnered, mainly those whose gardens had figured in Rosemary's television series, like the Carringtons, the Cavendishes, the Astors and the Tollemaches ... The next night some twenty gathered at the Garrick, a much cosier occasion and really far more enjoyable ... Still one must be grateful for Rosemary. One owes her so much and she soldiers on, a brave spirit.

Brave spirit indeed. I somehow knew, two years later, that when she went into Cheltenham Hospital with a perforated intestine that would be the end, and so it proved to be. During that anxious period I made a point of sending her a pretty postcard as often as I could, for the sick gain much from being remembered by those still caught up in the rush of daily life. Usually in no state to read, they gain joy from looking at the picture. In her case it was always one of a garden or a flower.

I was honoured and touched to be asked by the family to give the keynote address at her service of thanksgiving held in a packed church in Cirencester on 24 July 2001. This is what I said:

I only knew Rosemary from her sixties onwards. My lasting vision of her is of a lady in a silk dress, her neck swathed in pearls, her hair immaculate, a gracious if at times a formidable presence. To foreigners she fulfilled exactly their dream image of an English country gentlewoman, one who would then promptly don sensible shoes and a quilted jacket and traipse around the garden. I think that she was fully conscious of meeting such expectations for visitors to Barnsley. Although she always mourned the loss of David, widowhood in a way gave Rosemary a new lease of life, enabling her to respond fully to her role as a star of the horticultural world. And she loved every minute of it.

What were the roots of Rosemary's distinctive garden style? Her native Gloucestershire must rank high, for she lived and gardened in that part of England which had seen the creation of some of the great gardens of the Arts and Crafts Movement in the decades before 1914. Those impulses are summed up in Rodmarton Manor, in which all the threads that formulated that style are still entwined: memories of William Morris with his advocacy of native plants, the plea for formality of Reginald Blomfield, whose *The Formal Garden in England* held up the manor-house gardens of the Tudor and Stuart eras as his ideal, the horticultural inspiration of William Robinson with his love of naturalistic planting, and, of course, the creations of Edwin Lutyens and Gertrude Jekyll. Rosemary had no taste for Italianate formality of the type we find at Harold Peto's Iford Manor, or for Modernism, which impinged from the 1930s onwards, or, for that matter, for Dame Sylvia Crowe's stance that, even in the smallest garden, the model to follow was that of a 'Capability' Brown landscape.

Any glance along Rosemary's bookshelves provided a ready key to what triggered her style, for there were the works of William Turner and William Lawson, John Worlidge and John Evelyn, Stephen Switzer and Humphry Repton. She liked these authors to speak directly to her without the often dead hand of the academic historian intervening. But what all of this means is that her art was a reaching backwards in order, as she saw it, to go forwards. The English gardening tradition in the twentieth century had suffered two tremendous blows. The first, of course, was two World Wars. By 1945 gardens on a large scale were either abandoned or in retreat. Secondly, Modernism, and along with it public landscaping, had marginalized private garden making. Within that context her promotion of a style that was in essence a picking up of the threads severed by 1914 was all the more extraordinary. That it was successful was due not only to the ethos of the period but also to her response to present-day realities.

Although Barnsley was begun in the nineteen sixties it was the quintessential garden of what were the heritage decades of the last century, the nineteen seventies and eighties. These were the years often of social unease along with an acute awarenesss of the country's fall from greatness, a mood that fuelled a deep sense of looking back, which we find reflected above all in the country-house cult. The garden style of Barnsley firmly belongs to that, but its secret lay in the fact that it recast the elements of the past in terms of an accessible present. Garden elements which, up until then, were seen to be the prerogative of those only with lordly acres and many gardeners, were suddenly seen to be adaptable into quite small spaces in gardens where the owners were the only labour.

All the signature elements of Rosemary's garden style are quite small. They are stylish and elegant but never over-grand or pretentious: a tiny knot garden, a laburnum tunnel, a pretty potager with narrow brick paths, box-edged herb beds, a small classical temple reflected in a modest pool. Her designs were never wholly architectural in the sense of creating separate rooms. Rather she created spaces, ones whose success lay in contrasting structure and planting, one area smoothly eliding into another without any sense of visual disjunction. Rosemary had an extraordinary sensitivity to colour and detail which is one of the greatest attributes of women in the garden. Every visit to Barnsley, regardless of the season, was a lesson in planting in terms of shrub and plant form, flower colour and leaf shape. It was the richness of it that was always so breathtaking, plus the attention to the smallest detail so that one swathe of planting seemingly succeeded another effortlessly, although one knew it had been planned down to the last flowerhead.

The fact that she wrote, above all her book on *Classic Garden Design*, and even more that Barnsley was accessible to the public, meant that she opened the eyes of a whole generation of garden-makers tired of dreary island beds and groundcover planting. They came away rich and inspired and also, which was central to her vision, with an awareness that gardening was about style. The Verey style recast the English garden repertory of the decades before 1914 and transmitted it to a hugely expanded middle class hungry for style in the garden. That is no mean achievement. As a consequence Barnsley and Rosemary have a secure and honoured niche in the annals of this country's garden history.

In many ways the motivating ideas for Barnsley were not so dissimilar from those that formed the genesis of The Laskett. In different ways we had both gone back, both been concerned with evoking the timeless serenity of a vanished era in the terms of today. And yet the resulting gardens are as dissimilar as they are similar. Both cover the same acreage but orchestrate the available space quite differently. The result at Barnsley is that the garden appears quite small whereas at The Laskett the treatment of the same space makes it seem far larger than it really is. Rosemary never engaged with the world of ideas, seeking instead to create a unique and timeless atmosphere and to dazzle by means of pyrotechnic plantsmanship. In sharp contrast, behind The Laskett lies a world of allusion. Add to that an even larger and more fundamental divide. Barnsley was not a shared vision, for David, her husband, figured only marginally in the garden's story, whereas The Laskett from its inception has always been the work of two people with a single vision, one which, as the eighties gave way to the nineties, was to evolve and change.

But let me end with an account of her funeral, one of the most moving to which I have ever been. Such occasions are often a kind of summation of a person, a crystallization of the many aspects of a character threaded amidst time-hallowed ritual. It was so on that occasion.

We drove down on a dry but lustreless day to Barnsley for Rosemary's funeral. We arrived at about 11 a.m. and parked the car in the field near the house and made our way to the church. It was already almost packed. We were shown to a couple of seats in the north aisle. The church was beautifully decorated, as was appropriate, with garden flowers in the colours she loved, violet, lavender and purple with splashes of gold. The coffin sat in the chancel. At just before noon the Prince of Wales arrived and took his place in the front pew. . .

At the close of the service, which was of great simplicity:

We all followed out into that typical English churchyard and gathered around the grave for the committal. Each of the family threw a handful of soil onto the coffin. And then it was all over. I said to the cleric as we left: 'It was all as she would have wished it,' to which he replied: 'Yes. If it hadn't been, there would have been some knocking.'

The whole congregation was asked back to the house. There's always a certain poignancy about such occasions . . . We wandered through the garden which was really at its height, the panicles in the laburnum tunnel forming a water-fall of yellow above the purple allium flowerheads below. But the knot garden needed replanting. We walked to the potager, which was magical, surely her most original and beautiful innovation. Virtually useless as a kitchen garden, but as a work of art it cast its spell. I'm so glad that so many of the plants from her garden are at The Laskett, above all the clipped golden hollies in the Flower Garden, which stand as a testimony to our friendship.

It was a happy day with a dream-like quality, all about a vision of England and Englishness which now seems under siege and about to slip away. But its centuries-old ritual still exerts its power of consolation. As Charles Verey [her son] put it so well, 'Today we see her off on her journey.' I can't think of a better way to go.

GEORGE CLIVE WAS SOMEONE CLOSE TO US, BUT UNKNOWN TO a wider world. Let me begin with the account of his Service of Thanksgiving on St George's Day, 23 April 1999. He had died of cancer only ten days before:

We got up at 5 a.m. in London to drive down for George Clive's Service of Thanksgiving at Wormbridge Church. It was raining when we rose and it was raining still when we went to bed at 10.30 p.m. 'George, the bringer of rain', as he was known to us because every time he came to see the garden it poured, had lived up to his reputation. This was an occasion to remind anyone that the death of a shy, gentle man who loved trees and the countryside was not in vain. So many people, so much affection, a kaleidoscope of county and country, the grand and the humble, the odd and the ordinary, family and friends bound together to celebrate the memory of one man. It was a rite of passage of a kind only known in the country and to England and I give thanks for it. . .

. . .the church was wonderfully decorated. There were lilies on the altar flanked by huge branches of trees and the nave seemed, when I was able to glance in that direction, to be bedizened with the fresh green leaves of spring. At the back the font, I gathered, was adorned with some of George's favourite plants brought from Whitfield. Every seat was labelled. We sat on chairs in front of the choir stalls and there were more chairs on either side of the aisle . . . the service consisted of a few hymns, a reading from a psalm, another from Ezekiel about the cedar tree, very beautiful, and then one read rather badly by the Dean of Hereford from a book entitled *The Man who Planted Trees*, touching, then Thomas Pakenham's address . . . And then just everyone was asked back to the house afterwards. . .

It is always the same at these affairs, a terrible feeling of the 'end of something' engulfs me. As we walked up the steps to the front door I was seized with the memory of how we stood there on a warm summer night watching the great comet hurtle across the heavens. Opposite lay George's lakes and fountains stretching away from the house. How often we walked this ground to admire the waxen blossoms of his magnolias or the rarities of his secret garden. And now an era has come to an end.

This was a celebration of a much-loved man whose ashes had been scattered among the giant Californian Redwoods of his estate only a few days before.

George Clive had entered our lives through his cousin, Antonia Fraser, the historical biographer, an old friend who had signalled her aunt, Lady Mary Clive (one of the sisters of the head of the formidable Pakenham clan, the late Lord Longford), that we had bought a house not far distant from Whitfield. I recall the initial phone call from her asking us over and me saying, 'I know that you are the first hermit in Herefordshire, but you happen to be talking to the second.' But Whitfield quickly became part of our life and George, in particular, became a great friend stretching over twenty-five years. From what I have said it will already be clear that through his mother George was a Pakenham, an intellectual dynasty of which at least one other member had a horticultural passion. Dendrological would perhaps be the better word, for George's cousin Thomas, the present Lord Longford, who gave the funeral address, was not only a distinguished historian but also the author of the bestseller *Meetings with Remarkable Trees*. Thomas and George used to trump each other's aces over the trees they had seen and occasionally in the book George can be spied as the anonymous figure in the photograph, placed by his cousin to establish the scale of a particular tree. Green fingers were also inherited by George's sister, Alice, Viscountess Boyd, a member of the Council of the Royal Horticultural Society and the chatelaine of a five-acre garden at Ince Castle at Saltash in Cornwall. Through her marriage into the Lennox-Boyds we came to meet her sister-in-law, Arabella Lennox-Boyd, a garden designer of great distinction, the winner of a succession of gold medals at the Chelsea Flower Show and the creator of a remarkable garden of her own at Gresgarth in Lancashire.

But what of Whitfield? Whitfield was purchased by the Clive family in 1796. It had already been landscaped by that date with oak groves and a beech walk. Edward Bolton Clive was a friend of Uvedale Price, one of the major proponents of the new Picturesque garden style at the close of the eighteenth century. Tree planting must have run in the Clive family for the giant Redwoods at Whitfield had been planted by the Rev. Archer Clive in the year of the Great Exhibition, 1851, twenty of them, the biggest in any group in Britain. The seeds had only arrived in Britain in 1843, eight years before, and the tallest is now 148 feet high. In 1872 it was written that 'the great charms of Whitfield are to be found in the sylvan scenery amid which it is situated, and the pleasant air of tranquillity which pervades it'. That was still true of it under George's aegis at the close of the twentieth century. Educated at Eton and Christ Church, Oxford, the shy but stubborn George had come into this vast estate as a child. The depradations of death and tax had left it in a sorry state, from which his mother rescued it post-war, tearing down the two vast Victorian wings and returning it to its elegant Georgian proportions. George was to leave his mark not on the house but across the acres that surrounded it.

With George I found myself in contact with a very different tradition from the suburban gardening of my childhood or the garden-making of the kind I'd experienced at Reddish or King John's Hunting Lodge or at Oving. This was a man who thought in terms of landscape gardening, of planting woods, groves, copses, avenues as well as specimen trees over hundreds of acres. It was gardening of a vastly different kind from The Laskett, but that was irrelevant. There was huge exhilaration to be had from knowing someone who could still garden in the eighteenth-century terms we associate with 'Capability' Brown and Repton.

The area at Whitfield which we knew best, however, was that around the house. At the back French windows opened out from the library dining-room onto a stone terrace flanked by pleached limes. This led onto a large rectangle of immaculately kept lawn held in by an old yew hedge, topped by whimsical topiary. Beyond lay parkland. This was the site of what once must have been an Edwardian flower garden, long since grassed over, but to which George added a handsome fountain, which came from Copt Hall, Essex, as a focal point. Strange to say I do not recall ever having seen that fountain working. I always longed for him to put back a formal garden here once again, but, true to the thrust of his horticultural interests, he never did. It was not that he was uninterested in other forms of garden-making, quite the contrary, but his vision was firmly elsewhere.

I once recorded him thus: 'He was a large, fair-haired, blue-eyed man with a stammer which only left him when he spoke on the telephone. He was a born countryman, all tweeds and corduroy worn out of shape and totally unconscious of his appearance . . . He loved his garden and had a phenomenal knowledge of trees and plants.' To that one can add agriculture, contemporary literature and history, for he was hugely well read. In that sense he was the quintessence of the old country-house owner who was expected not only to know how to manage his estates productively but also to be a person of intellectual cultivation. The last fact explains why dinner at Whitfield was always an occasion to be savoured, for there was sure to be good and informed conversation, with an interesting assembly of guests. His talents were recognized, for he was on the National Trust's Estates and Gardens panels and was a great force behind the National Council for the Conservation of Plants and Gardens, acting for a period as its secretary for our part of the country. The estate itself was a pioneering model in terms of good husbandry and plant conservation, wild flowers being close to George's heart.

His creation we knew best was the approach to the house, for the drive was lined with a handsome avenue of mature lime trees, which he had planted as a young man and which had grown so well that he was able to take out alternate trees. Driving along that avenue, one caught glimpses to the left of his reordering of the terrain in the front of the house, which was sited on the summit of a gentle slope. There was already a pond in front of it, but in 1968, when he was still only in his late twenties, George enlarged that. Seven years later a canal was excavated to lead to a new, even larger pond, which was dotted with islands, on one of which there was a ruined castle and whose focal point was a large statue of a warrior silhouetted against the horizon. Much of this George had created with his own hands, lugging around huge boulders and siting them to effect. Standing in front of the house this was an extraordinarily bold, painterly composition: the waters, framed by trees, stretching into the distance shimmering in the light, and the eye taken even further by an avenue of poplars disappearing towards the horizon. In the middle of the first pond he had introduced a *jet d'eau*, thrusting up, I would guess, ten metres or so. As far as I could deduce, it was only put on for visitors. Sometimes he would forget to do it, and then say, 'Just a minute,' disappear, and then, suddenly, up it would shoot into the air. His last project had been a bubbling fountain in the forecourt of the house, which was to act as a source for the whole composition.

This was garden-making of a far different kind from any other we had so far encountered, reminding us that gardening is a many-roomed mansion. When The Laskett was opened for the first time for a few days to small groups, I suggested it was twinned with a visit to Whitfield, as the contrast was so very striking. It set our garden, by then billed as the largest formal garden to be planted since 1945, sharply into context. Compared with the rolling acres of Whitfield it was minute.

The interchange with Whitfield was constant, so much so that we took it for granted. Only once did I put pen to paper to capture something of it as a garden experience. The entry is for 15 March 1998:

Spring came remarkably early this year, February in fact, which, after weeks of deluge, was marked by warmth and sun on such a scale that by early March we found the peach trees already in blossom. So it was no surprise when we found a message on the answerphone from George Clive asking us to lunch at Whitfield. 'The magnolias are at their prime.' George Clive is a tree man and has a park to boot, for it is really no use being the one without the other. He's seen our garden since it was a blank field. When we came in 1973 I recall his mother, Lady Mary Clive, ringing and asking us for tea. She was there today, aged ninety, her brain as sharp as ever. . .

It's difficult to think that the house was abandoned in the thirties because of the disappearance of staff or that the Victorian wings were demolished. The effect is that it's always been like that, a spacious eighteenth-century house with symmetrical bow windows set high on a slope reflected in the lake in front of it. The lake was made by George and really the garden's the thing. There are some seventy varieties of magnolia, pink, white, magenta and every variable flush of one into the other. They were superbly planted, some thrusting up to be reflected in the water, others against huge tapestries of dark green yew. On arrival we all, bit by bit, fell out of our cars and wandered around, gaping and gasping with delight as the sun caught the water and the trees. Penny Graham [George's partner] . . . had to leave after lunch to go to a friend who was dying of cancer. I said, 'Live every day as your last.' She said, in reply, 'Live every day as your first.' And I felt the warmth of the sun on my face and I thought that this wouldn't have been a bad last day – friends, happiness, strolling through the explosion that is spring wrapt into its beauty. The magic of the country house, its park and garden never ceases to lose its hold on me as a perfection of life.

That vignette of one visit to Whitfield encapsulates an experience relived many times over the years that we knew George. He never wrote down the names of all those varieties of magnolia. With foresight, after his death, his sister Alice sought out the magnolia expert, himself ill, and got on record what was a precious heritage. The fact of the matter was George never needed to label the trees because he knew each and every one on sight. Seventy was a huge number, for there are only eighty species of magnolia in all. Those placed around the lake were of the deciduous variety which flower in spring. George's enthusiasm for them was shared by his cousin Thomas. Somehow what would seem an appalling wait for their first flowering – thirty years in some cases – was an attraction rather than a deterrent to them both. Of course, George had the commoner shrub-like magnolias, like stellata and its hybrids, which are met with time and again as the one flowering tree in a small garden, but soaring above them were varieties like *campbelli*, a stunning sight in flower, but one for which the owner must wait twenty to thirty years. Such trees demand a parkland backcloth to be set off to advantage, their pink goblet-shaped blossoms spangled to the height of a forest tree. As we tagged along behind him he would move from one magnolia to another, purring satisfaction as he inspected a solitary bloom, and mutter a name like 'Charles Raffill' or 'Kew's Surprise'. We could only listen in wonder. To none of this could we ever aspire.

Those visits were not one-way but two. The one I recall most vividly to our garden was when he brought over the novelist Iris Murdoch and her husband John Bayley, along with Grey and Nietie Gowrie. Grey for a time had been Minister for the Arts in Margaret Thatcher's government. Poor Iris and John looked like two refugees from Eastern Europe before the Iron Curtain fell. Their interest in gardens and their knowledge of the natural world was nil.

We also met George at the local meetings of the National Council for the Conservation of Plants and Gardens when he would arrive with a shooting picnic, producing hot baked potatoes wrapped in foil and good wine. These were extraordinarily enjoyable gatherings of local gardening types, everyone in wellington boots or cloggies and an assortment of tweeds, Barbours, woollies and rain-resistant clothing, not to mention headgear of a kind only to be seen in the English shires. Most began with a lecture in some crumbling icy village hall in which we picnicked, followed by a visit to one or more garden. One meeting I remember was at Berrington Hall, once the seat of the Lords Crawley but now a National Trust property, where in the old walled kitchen garden they were putting together a collection of historic Herefordshire apples. On a blackboard there was a list of the missing varieties. By the close of the meeting one had turned up.

Then there was the annual party held in amiable chaos in Whitfield itself with George shuffling around, giving everyone he talked to equal attention. Add to that the annual general meeting, at which he presided as a perfectly appalling chairman, and the annual plant sale to raise funds for the society. To that members came with plants they had propagated themselves. Often as not it was staged at Hergest Croft at Kington in the north of the county, which has a splendid garden and arboretum, the creation of four generations of the Banks family. There too one touches local gardening connections, for Lawrence Banks held office in the Royal Horticultural Society and his wife Elizabeth, another distinguished garden designer, garnered gold medals at the Chelsea Flower Show, running neck and neck with Arabella Lennox-Boyd. But in the country it was George's role to act as the catalyst drawing the Herefordshire gardening fraternity together.

He was himself, as can be seen, essentially a plantsman, and his own secret garden lay to one side of the first lake in front of the house. There he constructed an asymmetrical arrangement of large stones forming low walls and bays to offset a dazzling display of his favourite plants. Ferns he loved, and meconopsis. Always, when the latter were in flower with their intense blue, we would be bidden to make haste and contemplate the blooms in the gathering darkness before we went inside to dine. Once we gave him a great chunk of the Oman agapanthus, which I last saw thriving in what used to be an orangery but which housed his collection of camellias and opened on to the old walled kitchen garden. Our last gift to him was of a rare local apple, 'Herefordshire Beefing', which Julia had grafted from a tree in our orchard.

In turn our garden was enriched by him over the years. Once he arrived with a hunk of *Crinum* x *powellii*, which, I regret to say, failed to flourish. More memorable was his gift of a specimen tree, a sassafras. It came from the nursery of the Savill Gardens at Windsor. As I turn the pages of my books on trees it reads: 'Rare; a few gardens in the South of England' and 'Not suitable for the UK'. This is a real collector's tree and I am happy to write that, with careful nurturing, it has flourished here and is now over four metres in height, for it arrived quite tiny. It is planted along the walk at the back of The Folly, south facing. As the books say it has leaves of 'curiously varied shapes . . . all pale or deep sub-shiny green above a yellow-pink petiole . . . Autumn colours yellow-pink and finally orange.' Every time we pass it we salute what is known to us simply as 'George's Tree'.

There were no cowslips at The Laskett when we arrived here. On one of his many visits to us George arrived with a clump of them from Whitfield. Thanks to that one clump, and following Mollie Salisbury's advice on not cutting the grass until flowers have had a chance to seed, the garden is now carpeted with them in springtime. Not a bad legacy. In spite of the vast discrepancy between our garden styles, we miss that interchange, an intangible relationship to explain, for in many ways he was a taciturn man, quickly reduced to silence. Julia I think knew him better, for Whitfield being a house where the old courtesies still prevailed, I was always placed to his mother's right, and Julia to George's. I used to spy them at the other end of the table deep in garden talk, wondering what had transpired.

His was an affectionate and knowledgeable presence, a benign influence on our garden. Above all, during those years when we were struggling to establish it, never at any point did he view what we were doing with derision, as so many of our visitors, by implication, did. Knowing the nature of plants, he knew that our fledgling garden would grow and thrive, and his letters of thanks, after many an evening spent here with dinner prefaced by the inevitable garden tour, always explode with amazement at what we had managed to achieve since his last visit. It was wholly in character for him to have imagined a tour guide to Whitfield, spying George from afar heaving some vast sandstone rock in order to build a romantic ruin on one of his islands, saying, 'And there you can see Lord Littlebrain building his own folly.' Littlebrain he was not. And, if gardening be a folly, I can think of many far worse. For us his friendship remains a haunting and potent memory. Along with Rosemary and so many other friends he lives still in The Laskett garden.

HOW CAN I END THIS INTERRUPTION TO MY NARRATIVE? WHAT was it that these two people had in common which meant so much to us that I place them at the centre of this history? Both of them in their own way, like us, had made gardens from scratch, or almost from scratch. They understood what that involved. If I had to cite what hurt us most during all those years in which the garden grew, it was those who scoffed at us, usually behind our backs. Time and again we knew that was going on, even as we toured the garden with them staring at our sprigs of yew. The scoffers were of two kinds. The first those who knew nothing about gardens, and who had never made one. The second those with abundant financial resources, smiling condescendingly at our efforts to create this or that effect, with little at our disposal except our own ingenuity. George and Rosemary were never anything other than encouraging and understanding, knowing full well our resources in terms of money, labour and time and never despising them. Always but always they wanted to view the garden in every season, regardless of the weather, to see how things had grown, to inspect our latest project and to make helpful suggestions. And always but always too, after they had gone, we were left in a happy, grateful haze that we had been blessed with such friends.

Five

HOW DOES YOUR GARDEN GROW?

I LEFT THE READER IN 1977 WITH THE CREATION OF A GARDEN to mark the Queen's Silver Jubilee and, in the last chapter, I quoted from the first article ever published about The Laskett garden by Rosemary Verey in 1987. But what happened during the intervening decade? I am often asked, 'How long does it take to make a garden?' To that I can reply, thirty years on, with some degree of authority. The answer is fifteen years. By then, with careful nurturing, even the yew hedges begin to look as though they had been planted by Gertrude Jekyll. I go on to say that the first five years are agony, with everything barely a metre high and vast gaps between trees and shrubs. Inevitably no one understands the vision in your mind's eye. You, of course, see a mighty clipped wall of velvety green hedging, whereas all the visitor to your garden sees is a row of small straggly bushes at knee height. That, I can tell you, is a testing period. The pace quickens during years five to eight. The spaces between begin, at last, to diminish, trees start roaring heavenwards and hedging shrubs at last meet. From year nine onwards no one can deny that you are creating something that must just evoke an appreciative murmur from even the most horticulturally philistine.

In this account I pass over the never-ending battles against the enemies of horticulture – rabbits, moles, squirrels, mice, pigeons, to name but a few. Add to them the constant struggle against the elements, in this case flooding, wind and killer frosts. The moles, for instance, had decided to turn the Rose Garden into Clapham Junction and we could hardly cross it without a foot collapsing into one of their tunnels. Once we skimmed the surface turf off and stood astonished at the myriad passageways running in every direction. I pass over the rage felt at seeing large mounds of soil left on what was supposed to be well-kept grass. At last I found a molecatcher, an unlikely person, Josephine, a middle-aged lady from Rose Cottage at Mansell Gamage, who arrived dressed, I always thought, like a cavalier when she came to lay the poisoned bait. A few days later she returned to harvest the results of this horticultural ethnic cleansing, popping the creatures quickly into bags to despatch to whoever it was who wanted moleskin. Seeing this happen I used to recall the elegant coat I once wore at the close of the sixties with its soft collar of the fur, recorded in a photograph of me by Barry Lategan as the trendsetting flamboyant young director of the National Portrait Gallery.

We were overrun with rabbits, most of them invading us from the neighbouring farmer's fields. He, of course, stoutly denied he had any, in the same way that he flatly did moles, even in the face of his territory being covered with molehills. What farmers could not deny was the evidence of their sheep having pushed their way through the pig wire and hedging and run riot through the domain. In the rabbit war no ally was a greater one than our first cat, the Lady Torte de Shell. She belonged to a house along the lane, where she was having a rough time, and had decided that she wanted to move habitation. Up the wisteria she came day after day and through the bedroom window, jumping onto the bed and going to sleep on my head. She had clearly come to stay and I negotiated her transfer with the owner and ensured that she was cared for by the Bevans in our absence. From the start she was my cat rather than Julia's. Torte tolerated my wife, but I would wake up in the middle of the night and find one paw on each shoulder and her green eyes blazing affection at me. That's how it was, but she was a formidable rabbiter with the unattractive but inbuilt feline trait of bringing her bag into the house via the cat-flap for us to see. When that entailed a live rabbit running around the bedroom we were less than enchanted, but she did valiant service. When the end came, in 1984, we were both grief-stricken, but, by then, she had a redoubtable successor in the Rev. Wenceslas Muff (of whom more later). As I wrote in my diary: 'I loved the Lady Torte de Shell more than many, many human beings.' She was to be the first of our cats to be laid to rest in the garden. She awaits a monument, but sleeps beneath spring flowers in a quiet glade just beyond the Yew Garden, where I still pause and bring to mind all the happiness and love that that beautiful and capricious creature brought us.

MAKING A GARDEN I ALWAYS THINK IS LIKE THAT MAGIC MOMENT in *The Sleeping Beauty* ballet when, the heroine having been cast into an enchanted slumber by the wicked Carabosse, the redeeming Lilac Fairy appears. To Tchaikovsky's thrilling score the palace and its gardens are slowly enveloped as greenery spirals its way upwards, engulfing the scene. If a camera had been run on The Laskett garden for the whole fifteen years from its inception and the film then projected at vast speed, that is precisely the kind of visual experience we would undergo. Before one's eyes walls and ramparts of yew would arise, verdure tapestries of a myriad of shades of green unfurl, a tracery of branches and twigs would pierce ever upwards, the whole composition eventually perforating the skyline (so important a feature of any really good garden) with contrasting shapes and forms from the solid to the transparent. Only when that moment comes do you have a garden, have, at last, the infrastructure upon which to embroider. No longer can everything be seen at a glance. All the 'rooms' are there, the twists and turns bringing vista and surprise, the living architecture which controls the eye and physical movement of the visitor through the domain. I cannot express fully the excitement and sense of achievement that this brings. When Rosemary Verey wrote of our garden that 'the stories will accumulate and the garden will develop', she never wrote a truer word.

What might be called the growing period coincided almost exactly with my fourteen years as Director of the Victoria & Albert Museum, running from 1974 to 1987. In retrospect they may have been years of achievement, but, at the time, they were often far from easy ones. As a consequence of this the garden was to grow in another sense. It became more and more that blessed haven from the blows and buffets of public life. Here was our own patch of God's earth to cultivate, untouched by government cuts, the caprices of Arts ministers, the ignorance of trustees, the perfidy of staff or the cruelty of the media. Never before or since have I felt so hurt or so vulnerable as during those years when I struggled to preserve the best traditions of that museum and, at the same time, reform it in order to meet the needs of a changed society in what, all too soon, would be a new century. Time and again the opening lines of John Donne's *Twicknam Garden* summed up for me my relationship with the garden:

> *Blasted with sighs, and surrounded with teares,*
> *Hither I come to seeke the spring,*
> *And at mine eyes, and at mine eares,*
> *Receive such balmes, as else cure every thing. . .*

His was the cry of a lover in distress, mine the one of someone who felt utterly alone, but for Julia, amidst a sea of troubles.

The garden too took on another dimension during these years. It is always, I believe, greater to create than to write about creation. By that I mean, in the most rudimentary sense, that it is better, for example, to be Rembrandt than an art historian writing a book on him. Suddenly, through the garden, my urge to create in aesthetic terms, denied through circumstance in childhood, found expression. The Laskett garden was never to me anything other than a work of art in the making, one that called for vision, the exercise of the eye, the application of taste, discipline, patience, craft and knowledge over a sustained period of time to conjure up an unforgettable experience through the time-honoured application of art to nature. It was always viewed with that higher vision in mind, one of a kind I learnt about through studying garden history. There I read that any great garden was not only an arrangement of plants and artifacts in terms of design and composition but also a tissue of allusions and ideas. In our case to wander in The Laskett garden was a journey of associations. On a superficial level the garden set out to delight and surprise but, on a deeper one, for us the resonances have always been far more complex.

APART FROM THE SILVER JUBILEE GARDEN, 1977 SAW A NUMBER OF other significant changes. In the middle of February I wrote in a staccato way:

This week the hedge between Paine [the neighbouring farmer] and ourselves was reduced, cleared and tidied, gaining us at least twenty feet more of land. We look exposed! The poplar trees have been moved here as a screen. During December we replanted Elizabeth Tudor with *Nothofagus nervosa*, the first half of Mary Queen of Scots [now the Beaton Bridge leading up to the Hilliard Garden] with *Chamaecyparis lawsoniana* 'Columnaris Glauca' and turned the second half into a maze of specie roses, nearly all 'Lord Penzance' briars from Hilliers. We planted the walk parallel to the drive to the house with *Robinia pseudoacacia*. The amelanchiers were planted in the Rose Garden and look marvellous. I enlarged the central bed and planted it thick with huge grey plants: *Brachyglottis* (Dunedin Group) 'Sunshine', *Senecio cineraria* 'White Diamond', lavender, pinks, etc. ... The roses have been trimmed into pillar roses ... we planted in front of the house thuja and laurel to hem ourselves in after a cow had careered through the garden and eaten the top off the arbutus.

Poor arbutus. It never survived. And that was sad, because it was one among a trolley-load of plants I had been given as a farewell present by the staff of the National Portrait Gallery early in 1974. A party was held in my honour in my beloved Tudor gallery presided over by the famous 'Ditchley' Portrait of Elizabeth I, a silvery vision in a farthingale standing on the British Isles. On the trolley were other plants, all of them bedizened with scarlet ribbons tied into bows. One in particular thrived because it was planted in a sheltered spot, and that was a bay tree, which, trained over the years into a large but vague cone, now soars up to four metres in height in the Spring Garden. Its leaves have enriched many a dish I have cooked over the years, a reminder always to plant a bay within a short walk of the kitchen.

That February diary entry records that what we had been up to during the winter months was righting mistakes. In August some old friends, David and Nancy Perth, came through on their way up to Scotland to see what we had been up to. David was a keen gardener at Stobhall, the castle of the Earls of Perth, which he had purchased back for the family, not far from the city of the same name. Sited up on an eminence above the river Tay, it boasted a beautiful topiary garden in the manner of James Lorimer, the late Victorian reviver of the Scottish pleasance. This was my type of garden, very much in the format of Levens Hall, Westmorland, with large drums and cones of yew dotted amidst box-edged beds filled with roses. Elsewhere there was a beautiful sundial, which David had commissioned from Henry Moore.

I recall their visit to us young gardeners so vividly for two things. One was the voice of the irrepressible Nancy, American by birth, as she trudged her way across the expanse of our garden notching up how many gardeners we would need to maintain it when it was fully grown: one, two, three, four . . . she ended with ten. We hadn't one. It was David, however, who pointed out the folly of the poplars. We would curse having planted them. Their suckers would push up everywhere (they already were; poplar suckers are capable of erupting through layers of tarmac), and these were trees with only a twenty-five-year lifespan and we would have to fell and replace the avenues in our lifetime. (In fact, he was wrong. Pollarded poplars can last up to three hundred years. Moral: always check any horticultural advice given to you.) He recommended planting instead *Nothofagus nervosa* (syn. *N. procera*). Their origin was Chile, but they had the virtue of being quick growing and having handsome autumn colour. One of my tree books lists them among 'the hardiest of *Nothofagus* varieties, and most suitable for garden planting'. Alas, that proved not to be true for virtually all of them were killed outright by the vicious frosts of the winter of 1981/2. The poplars therefore were all dug up and moved that winter and replanted along the boundary hedge parallel with the main road as a windbreak. They had been an expensive if innocent mistake.

So Elizabeth Tudor remained an avenue, now of *Nothofagus*, but already what had been called Mary Queen of Scots changed character. The lower end was given a stately Italianate vista of *Chamaecyparis lawsoniana* 'Columnaris Glauca', pillars of greyish blue-green foliage leading up to the new Hilliard Garden. This too was to prove a doomed avenue, for part of it was fated with that gardener's curse of 'dead earth', a spot where nothing, regardless of what you do, will ever grow. One of these elegant conifers was replaced no fewer than three times, but to no avail. Nonetheless, we were to struggle on with this planting until 1988. Most of the backing shrubbery, however, remains still intact and vigorous to this day, not the *Philadelphus* varieties, 'Belle Etoile',

'Burfordensis' and 'Virginal', but the eight *Viburnum opulus* (guelder roses), four each of 'Fructu Luteo' and 'Notcutt's Variety'. The latter all quickly rushed up to four metres, their branches meeting across the avenue and therefore demanding to be savagely cut back from time to time. But they are good value shrubs with deep-green ribbed leaves, small frothy pinkish-white flowerheads in late spring and, best of all, beautiful autumn fruits which, sadly, are speedily devoured by the birds.

Beyond the Hilliard Garden, where so far we had planted the yew bay known as the Ashton Arbour, a very different planting was made, one which was loose in character as a foil to the formal accents in the making there. The roses I ordered I knew grew quickly to a vast size and the list of those that came from Hilliers Nursery is headed by *Rosa rubiginosa* (syn. *R. eglanteria*), a monster which rapidly expanded up to three metres in height, but which, in late to mid-June, was a glorious spectacle dappled all over with deep clear pink flowers, each one with a golden centre. That rose shared a bonus with several of the others I ordered, for its feathery foliage was scented. So too was that of the *R. rubiginosa* hybrids 'Lord Penzance', 'Meg Merrilies' and 'Flora McIvor', whose blooms were rosy-yellow, crimson and blush-pink. Mrs Bevan, living opposite in the stone-built bungalow Withy Brae, was a Scot and it became her delight to come and sit among these hybrid sweet briars at their zenith, most named after characters in Walter Scott's novels, and think of her homeland.

To these I added others that were also mighty growers, among them the white rose of York, *Rosa* x *alba*, pale creamy-yellow *R. xanthina f. hugonis*, white *R. soulieana* with its stunning glaucous grey foliage, *R. forrestiana*, another with striking foliage, this time bright green, and *R. macrophylla*, which, each autumn, produced brilliant orange-scarlet hips no less than three inches long. That feature of hips was shared by the others, a great bonus, for the flowering season lasted only two or three weeks.

From that the reader will have gathered how profoundly changed in character that whole area became from being a mere circle of yew in the field grass interrupting a parade of poplars. What I have not dwelt upon is the fact that this north–south axis was cursed from the outset by one almighty eyesore. In the Kitchen Garden was sited an electric junction box from which wires descended south to Laskett Cottage (The Folly). For this facility the Midlands Electricity Board paid us an annual pittance. The junction box we successfully obscured with the fast-growing x *Cupressocyparis leylandii*. The main axis presented appalling problems as I had some-how to site trees and shrubs to deflect the eye from the electric poles and overhead cables. Once, early on, I asked a representative of the electricity board to contemplate the full horror in the hope that he might take pity on us and re-site the poles in the adjacent farmer's field or bury the cables. Alas, the man who came was overbearing and officious and, far from hold-ing out a ray of hope, instead berated me as to their right to mutilate and prune any tree or shrub of ours which dared impede access to their poles or junction box. In addition, he demanded a pathway wide enough for their lorry to career through the garden. I was both mortified and defeated.

At the time it never occurred to me to question the board's right to cross our land. It was not until over a decade later that I was to learn that the authorities, far from having the rights they claimed, were actually bound by law to provide electricity even if way leave was withdrawn. And that, in the end, was what we did. This time another of their officials appeared, someone quite unlike his predecessor, indeed who was positively benign, who was entranced by the garden and arranged for the poles to be removed and the cables buried at their expense. Ever since we have been on the best of terms with the Midlands Electricity Board. We owe this triumph to

George Williams, a doughty Welshman who was creating a marvellous landscape garden in a Welsh valley near Crickhowell. The garden included a natural winding stream, a magnificent laburnum tunnel and a Chinese Chippendale bridge leading to a delightful pavilion designed by Quinlan Terry. George had already achieved the removal of similar eyesores by the simple expedient of getting a solicitor to write a letter to the electricity board withdrawing way leave. It was a tip which in my turn I was able to pass on to another garden-besotted friend, the novelist Susan Hill. In her case there were horrendous poles and cables swagged all the way up her long drive. I am pleased to say they are no longer there, and her victory was signalled by the arrival of a crate of champagne at The Laskett.

'THIS YEAR WAS EXCEPTIONALLY GOOD FOR GROWTH IN THE garden,' I wrote in my diary during the summer of 1978. 'The Orchard had real fruit, apple trees bent low with the weight of it . . . The urn which had stood on the front lawn at Bride Hall was placed at the end of the *Die Fledermaus* Walk [Julia had done a production of this opera at Covent Garden]. It was always called "John Taylor's Monument" and we found out why when we moved it. The slab of stone it sat upon, when turned upside down, was his headstone! No time for great garden works.'

This entry records the passing of yet another member of a generation of my wife's family, in this instance her aunt, Carola Oman, Lady Lenanton. Four years later, early in 1982, my father-in-law, Charles Oman, was to follow her. Both losses brought enrichment in the form of handsome stone ornaments. Indeed, we were very much aware that one day some of these artifacts would come our way, and so we had planted accordingly. Carola, known to the family as Betts, lived at Bride Hall, Ayot St Lawrence in Hertfordshire, a stone's throw from Bernard Shaw's house. Bride was a small

E-shaped Elizabethan house of rose-red brick, its facade rich in climbers. 'I'm your period, E-shaped,' she once said to me. Carola was a remarkable woman in her own right, for she had made her way as an acclaimed biographer (her *Nelson* won a major literary prize) in spite of, rather than because of her father, Sir Charles. He did not believe in education for women. She entered my life as one of the trustees of the National Portrait Gallery, a formidable, reticent *grande dame*, but not devoid of a certain kind of humour. When I had to ring her up and tell her I had eloped and married her niece, she said, 'About time too,' and her wedding present included a copy of Browning's works. Not for nothing had she once written an historical novel entitled *Miss Barrett's Elopement*. She left me half her library and I write at her desk still, but what of 'John Taylor's Monument'?

Bride Hall was set on a platform, its entrance approached by way of a flight of steps. In front of those was a carriage drive around an oval of greensward, in the middle of which sat what Carola always referred to as 'John Taylor's Monument', an urn in the classical style, probably eighteenth century, attractively weathered and gathering moss and lichen. It had come from Crowther's, the long-established dealers in antique garden ornaments, after the war. Whether they also provided the slab on which it sat I know not. That summer it reached its final destination here, not at the close of the *Die Fledermaus* Walk as originally envisaged but perfectly sited at the centre of the Rose Garden, where it has been ever since, a key focal point in one of the garden's grandest vistas. I might add that this was a rare instance of an ornament finding its final resting place almost at once. David, our contract gardener, always used to say, on placing any new addition to the garden of this kind, 'We won't cement it down, Dr Strong. We know you, you'll move it.' Years after we used John Taylor's headstone, the inscription side up, on the landing of the steps leading down to the Silver Jubilee

Garden. We agreed that if anyone asked who John Taylor was we would reply, 'Oh, he was the man who built the house.'

The death of my father-in-law brought two far more significant and meaningful ornaments, both associated with his father, Sir Charles Oman. He was one of the most brilliant intellects of his generation, elected a scholar of Winchester and New College, Oxford, winning the first place on each occasion. In 1883 he became a Fellow of All Souls, which he remained until his death in 1946, and in 1905 he was appointed as Chichele Professor of Modern History. He was to be an historian of polymathic range and prolific output, his acknowledged masterpiece being a seven-volume history of the Peninsular War, over which he laboured some thirty years. But he was also a man of public affairs, sitting as burgess for the University of Oxford in the House of Commons from 1919 to 1935. The range of information retained in his memory was recognized as being both extraordinary and almost eccentric, as any reading of his own part autobiography, *Memories of Victorian Oxford*, reveals. The attribute of total recall Julia has inherited, as well as the Oman cast of countenance, a pale handsome face with a noble brow, the features tending to small-set within it. But had Sir Charles any garden credentials?

The answer to that is no, or at least, not any beyond a passion for keeping hens and the planting of runner beans. His wife, Mary Maclagan, in fact disliked both gardens and flowers, an indifference that probably descended to her daughter Carola, for Bride was no horticultural paradise. But the two ornaments which came to us and which began their life in the unloved garden of Frewin Hall in Oxford played a different role in the scheme of things. They stood there less as garden ornaments and more as mnemonics. The first was a lion from Barry's Houses of Parliament, acquired in 1933 when restoration work to the House threw up items that had to be replaced. A letter to Sir Charles dated 13 March reads: 'Your carved stone Lion has been despatched to you to-day per G.W.R., Goods Train, Carriage forward. The price is £5.' It was placed at the far end of the Frewin garden, sitting upon a medieval fragment of what family tradition holds is a piece of Christ Church. Supporting a shield inscribed in honour of Queen Victoria, VR, the lion found its home at once as the focal point of the Yew Garden.

The second was a tapering pinnacle from All Souls which, on first sight, could be taken as fifteenth-century Gothic, if it were not recorded as part of the restoration of the college by Nicholas Hawksmoor in the eighteenth century. It is of the stone one associates with Oxford, wonderfully creamy yellow, soft and all too easily eroded, which is why it now passes its winter shrouded to protect it from any further damage from frost. It was drawn by my father-in-law as a child of eight, soon after its arrival at Frewin. The drawing, dated 1909 and touchingly framed by his proud parents, shows the pinnacle with climbers struggling their way up it. Photographs in family albums record its siting in an oval flowerbed directly in front of the main facade of the house, flanked by two Doulton urns which had come from another Oman connection, James Anderson Rose, the solicitor for the Pre-Raphaelites and the lawyer who had won the famous case Whistler brought against Ruskin. One of these urns is today at The Laskett. These faded sepia-tinged photographs evoke a reverie of the secure world of before 1914, catching a dog romping its way across the front lawn or Carola Oman and her friends attired in medieval dress standing en tableau in front of the house. And, perhaps the most touching of all, one of Carola hugging the beloved dog Patch sitting in a child's wheelbarrow, the pinnacle behind her.

That now stands at the end of the *Die Fledermaus* Walk within an apse of yew, which I trained upwards either side to incorporate echoing pinnacles of greenery. Later we lifted it up onto a reconstituted-stone pedestal and Julia commissioned the circular slate plaque bearing the Oman arms and motto, *Homo sum* (I am a man), and the initials and dates of her father and grandfather. Her father was to become this country's greatest expert on silver and all kinds of European metalwork and jewellery, a distinguished antiquarian and a member of the staff of the Victoria & Albert Museum for almost half a century. One of his most important initiatives led to the founding of treasuries in the country's great cathedrals. Every time I pass the pinnacle I think of that lost world of the Omans, whose last childless representatives are Julia and my brother-in-law, another Charles. This is a memorial to a dynasty with proud achievements.

ON THE EARLY PLANS OF THE GARDEN IN 1975 I HAD DRAWN A circle in the middle of what was designated Hartwell Grove in acknowledgement of Pam and Michael, that area which formed the junction of the two great avenues. It meant that I knew something important was needed as a focal point for the two vistas which went the whole length and breadth of the garden. I was training two topiary pieces at the end of Elizabeth R to frame whatever it was, and also a backcloth of conifers, common laurel and *Viburnum tinus* (laurustinus). Inevitably, in desperation, the nomadic sundial found its way there for a time, but, in 1980, something happened which resolved the yawning gap. I was awarded the Shakespeare Prize.

That prize is given annually by the FVS Foundation of Hamburg to the person considered to have contributed most to the arts in Britain. It was an incredible honour to receive such an award. The list of recipients, Henry Moore, Margot Fonteyn, David Hockney and Harold Pinter among them, reads like a roll call of those who have contributed to this country's culture during the second half of the twentieth century. I still remain the only museum person ever to be given it. The prize involved a ceremony in the town hall in Hamburg, speeches, the presentation of a medal and a handsome cheque. At the lunch given afterwards, I spoke a second time and said how I intended to commemorate this auspicious moment in my career – the first public recognition I had ever had – in the garden. And so it was that in the autumn of 1980 the Shakespeare Monument arose.

It was a reproduction in reconstituted stone of an urn designed by William Kent for Longleat House in Wiltshire. I placed it on a stone platform two steps in height. From Elizabeth R it was seen straight on, while from Mary Queen of Scots it was seen at a diagonal. In all, the urn is about three metres in height, and testimony to my fervent belief that garden ornaments should be on a large scale if they are to make any impact. From the moment we got it up I was thrilled with it. Suddenly our grand avenue had a point, for it actually led somewhere. The following spring there was real satisfaction to be gained from the vista along the sixty-yard walk of Elizabeth R. This was the most theatrical spectacle so far in the garden, the long grass either side of the walk filled with yellow daffodils with the beech trees emphasizing the perspective.

Much later, in the early nineties, we were to embellish the Shakespeare Monument. Reg Boulton, the sensitive artist craftsman who had carved the circular slate plaque for the Oman pinnacle, carved two more oval ones, which he inset into the pedestal of the Monument. On one there figured the logo of the FVS Foundation, a fountain, together with the date, 1980, while on the other he did a bas-relief of Shakespeare with the initials WS and RS below, perhaps getting a little carried away with it all. Later still we were to gild the finial and add blue and honey-yellow colour washes to delineate parts of the urn and pedestal. From the moment of its erection this has remained a highly dramatic linchpin of the garden's composition.

*

THAT SPRINGTIME TABLEAU LASTED PRECISELY ONE YEAR. IN MY garden book, into which I had gathered all my drawings and plans and which, from time to time, I annotated, comes this entry for the winter of 1981 to 1982:

> February was the great frost, minus 24 degrees in Herefordshire, only to be exceeded by twenty-seven in Shropshire. Seven feet of snow fell on one side of the house, four on the other. This took a terrible toll of the garden. The beech avenue, Elizabeth Tudor, fifteen feet high, was killed outright. All our standard roses, bar eight, were killed, all the elaeagnus, escallonias and even common laurel were obliterated to the ground. The tender buddleias and daphnes were completely killed, as was the old bay tree near the garage. Some of the conifers also succumbed. It took all of 1982 to recover.

This brief painful paragraph captures something of the appalling toll this icy visitation exacted. It took us several days to dig ourselves out, and it was not until the snows melted that the full horror of what had happened was taken in. Common laurel is very tough, but shrubs two metres and more high were wiped out to the roots. They did, of course, spring again, but suddenly, in many areas of the garden, we were back to square one. Mercifully, yew is frost-resistant and a large number of the other plants recovered remarkably quickly. But a great number did not, among them the beech that had formed Elizabeth Tudor. For the third time we had to plant that avenue.

On Boxing Day 1982 I wrote to Jan van Dorsten: 'It was sad to fell the beech avenue fifteen feet high after being killed by frost, but I've got twenty lime trees coming in March and I'm determined to have a great avenue of clipped limes as at Hidcote Manor.'

This records my initial concept for the new planting, an

aerial hedge of *Tilia platyphyllos* 'Rubra', the red-twigged lime, a garden feature in imitation of the famous one at Hidcote and, equally, of the one which articulated John Fowler's garden at King John's Hunting Lodge. That was how it started, but it was George Clive who, on one of his visits, pointed out that I needed double the number of limes I had planted and also a frame along which to train them. I had to wait until the following winter to double up the avenue, by which time an article had appeared in the Royal Horticultural Society's magazine *The Garden*, which included a diagram showing how to pleach limes. What attracted me was that the pleaching could be achieved, not by the addition of a vastly expensive custom-built iron framework, which I could not afford, but by the simple method of using ten-foot bamboo canes tied onto the tree stakes and then adding a further series horizontally. The article also presented the possibility of either training the limes as a hedge or securing branches along tiers of horizontal bamboos and creating a rival to the Lime Walk at Sissinghurst.

That walk, which was Harold Nicolson's particular garden and his pride and joy, was planted in 1936, an avenue of thirty lime trees, fifteen each side. Behind was added a beech hedge and later the walk was paved and the area between that and the hedge made into borders crammed with spring bulbs and flowers designed to provide a dazzling display in March, April and May. To the influence of that I must add one nearer home, Rosemary Verey's lime walk at Barnsley. That had only ten trees either side and Rosemary let the twigs remain on the trees, once the leaves had fallen, through into the spring, so that during winter the espaliered branches sported a haze of crimson. Here again the underplanting is of spring flowers. I decided that that was the effect I would plump for. Our lime walk boasts nineteen trees each side, eclipsing both Barnsley and Sissinghurst, but for what was to prove in the long run a very different effect.

The limes were planted by David and Wilf with the instruction to place them ten feet apart, but since David never measured anything except by the length of his wellington boot the resulting spaces were inevitably variable. There has had to be a great deal of fudging to conceal the irregularity. Initially there were four tiers of branches espaliered the length of Elizabeth Tudor. It was my delight each winter to prune the limes, in our case, as against Barnsley, cutting off the red twigs and tying in the branches along the bamboos. To prune them in spring as Rosemary did would have meant trampling down a forest of daffodils in bloom. I had no idea how to join up the branches of two trees when they eventually met, so that when that occurred I merely bound them together with garden string and wire, hoping for the best. And it worked. As I suffer from vertigo I quickly found that top tier too much, so fairly early on I sacrificed that. Even then, up until we had a gardener, I found pruning the upper reaches, perched on a pair of steps which would suddenly lurch unexpectedly to one side plunging down a mole tunnel, an unnerving activity.

Something of my excitement about the new avenue is caught in a letter I wrote to Jan on 8 May 1983:

Here we have been in a sea of water, rain, rain and more rain. Everything is sodden. There has only been one weekend when the sun shone and then it was gorgeous. We have been enjoying your four amaryllis which Julia planted and which shot up, although it is odd that the firm seem to have cut the shoots that produce leaves off! At any rate they are giving us pleasure and the flowers are to come. There are also the 'Dillenburg' tulips [his gift too] in the Hilliard Garden far away from the house which are still going strong after years. It has been, however, the most wonderful spring for flowers. The great avenue was thick with daffodils for over a month and we await the newly planted lime trees, twenty of them, to leaf for the first time. Pray heaven that they last as that's the third planting so far. The banks are covered with hyacinths and primroses. And the Rembrandt tulips, which I'm crazy about, are beginning to come into bloom in the Rose Garden.

Julia has always been in charge of bulbs and here you can tangibly sense how much she had already achieved by the early eighties, just by diligently adding each year new plantings. She would always consult me about those she ordered for the Rose Garden, and Rembrandt tulips were understandably my passion because they are the nearest ones available to those seen in seventeenth-century Dutch flower paintings. Their striped and multi-coloured petals I find irresistible.

The saga of this third avenue did not end there, for as the trees grew it became increasingly apparent that something was radically wrong. I explained the problem in a letter dated 11 July 1988 to Mr Dyter of Notcutts, who had supplied them:

The avenue of about forty trees is now established with the cane framework and pruning to shape. All the trees have done splendidly, except seven. Their trunks remain thin, their growth slow, their leaves yellowy and they always have seed-pods dangling. The others do not, but are vigorous in growth and green in colour with largish leaves. The seven are not all together. I got the tree surgeon to look at them last year and he suggested feeding them with Vitax Q4. I did. No improvement.

It could be that their growth is impeded by underground water streams (we've had that trouble before) and we can insert drainage this winter, but it could be something else. Your colleague suggested I send a branch to you upon which to pronounce. As you can imagine the loss of seven trees in a pleached-lime avenue of some years' standing is a major blow. I do hope that we don't have to replace them. But they look strangely different, so I wondered whether we had been supplied with seven of a different type.

We had, and back came a letter of abject apology from Mr Dyter: 'The specimen you sent us is from *Tilia cordata*, which explains why it is different from the other limes which you have established successfully, why it is a smaller grower and of a different shape.'

I cannot fault the nursery's reaction, for I was asked how many replacements were needed and the height to which the other trees had grown and that winter they were delivered. When planted they were a perfect match.

So in 1989 we were back on track, but it was not to be the last change to Elizabeth Tudor, for, during the following decade, further additions were to give it its own identity and remove it from being a pale imitation of Sissinghurst or Barnsley and finally render it, I believe, unique as a garden experience in this country. The first came in 1988 when we added a beech hedge joining up the limes which, as it grew, was trained into decorative swags the whole length of the avenue. This added to the winter interest, for during those months the architectural splendour was enhanced, the rich dark-green sentinels of Irish yew, cut off at the level of the first tier of the limes, set against the coppery russet of the beech leaves from which arose the intriguing decorative screen of the pleached limes plunging into the distance. But the most spectacular addition of all was only to come at the close of the 1990s.

BY THE CLOSE OF THE SEVENTIES SOME OF THE YEW WAS ALREADY reaching maturity. On 25 July 1979 I had written to Jan: 'The hedge around the Rose Garden is nearly everywhere six feet high and one sits within it enclosed, a *hortus conclusus*.' The following year I wrote in my Garden Book: 'The yew hedge up to seven feet most sides and the decision as to buttresses made and cut,' something I did in September. For anyone who plans to plant a yew hedge this is the magic moment. At the same time there is something faintly comic about it, for all it means is that you can sit down in a yew-hedged garden room and not see out. Standing up, of course, you can still easily see over the as yet feathery top. It had taken eight years to reach that stage and its rapid growth had been aided both by the Herefordshire soil and by an annual dressing of bonemeal which guaranteed at least a foot of growth each year. Nathaniel Lloyd's book, recommended to me by Rosemary, was my only guide and that called for the hedge to be battered, that is, cut with sloping sides, advice which, I regret to say, I ignored. Nor is the hedge as full at its base as I would have wished. Nonetheless it is handsome, providing a magnificent frame for the Rose Garden.

It is extraordinary how few people who plant any form of hedge ever think of doing anything with it, other than cutting it off in a boring straight line when it reaches the required height. Even at Highgrove, Mollie Salisbury had planted seemingly miles of yew hedging with no scheme as to what to do with it, which was why Rosemary brought me in to sculpt it into shape. My Garden Book contained sketches from quite early on of what I intended to do with the Rose Garden hedges and the turf was cut indicating where the buttresses would fall. The final result, I admit, is not exactly symmetrical, a fault going back to David and Wilf's rhomboid planting, but few people ever notice the irregularities. A hedge doesn't just divide and conceal, it is living architecture. The buttresses broke up the monotonous surface and, when formed, were fully responsive to the fall of light, casting shadows and animating what otherwise would have been a dull and flat expanse of greenery. In the same way, cutting the top into what, in effect, was crenellation added a dramatic silhouette to the garden's skyline.

Hedges to most people are a burden. To me they are a joy. If I had to simplify The Laskett garden I would indeed sweep away everything and leave just the hedges and topiary. They endow the garden with its romance and mystery, evidence too that garden design is as much about placing human beings in space as are architecture and theatre design. It is not for nothing that I sometimes like to shock an audience by saying to them, 'Remember, flowers are a sign of failure in a garden,' a remark that is always guaranteed to produce a reaction. During those years at the museum, each August I would spend the morning in my writing room and then after lunch, clutching my shears and a radio, I would head for the garden and snip away. As the hedges reached their full height I moved on to using petrol-driven shears for the larger surfaces and hand shears for anything intricate. It always gave me a deep sense of pride to step back at the end of the day and admire what I had sculpted, noting with pleasure how an arch was about to be formed or a gracious curve was there in all its fullness.

In hedge making I urge the extreme importance of wielding a camera to record progress. It was not until the eighties that I had a camera of my own, which Julia gave me; up until then she was the sole photographer. A series of scrapbooks now running to well over a hundred, plus a garden archive of some sixty volumes, are evidence of her sense of organization and documentation. At the early stages, it is wonderfully encouraging to turn back and trace how much a hedge has grown year by year. I would always pull last year's scrapbook off the shelf and see where this or that part of the garden's green architecture had got.

Not that we have ceased to add more. Indeed we are still planting yew even today. Early in September 1979 I had written to Jan: 'The orchard is to have a yew hedge around it this autumn.' It was something which, as I have already noted, I had had in mind for some time. To reveal my full ignorance I will confess that the desire for a hedge was to screen off what I regarded as something of a service area in the garden, the Christmas Orchard. There, I've written it, revealing my own foolishness. It was only when the hedge reached its maturity that I was aware of my stupidity, that in fact the Orchard was quite beautiful with its flowers and fruits. This was to be a hedge with a history, for its start was not an easy one, since no sooner had it been planted than, in the following April and May, it was threatened with extinction by drought. My most abiding memory of that period was of arriving from London exhausted, staggering out of the car and watering the young plants or else they would have died. That hedge was never fed, nor was there ever the labour to clean the beds under it, but up it went until, in July 1987, I was able to begin clipping it into the swags adorned with the cake-stands and pinnacles which are there today. On 10 October I noted with satisfaction: 'R. finished sculpting Orchard hedge.'

The garden's main topiary set piece was in the end to be in the area called Covent Garden, after the Royal Opera House, to which Julia had contributed six productions. It was appropriately directly opposite the Ashton Arbour. In the early plans it can be seen as little more than four symmetrically placed yews planted to frame a vista from the Arbour into the Orchard. The re-labelling occurred during the winter of 1978–79 when the area was simply paved, incorporating the yews, and given a framing planting of shiny green common laurel behind a proscenium arch of two *Sorbus cashmiriana*, which had been planted in 1976. We had been introduced to those beautiful trees in the November of that year by Sir Richard Cotterell of Garnons, who had taken us up to Queenswood, just north of Hereford, which he had created in honour of the Queen's coronation in 1953 and where there were handsome specimens which took our fancy. In spring the branches bear pink or white flowers and in the autumn there are beautiful pink-tinged berries which turn white, hanging on the trees long after the leaves have fallen. In between the yews I planted *Elaeagnus pungens* 'Maculata', which, on account of the brilliant splodges of yellow on the leaves, formed a contrast with the even-textured surface of the clipped yew.

My Garden Book traces the evolution of those yews into topiary. My initial drawing shows the original intention for their shape, copied directly from the row of phallic yews at Hidcote. After the paving was laid follows a second drawing, in which they were to grow right up to about three metres in height, like stage wings, and, in effect, create in that area what the Italians call a *teatro di verzura*, that is, a green theatre. These were to set off a symmetrical arrangement of phoney statuary, two elegant planters in the classical style and busts on tapered plinths of a male and female satyr who were promptly called Pyramus and Thisbe.

By the middle of the eighties I had abandoned that scheme and decided finally to cut the four yews into cubes and allow a leader to go up which I would train to form a peacock. All I had to go on in this exercise was a series of photographs in Lloyd's book which made use of strong fencing wire to tie shoots, and that is what I did. Gradually the birds took shape year by year, but most of the training had to be improvised. Topiary at this period was completely 'out', regarded as hugely labour intensive, and I was keenly aware that I was a pioneer enthusiast for the art, so much so that I began to be called upon by newspapers to write about it, contributing, I believe, to its return to fashion as a delightful feature in any garden. It was only in 1987 and 1988 that two books at last appeared which dealt in depth with the planting and training of both hedges and topiary. They were in fact the first for over sixty years.

BY NOW THE READER WILL GET THE IMPRESSION OF A SORT OF creeping colonization of the acreage, in a sequence moving inexorably from mown grass to some kind of wild planting, which generally lasted a few years, and then, hey presto, an influx of cash would incite us to embark on yet more hard landscaping. In 1985 I reached my half-century. At the time Julia was working at Chichester designing a production of

Robert Bolt's *A Man for All Seasons*. On the long car journey to and fro, as she circled Arundel, her eye was caught by an array of garden sculpture in an establishment which traded under the unlikely name of Fagin's Den. There she found four Vicenza-style putti of the Seasons which she purchased for my birthday and which triggered two things, the paving of the Hilliard Garden and the creation of the Birthday Garden leading off it. This was the first indication that what had begun as a grass avenue was piecemeal to be transformed into an architectural ascent.

The paving of the Hilliard Garden meant that the yew hedges were all out of true and we had to wait a few years for them to even up to the new horizontal. The *Rosa* 'Cantabrigiensis' stayed in place encircled by a box hedge while, to the south, a small flight of steps led down to the new Birthday Garden. The drawing by Julia was of an octagon made up of a mixture of ordinary paving stones and old brick with little beds left for box topiary. The putti were to be inset into tall yew niches and the hedging otherwise was to be kept low in contrast to the mighty walls of yew, six feet wide in places, of the Hilliard Garden. In the latter you could not see out other than through the entrances, whereas in the Birthday Garden there was no such feeling of enclosure. Outside its crisp green walls I trained pillars of the luscious apricot-pink David Austin rose 'Compassion' and, on one side, a *Rosa* 'Wickwar', a waterfall of single white blooms each June. At the foot of each statue there was a bouquet of pink *Bergenia cordifolia* and on either side, facing each other, were sited two garden seats, for in the end the garden was to celebrate both our half-centuries.

It was when I was fifty that I decided I would resign the Victoria & Albert Museum directorship, a decision which took two years to expedite. That was finally announced to the public in January 1987 and I left at the end of the year. Fourteen years of my life, I suppose those of what will be regarded as the apogee of my career, were spent in that post and as such they cried out to be recorded and celebrated in the garden. That was made possible by the gift from the museum's fund-raising body, which I had founded, the Associates. At my request they commissioned the sculptor Simon Verity to create something appropriate. Simon's work I had first seen in Rosemary's garden at Barnsley, including the charming pair of naive figures which flank the gate leading towards the potager. Later I commissioned him to inscribe in carved letters like flames of gold the name of the new Henry Cole Wing of the museum.

By then I had decided that we would mark the V & A years with a temple. Even in reconstituted stone such a garden building is not cheap, but in our garden visiting I had seen what I set out to copy at Painswick, the restored rococo garden in Gloucestershire. There, walking the circuit, I came across a temple of sorts consisting of two columns and a pediment and a back wall. Simpler it could not have been. With that in my mind I ordered the necessary columns and pediment along with materials to build a back wall and to construct two steps as an approach. The wall would be adorned with a suitable commemorative plaque.

I recall Simon sketching a number of alternatives, but the one I found irresistible, because it made me smile and still makes every visitor to the garden smile too, copied a medal of Victoria and Albert sandwiching my bespectacled and moustachioed profile between them. On 17 December the Associates staged a small party, at which the plaque was presented. I had arranged for a board to be set on an easel. Onto it I had pinned a photograph of where the temple was to be sited, as the culmination of the north–south vista replacing a solitary and inadequate obelisk, and sketches of what was intended. Three days later Simon Verity delivered the plaque to The Laskett and the day after the Temple arrived in pieces and Wilf and David dug the foundations. Gradually it went up through the opening months of the new year and by early summer the plaque was in place with a comfortable stone bench beneath. Something then happened which, I feel, was fated. I had been in contact with Crowther's about garden ornaments when they signalled that busts of Victoria and Albert had just come in. They were marble and by the sculptor John Francis. Weathered they were, but pleasantly. These I felt were destined for this garden and to it in May they came. Now they stand flanking the Temple.

That composition called for enrichment and softening by planting. Behind the Temple already soared a weeping birch, the gift long before of the sculptor Angela Conner and her husband, the photographer and filmmaker John Bulmer, who lived on the other side of Hereford at Monnington. On one side the Himalayan Musk Rose (*R. brunonii*, syn. *R. moschata* var. *nepalensis*) extends its tendrils over the Temple and into any neighbouring tree. Facing south and with room to expand this was ideally sited and when in flower is a great spectacle weighed down with showers of creamy-white flowers. Through it runs the pale-pink *Clematis montana* 'Elizabeth'. On the other side there are vines for autumn colour, including *Vitis coignetiae*, which turns bright red, and another rose, 'Veilchenblau' ('Violet-Blue'), the nearest thing there is to a blue rose, although in truth its blooms run from purplish to bluish-violet.

This building remains the climax of any tour of The Laskett garden, a tour which takes on almost a spiritual dimension with the inscription we added later in Greek across the pediment, which in translation reads: 'Memory, mother of the Muses.' The Muses lived in a museum and memory, Mnemosyne, is the key to the garden, memory of family and friends and events which have shaped and touched both our lives. Appropriately there are heavy swags of rosemary for remembrance on either side. Mnemosyne too is the only word inscribed above the entrance to the institution to which intellectually I owe most, the Warburg Institute in the University of London. Its scope is the history of the classical tradition in the West and it was there that I spent three extraordinary years having the eyes of my mind opened under the aegis of the late Dame Frances Yates, one of whose most brilliant pioneering books was an attempt to trace the classical art of memory from antiquity to the age of the philosopher Leibniz. I owe her an incalculable debt, even though our relationship, that of professor and pupil, was not always an easy one. So the reader can understand just how complex the thoughts that assail my mind every time we sit here.

On a summer's evening we sometimes take a basket with a bottle and two glasses and make our way to the Temple. There we sit, our eyes turned towards the great sweep of the axis down to the Shakespeare Monument, whose gilt finial glints in the distance. Wine may fill the glasses but memory our minds, above all in my case, the recollection of all those years as director of the museum I fell in love with as a child and which it was my privilege to direct for fourteen years during the second half of the twentieth century. There we sit, not saying very much to each other but in perfect accord, watching, as Lindy Dufferin told me to, our garden grow.

In June, not long after the Temple was finally up, Anne Scott-James came over with Rosemary Verey to visit the garden, see what she had never seen when she had written her article and discover whether I had come to terms with squirrels as vermin. She wrote a letter to her daughter Clare describing the experience in her delightful book, *Gardening Letters to my Daughter* (1990).

> Yesterday I saw a lovely garden which is quite shaggy, a garden which I had written about fifteen years ago, when it was nothing but a field and the planting was all in the mind, Roy Strong's garden in Herefordshire. Today it is a dream of green, the many greens of trees, hedges and topiary, of long meadow

grass and grassy walks, some straight, some meandering, but each one leading to some charming piece of statuary – a pinnacle from All Souls or a little Victorian temple with (appropriately for Roy) period busts of Victoria and Albert. It is a relaxed and happy garden, hedges sprouting wildly, hairy topiary shrubs patiently waiting their turn for the clippers, long grass not cut until the end of July, paths mown once a fortnight. Not a herbaceous border anywhere, the whole garden is non-Jekyll. Roy and Julia and I wandered down the long alleys and through the hedged enclosures and down the pleached lime walk for two hours while I gulped in the greenness and freshness.

I think I can say that by the opening of the last decade of the twentieth century we had passed muster.

Six

PORTRAIT GALLERY

THE EIGHTEENTH-CENTURY BOTANIST PETER COLLINSON once wrote as follows to the equally great American botanist, John Bartram: 'As often as I survey my Gardens & Plantations, it reminds mee of my Absent Friends by their Living donations. . .' He then takes Bartram on a tour of the trees and plants of Ridgeway House, north of London, in terms of the people who gave them: '. . .look yonder at the Late benevolent Duke of Richmond, His Everlasting Cedars of Lebanon, will Endure when you & I & He is forgot. . .' Anyone who gardens knows the truth of Collinson's senti-ments, prophetic of The Laskett garden as of so many others.

The word 'memory' has already peppered these pages and so it should, for my mother-in-law equally saw her garden in this way and referred to it as her 'Garden of Remembrance'. The word 'ghosts' also comes to mind and indeed might be the better word, for there is a haunting quality to this garden, or at least so for its owners. At each twist and turn spectres arise, images of people – some long gone but still loved and cherished – as well as recollections of garden experiences that have enriched our consciousness and contributed in their way to the garden here. All this kaleidoscope of recollection lives on, triggered by a glimpse of this or that in The Laskett garden. When we also become two of those ghosts whose presence will haunt these acres that pattern of association known will inevitably be lost. In that as well as in many other senses, a garden dies with its creators. Only we, for instance, could think of the art historian Hugh Honour and his life-long partner, John Fleming, each autumn when the cyclamen flower up the drive, recalling that they came from their garden at the Villa Marchio, near Lucca. I had known them from the late 1960s and stayed there happily many times. Or that we owe our violets to Sylvia England, the eccentric but lovable lady who devilled for me in the Public Record Office in the 1970s, and whose estate now finances a scholarship in Renaissance Studies at the Victoria & Albert Museum. Or that what we were told were Dragon's Teeth (*Dracunculus vulgaris*) and a certain pretty, pale violet-blue flecked with white *Geranium pratense* 'Striatum' we owe to Joanna Drew, the redoubtable head of the Art Department at the Arts Council. They came when we were just starting in a large box from her garden at Wallingford. Later, in the eighties, I was to work with her as chairman of that department. Such details are locked up only in the minds of the makers.

To them I might add Joan Henderson, who taught me history as a schoolboy at a grammar school on the fastnesses of the North Circular Road and who set me on my path as an historian. Every year she would touchingly send me a cheque saying it was to be spent on something for the garden, as indeed it was. Two fastigiate golden yews flanking the steps of the Beaton Bridge I always particularly associate with her. They act as a mnemonic, recalling a shy and awkward grammar school boy in the early 1950s and the incalculable debt he owed at that period to an inspired teacher.

Along what we call the Canal to the left of the Yew Garden still each spring appear white primroses which first came to The Laskett in a basket from the couturier Jean Muir. No gardener, Jean, but someone I still acutely miss as one of life's originals and an inspiring and loyal friend. Her death came as a great shock, for she had concealed her illness from, it seems, everyone. How touching it was that when the sad news broke, certain shops emptied their windows and placed at their centre a solitary vase of white lilies in tribute.

I can't list all our many ghosts, but some we've met already. So far we have had rosemary from my mother-in-law's beloved nanny, Dooks, the quince and white jasmine from the

Omans at Frewin Hall, the catalpa known as the Second Lord Plunket, the house leeks from John Fowler, the 'Albertine' rose and herbaceous plants from my parents-in-law's Putney garden, Beaton's white willowherb, George Clive's sassafras, as well as a small cornucopia of plants from Rosemary Verey, above all the 'Golden King' hollies in the Flower Garden, which I clip each year thinking of her and beloved Barnsley. From these alone the reader will gather that plants are cherished in this garden not only for their own intrinsic qualities, but also because they are precious in terms of memory.

In the early days of making a garden, gifts of plants are warmly welcomed. It is only later when they can become something of an embarrassment, one akin, but far worst in its consequences, to those acquired through the folly of impulse buying. At least, in the case of the latter, it has been your own fault and, if the worst comes to the worst, you can dump the plant. But in the case of plant gifts, whether you like it or not, a space somehow must be found, for the donor will expect, on his next visit, to be shown how it has prospered. Of course, as a last resort, plants can be mysteriously disposed of, victims, you will tell the donor, of some ghastly weather aberration which struck this particular area of the country but nowhere else, or of some unexpected and strange disease, when you know full well it is yourself that has arranged its fate.

So here in this chapter I intend to pause once again and cast my mind, as any other gardener would, towards certain plants, artefacts and experiences which have left indelible marks, small as well as large, on The Laskett garden, those with a story, or, rather, a story for us. At my age they are truly remembrance, for the people they represent have, in most cases, long since gone, but their memory is treasured. I can't think that I am alone in strolling along paths and recalling this or that person or garden as my eye catches this or that plant throwing forth shoots or bursting into flower. In that way a garden becomes peopled, in my wife's case as far back as the Second World War. Those years were spent by her in Wokingham in Berkshire and she still recalls that it was a Dr Ernest Ward who gave her mother some golden feverfew (*Tanacetum parthenium* 'Aureum') and common green fennel (*Foeniculum vulgare*), whose descendants thrive here today. But there are others about which there is so much more to tell.

IN THE KITCHEN GARDEN, OVER AN ARCADE OF ARCHES THAT forms its focal point, sprawl two plants, one a honeysuckle, the other a rose, each of which has a history. The honeysuckle is a memory of the childhood of my mother-in-law, Joan Oman. As she lay dying of cancer, her oldest childhood friend, Betty Clutterbuck, came to see her clutching a simple posy of flowers gathered in the garden of the old rectory at Wootton, not far from Oxford. Betty was the daughter of Canon Frank Marriott, brother of the historian Sir John Arthur Ransome Marriott, known as 'Jar'. This was a rectory of the kind one dreams of, large, rambling, Georgian in date, with spacious, light-filled rooms and passages, the atmosphere fragrant with beeswax and wood smoke. In fact, the type of interior which *Country Life* celebrated and promoted in its early days, the epitome of Englishness, continuity, comfort, unassertive and, in its way, unpretentious. But the garden was the thing.

This was a plantsman's garden of a kind, when I made my solitary and only visit shortly after marriage, I little understood. But I recall the tender climbers which clambered up the house and over which huge wooden frames were carefully placed in winter to protect them from the frost. Betty's father, Frank Marriott, belonged to the era of the great parson plantsmen who adorned the Church of England in the Victorian age. He takes his place alongside the likes of Canon Henry Nicholson Ellacombe at Bitton in Gloucestershire, whose book *In a Gloucestershire Garden* remains a good read to this day, or Dean Samuel Reynolds Hole of Caunton in

Nottinghamshire, latterly Dean of Rochester, the great rosarian. These men imported plants from abroad and created gardens which gained world renown. Frank Marriott fits neatly into this gallery of green-fingered clerics. He was a great fisherman and went to Norway to fish each summer, returning from there plant-laden. But why was the honeysuckle so meaningful?

Joan Oman was effectively motherless and Betty's mother took her under her wing. Joan and Betty would spend the week in Oxford in Marstonferry Road, the home of Sir Ernest Trevelyan, while attending Miss Batty's school, Wychwood, the 'Batty Hole', as it was known, and then, each weekend, the pony and trap would deliver them to the rectory at Wootton. Joan Oman called old Mrs Marriott 'mum', an indication of the loving bond that existed between the two. So we may guess what thoughts must have tumbled through her mind as she gazed upon that posy gathered from the haven of her childhood as she lay on what was to be her deathbed.

After she died, Julia took the sprigs of honeysuckle, which had sprung roots in the vase, down to The Laskett and planted them. With careful nurturing the honeysuckle was quickly clambering up a little arch of larchwood near the house and, later, found its resting place in the kitchen garden. As far as I can judge it is the common *Lonicera periclymenum* with its pretty fragrant white into yellow flowers, but that is beside the point. Who could not be touched by such a clutch of memories taking one back to a reverie of childhood tragedy and happiness in the golden days before the deluge of 1914?

The second plant, the rose, is a mystery. We were presented with it as 'The Gardener's Rose' and as having come from Margery Fish's garden at East Lambrook Manor in Somerset. We've visited that garden a couple of times, but we've not spotted it, although we have never come away empty-handed, for the creator of that garden was the mistress and pioneer of ground-cover planting and also of gardening in the shade during the post-war years. Her book, *We Made a Garden*, still remains a classic. Our first visit was on 15 April 1993 and it made a great impression, even though its creator had long since died, for I wrote about it in my diary:

> We went to Margery Fish's garden at East Lambrook. It was a little untidy due to lack of labour, but it was such an exciting garden with dramatic changes of level deployed to stunning effect with a cornucopia of plants. The garden was in fact quite extraordinary with a winding, intimate quality like a child's picture-book, a magic garden . . . terrific underplanting which inspired me.

Two years later we returned and I was equally impressed, noting, however, that the photos exhibited of Mrs Fish showed her looking tough and someone told us that she'd poisoned her husband with weedkiller! The range of hardy geraniums she had was enormous, over a hundred, and our garden is the richer for many varieties as a result of those visits. But what of the rose? 'The Gardener's Rose' is one of those monsters which may not be so all-consuming as the legendary 'Kiftsgate', which can swallow a house, but it is certainly explosive. It is not repeat flowering, but few garden sights are as splendid as this rose at its height in mid-June, powdered all over with pale pinkish blooms tinged deeper at the petal rims. A second now erupts up and through an old apple tree in the tiny Folly garden. That was quite slow to get going, but once it had, there was no stopping it.

We owe this rose to one of my wife's oldest friends, a lovable, larger-than-life eccentric called John Vere Brown. Julia remembers him from her first day at the two terms she spent at Kingston School of Art in the late forties where, fresh from a repressive girls' boarding school, she had found herself in a world peopled also by young men. That leap was made the easier by the cheery 'Hallo' from John. A talented photographer and a not untalented painter, John was to work his way through a large fortune matched by a slow descent from a moated manor house in Kent, where the rose flourished, through endless moves, to the only residence of his I recall, a modest flat in Redcliffe Gardens presided over by a melancholy portrait of Charles I, but which had a garden. John, or 'Beige' as he was nicknamed, was born with green fingers, for on our visit there even this minute garden was filled with hellebores in flower and Julia asked for seed. Through the post a little later came a jiffy bag stuffed full of seed-laden flowerheads. Their descendants grow here to this day. 'The Gardener's Rose' came shortly after a visit to The Laskett, for he had to secure rooted cuttings of it from the new owners of his moated Kentish manor house, where he had planted the East Lambrook rose.

This was a man of mad enthusiasms, someone whom people took advantage of and whose life skidded from one catastrophe to the next, but whose capacity for friendship was real. After he died, we drove all the way down to a remote church on the Sussex–Kent borders for the interment of his ashes. It was a golden summer afternoon and we had difficulty finding the place, arriving late, creeping in at the back of the tiny church. There gathered together were about a dozen of his friends scattered in the pews. One by one they were called upon to say a few words about him. I'd never seen that done before and was much moved by the simplicity and truth of it, for what was said brought fewer tears than smiles and laughter. Then out in a straggly procession we went, arranging ourselves in a semi-circle while his ashes were carefully lowered into a hole in the turf close to the crumbling churchyard wall. Everything was calm and beautiful in that most English of settings and yet true to a man whose nature was to be a permanent firework display, not unlike his rose which erupts into flower each June in The Laskett garden.

*

THE GARDEN YEAR AT THE LASKETT BEGINS WITH SNOWDROPS. No, not just snowy drifts of them in shady places, which of course we have in abundance, but something much more special, the hidden snowdrop garden of my wife's. There from mid-January on her collection unfolds, each variety with its label, until it reaches a climax of beauty and then embarks on a dying fall. On a last count she had something like fifty varieties, which would hardly qualify her as being a galanthophile, plant collectors of a highly predatory nature. Her far more modest interest goes back to one person, Bill Bishop, and the visit we made to his garden at Putley in Herefordshire not that far from us.

That visit came as part of one of those local meetings of the National Council for the Conservation of Plants and Gardens late in February 1988, not long after I had left the V & A. We met in a decrepit church hall to listen to the great galanthus man, Mr R. D. Nutt, deliver a lecture on snowdrops while we sat huddled up in the cold looking forward to our picnic lunch. George Clive was, of course, there and also, on this occasion, old Dick Banks, father of Lawrence, of Hergest Croft and a major tree man. He too was a galanthophile and had brought items to sell in aid of the NCCPG, Julia purchasing three bulbs of *G. nivalis* 'Viridapice' and two *G. ikariae* for the princely sum of £2.

And then there was Bill Bishop. He was the former superintendent of Harrogate Parks Department and a well-known plantsman. He must then have been in his seventies, a stocky figure with a moustache and large glasses, so inseparable from the flat cap on his head that he must have gone to bed in it. After lunch we all made our way to his cottage at Putley to see his snowdrop collection. This was a plantsman's garden, one whose central concern was to create habitats in which the snowdrops would flourish, so the house was surrounded by paving followed by a small irregular swathe of grass accommodating trees and shrubs held in by a clipped hedge. The snowdrops were planted in pools of dazzling white, lighting up the shade. Up until that lecture I was unaware even that snowdrops existed in varieties, but here they were and interest seized Julia in such a way that Bill Bishop was impressed and offered to put together a small collection for her from his own once they had died down. Snowdrops of course have to be split and planted in the green.

So it was that on 5 May Mr Bishop came, hat on head, to The Laskett bearing a box of snowdrop varieties. He gave my wife about a dozen in all. Some were of well-known varieties like *G. nivalis* Scharlockii Group, which has slender flowers, *G.* 'Mighty Atom', which has large ones, and the venerable *G.* 'Hill Poë', which is recognized to be one of the finest and a great favourite of all galanthophiles. E.A. Bowles was growing it at Myddelton House as early as 1917. Others bore names like 'Mrs Backhouse No. 12' and 'from Mr Nutt', evidence endorsing what the latest definitive work on snowdrops confirms, that the varieties run into hundreds and the subtle variations and mutations are never-ending. As I walked Mr Bishop around our garden he seemed a sad man, for his wife had recently died, and, although he was to live another decade, I felt that he had chosen Julia as one of the heirs to his collection. In that he had selected well, for she initially carefully planted and labelled them with a plan in the Kitchen Garden. Only after they had multiplied and prospered and she began to increase the collection did she embark on her secret spring garden for their display.

It gave me joy to read that in Bill Bishop's garden in 1999, just before he died, an early-flowering variant of 'Mighty Atom' was discovered. That other great snowdrop authority Chris Brickell suggested that it should be called 'Bill Bishop' and so it was. But that initial kindness of his had set Julia on her way to form her own collection and take a keen interest in snowdrop varieties. Her firm rule is that her snowdrop beds are sacred, not to be touched by the likes of me or indeed Shaun. Until a particular bulb has multiplied none are moved out of its precincts to be naturalized elsewhere in the garden.

So much for Bill Bishop, but spring is also signalled by a scattering of buttery yellow aconites at the top of the drive, planted at the foot of the great beech tree we had to fell after the 1976 drought. We owe them to another great character, always known to the art world as Lady Charlotte Bonham-Carter, a form of address to which she had no right by birth, for she was a colonel's daughter. For decades this extraordinary, minute, wrinkled, bent and cheerful soul would turn up everywhere. In one evening she would manage the private view of an exhibition, tuck in a party and pop up in a box at the opera house. Her appetite was as insatiable as her generosity of spirit, and she always lit up with a smile and an exclamation of pleasure at absolutely everything and everybody. Her dress, which consisted of an arrangement of shawls, recalled Augustus John depictions of gypsies in the 1920s. As she made her way from one event to the next she could be caught disappearing behind a bush to achieve a quick change for the next encounter. Her house in the country, Wyck, was in Gilbert White's village of Selborne in Hampshire where, every year, she staged what she called her aconite parties.

We never actually got to one of those parties, but every time we met her she knew of our purchase of a house in the country and that we had set out to make a garden. 'Oh, my dear, the aconites!' she would exclaim, always promising a box of them, for at Selborne they apparently grew like weeds, carpeting what was known as the Aconite Walk. And then, one day, I returned to my office in the museum and there it was, the box of aconites. I can't recount my delight, for that was quite early on in our garden-making. We planted them on the green bank at the top of the drive deliberately so that we would get full joy of them in springtime. And, although over the years the numbers have diminished, they are still there, a memory of someone who just failed to make her hundredth birthday. I can hear her now saying, 'Oh, my dear, how perfectly marvellous!'

IN THE REMOTEST PART OF THE FIELD, DELIBERATELY PLANTED TO be as it were 'lost', a pink cherry tree soars fully upwards. It has never done particularly well, nor has it been loved. That it was sited as close as could be to oblivion is at least a hint that it embodied some memory which I wished to obliterate from my mind. With the passing of the years its story can now be told.

One of the reasons which brought me to Hereford was to remove myself as far as possible from my own family. I had never got on with my father, who was quite unfit to have sired children as he was wholly devoid of any sense of responsibility for them either in terms of their upbringing or their education or what was to happen to them. Early on I learnt that in order to survive the wisest thing to do was to steer clear of him. And it was he who brought me that tree, thus endowing it with a potency of recollection of a kind I sought to avoid. The unhappiness of childhood can only be comprehended in retrospect, but in my case it was compounded by being raised in a house with a broken marriage. How often I recall as a child the injunction, 'Whatever you do, don't tell your father.' Add to that the possessiveness of my mother, who wanted none of her three boys ever to marry and leave her, and the picture is further heightened.

It is not an accident therefore that this book began with an elopement, a secret marriage, not in fact the first in the case of the three brothers. My mother was never really to come to terms with the fact that my prime affection was now for another woman. That was her loss. Nonetheless, once a year my parents used to make a visit to The Laskett. It was a day we dreaded, one somehow to be got through and, as is the case with so many families, one to be got through hopefully with nothing untoward said. It was on such a day that my father arrived with that cherry tree, one which had self-seeded in that north London suburban garden. Poor plant. The gift I know was well meant, but at the time all I could see before me was something which would forever bring to mind everything from which I had sought to escape. But I was caught. There was no way that I could throw it away. Next year they would be bound to want to inspect its progress. So the only solution was banishment to a remote corner engulfed by conifers, an area I visited only rarely.

When I came to write this book I asked my wife whether the fatal tree was still there. The reply was yes, it was, an index of just how much I had tried to blot out its existence from my mind. That day I strolled to find it. There it was, a lanky, awkward specimen fighting for light. It wasn't at all beautiful. Somehow I wished that it had been, as if by some miracle it had been transformed. I stared at it and asked myself the questions I had asked so often asked and to which I had no reply. Why had things been like that? Why did some families breed within themselves such destructive emotions? In what way had I contributed to the failure? Both parents are long since dead and gone. Reconciliation is one of the most difficult of all the virtues to practise fully. That tree stands as a perpetual reminder of that sad fact.

NEITHER OF US IS OF THE TYPE WHO WOULD SURREPTITIOUSLY take a cutting from someone's plant when they weren't looking and pop it into one's pocket, but picking up a chestnut or a fir cone is another matter. And that Julia always has done over the years, and so does another friend, Gillian Sladen. As a consequence of that we have a chestnut tree slowly growing which came from the celebrated late-eighteenth-century French garden the Desert de Retz, not far from Paris, which we visited in the nineties. This is one of the greatest of

The crown to mark the Queen's Golden Jubilee, 2002

Autumn tableau: The Victoria & Albert Museum
Temple glimpsed through fruit-laden branches

TOP: *The pleached-lime walk Elizabeth Tudor*

The Triumphal Arch in the Rose Garden

LEFT: *The recumbent Stag in the Orchard, with the inscription from Milton's* Paradise Lost

BELOW: *The Hilliard parterre at its height before it was destroyed by box blight with J and R at the centre*

OVERLEAF: *A plan of the gardens*

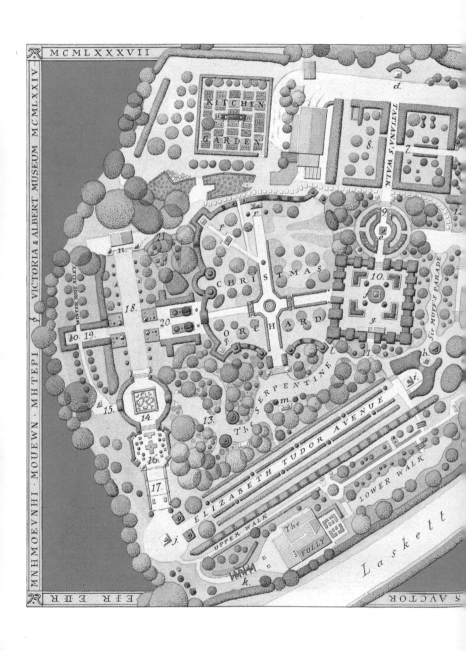

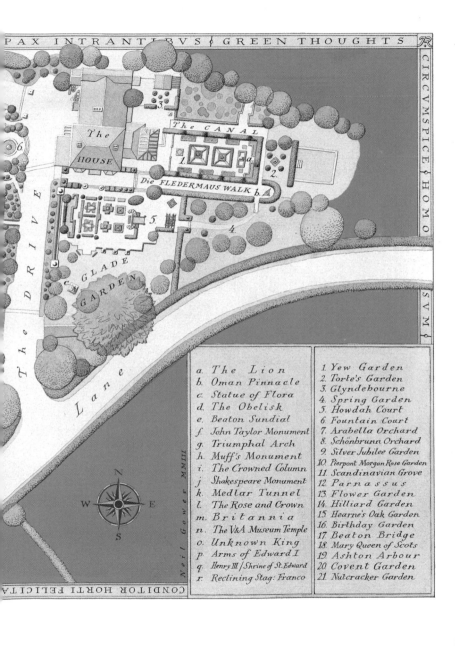

CIRCVMSPICE ✦ HOMO

SVM

The CANAL

The HOUSE

Die FLEDERMAUS WALK

GLADE GARDEN

The DRIVE

Lane

Neil Gower MMIII

N
W   E
S

a. The Lion	1. Yew Garden
b. Oman Pinnacle	2. Torte's Garden
c. Statue of Flora	3. Glyndebourne
d. The Obelisk	4. Spring Garden
e. Beaton Sundial	5. Howdah Court
f. John Taylor Monument	6. Fountain Court
g. Triumphal Arch	7. Arabella Orchard
h. Muff's Monument	8. Schönbrunn Orchard
i. The Crowned Column	9. Silver Jubilee Garden
j. Shakespeare Monument	10. Pierpont Morgan Rose Garden
k. Medlar Tunnel	11. Scandinavian Grove
l. The Rose and Crown	12. Parnassus
m. Britannia	13. Flower Garden
n. The V&A Museum Temple	14. Hilliard Garden
o. Unknown King	15. Hearne's Oak Garden
p. Arms of Edward I	16. Birthday Garden
q. Henry III / Shrine of St. Edward	17. Beaton Bridge
r. Reclining Stag: Franco	18. Mary Queen of Scots
	19. Ashton Arbour
	20. Covent Garden
	21. Nutcracker Garden

The Shakespeare Monument

gardens in the style designated *anglo-chinois*, a fantastic, eerie landscape, the nearest experience I know in horticultural terms to Mozart's *The Magic Flute*, which includes a house that is the stump of a vast ruined column and a metallic blue and gold tent. I am glad to have that tree as a mnemonic, for the Desert de Retz was an unforgettable experience, another powerful reminder, in the tradition of Bomarzo, that the garden has room for madness.

Julia picked up her pine cones in Italy in the gardens at Landriana and La Mortella. There is a link between the two, for both gardens were creations of one of the great designers of the last century, Russell Page. He had entered my life in 1979 when the exhibition *The Garden* was staged in the V & A. It had been one of my aims to make a distinguished garden in the museum's quadrangle, which had been planted in the immediate post-war period with municipal pink cherry blossom. Russell Page prepared a brilliant scheme, but the staff bitterly fought against the felling of the ghastly cherry trees and I lost the battle. Page's garden never happened, but I'm proud to have met him, a large man carrying a capacious canvas bag stuffed with plans.

The Giardini della Landriana we visited at the close of the nineties. It is south of Rome near Anzio and was the creation of the Marchesa Gallarati Scotti with the aid, from 1967 onwards, of Page. This is a meandering site with formal accents, treasured for many things, but one garden held for me an especial magic. Enclosed by olive trees with their chalky grey-green leaves there was a garden of a kind that could never survive in northern climes. At ground level it was scattered with myrtle clipped into crisp balls. From these arose a network of maples (*Acer platanoides* 'Globosum') shaped into mopheads, each one surrounded by four bitter-orange trees, again clipped into globes. The ground was carpeted with golden *Lysimachia nummularia* 'Aurea' and an unidentified bluish flowering weed. This composition, the marchesa's own in an area Page had used for a rose garden, ranks high on my list of unforgettable garden experiences, the atmosphere luminous and mysterious, the repetitive use of the same globular shape at different levels and of slightly differing sizes of a haunting beauty. The marchesa, who played a great part in the revival of gardening in Italy, died not long after our visit. I am glad to have met her, a huge enthusiast, and have at least a memory of her and her garden in that burgeoning umbrella pine, planted in proximity to The Folly.

Far more serious is the other pine, now three metres in height and pushing its way skywards along the walk to The Folly. In 1994 we were asked for the weekend to La Mortella on the island of Ischia as guests of the Walton Foundation at the behest of the redoubtable widow of Sir William Walton. There Susana with the help of Russell Page had also created a remarkable garden, one which left its imprint on me in that I wrote about it in my diary:

This is a marvellous garden hewn out of and wedded to the rock. It is quite wonderful with an oval pond below from which arises a vast jet, a number of smaller fountains and a charming rill. This 'architecture' was due to Russell Page . . . Trees are her real obsession and up they soar to a great height: pines, ginkgos and jacarandas. Below them sprawl huge drifts of groundcover plants, hardy geraniums, ferns, hemerocallis, begonias, hellebores. . . One of the problems is that the garden is split in two. The one above is really above, a huge ascent on foot (there's also a funicular from the back of the house whereby to reach it). There one finds 'William's Rock', in which the composer's ashes rest, and higher up still there are ponds and cascades surrounded by grey foliage plants and beyond them a Thai house made of wood, which had been shipped from Bangkok . . . It was so interesting to meet someone who had made a garden the same size as ours but so very very different.

One result of that visit was my wife's suggestion to Susana that she copy the mask from John Piper's design for *Façade*, which hung on her walls, as a source for the garden's waters. I was made to stand where this was to be placed right at the garden's summit and be photographed by Julia. That I hear is now in place as La Mortella's *bocca*. The parent fir cones from both Landriana and La Mortella still adorn our hall table as still-life today, reminders of the inspiration to us of two great late-twentieth-century gardens.

AT THE CLOSE OF WHAT IS CALLED SIR MUFF'S PARADE THERE stands a solitary yew, shaped like a sugar loaf and about three metres high with the summit trained to form the arches of a crown. In spring it is surrounded with a garland of white and blue hyacinths while nearby there are swathes of Lent lilies, primroses and hellebores at the foot of a short avenue of pollarded acacias interplanted with *Malus*. This yew came from Sutton Place in Surrey at the time when Sir Geoffrey Jellicoe was busy creating what he had hoped might be his greatest private garden for the multi-millionaire Stanley Seeger.

Seeger had acquired Sutton Place in 1980 and called in Sir Hugh Casson to work on the house, and it was he who recommended Jellicoe for the garden. At about the same time a Trust was established peppered with various eminences including the likes of John Julius Norwich, David Starkey and myself. What was striking about the project was that money seemed to be no object, and I vividly remember on my initial visit seeing drawings by Jellicoe scattered all over a table's surface. I was hypnotized by them. Jellicoe was the most exquisite draughtsman, each drawing a work of art in itself, but what astonished me was the scale of the garden, a vast domain with a lake dominated by the largest Henry Moore sculpture ever cast, a garden music room, a moss garden in the manner of Japan, a swimming pool based on Miró, a Paradise Garden, a kitchen garden with a Magritte Walk, not to mention the southern cascade or Avenue of Fountains which swept down the hillside behind the house. All of this was within a decade to founder, as I understood it, on the topic of taxation. Much, like the great cascade, was never built. But through the eighties work went galloping forward with all the resources which money could buy to achieve more or less immediate effect. And into that saga came our solitary yew.

As I was walked around the garden I recall sighing, 'Ah, I wish that I could afford to plant yews that height.' The yews in question were two metres high and had been imported by the hundred from Italy and, on being planted, formed an almost immediate mature yew hedge. In 1980 ours had just about reached half that dimension. So it was that one day a lorry came all the way from Sutton Place to The Laskett with a solitary yew. I was touched by the gift. I have to admit that it would have been far easier if there had been two, but, alas, there was only one. In desperation I planted it where it can be seen today, a perpetual reminder to me of Geoffrey.

In April 1988 Geoffrey and I were asked to do a double act on the future of gardening, arranged by the Palace Academy and staged before Queen Beatrix and appropriate Dutch horticultural worthies in the royal palace in Amsterdam. Geoffrey was a jovial rotund man whose gardening ideas, rooted in the study of Jung, were way beyond his audience. His main concern on that occasion was for his poor feet and would the Queen notice that he was wearing slippers? I said of course she wouldn't, but, as he would lecture without rehearsing the slides, it was all a bit of a muddle. And he would also only talk about his Moody Gardens project in Texas. I was seated next to Prince Claus who, at the end of Geoffrey's paper, turned to me and said, 'Pure Disney.' And, in a curious way, he was right.

The last time I saw Geoffrey was when I was filming the television series *Royal Gardens* at Sandringham in 1992.

Surprisingly it was the first occasion that he had clapped eyes again on the garden he had designed for George VI and the Queen Mother in 1947, a long rectangular flower garden with box-edged beds, containing walls of yew and elegant flanking walks of pleached lime. Geoffrey was then a splendid ninety-one-year-old with a mind less on the garden he had made all those years ago than on the large gin and tonic which had been promised him before lunch. It was only later that I was to see what I consider his greatest private garden, Shute House in Wiltshire. But how lucky I am to have known him at all and that through that solitary yew, in an eccentric way, he has been gathered into our garden.

THE REASON THAT YEW IS TOPPED BY A TOPIARY CROWN GOES back to Rosemary Verey, who, as I have said, suggested to the Prince of Wales that I should design the hedges and topiary at Highgrove. It was on Friday 9 June 1989 that we drove over on the first of several visits to Highgrove and not long after that I presented a dossier of designs for training and cutting the yew hedges. The Prince is a passionate and knowledgeable gardener, but the story of those hedges and my other contributions to his garden are tangential to The Laskett narrative, except that in a strange way the gardens are linked by a common hand, mine, at least in respect of the swagged and pompommed hedges. For the first few years I went and cut the Highgrove hedges myself, taking one of our gardeners, Wilf, with me, and now they are very capably clipped by the Prince's gardeners. But I do, every so many years, like to see how they have progressed and on each occasion I confess to being well pleased.

The result here was that our garden became an experimental laboratory for the Highgrove topiary. On one of the designs I had cheerfully drawn two pillars of clipped yew topped by the Prince of Wales's triple feathers. I had no idea at the time as to whether such an effect could be achieved, but, for a few years here, I attempted to train the yew sentinels flanking the approach to the Flower Garden with those feathers. They were not a success and, in the end, I lopped them off. But the crown I trained on the Sutton Place yew was another story and was until I recently re-sculpted it recognizable as such. The odd thing is I never actually did one at Highgrove.

The fact that I had contributed to the creation of the garden of the heir to the throne I felt needed some kind of commemoration here, and the opportunity came when I was trying to suggest to the Prince how to pull the great garden at the back of the house together. Highgrove lacked virtually any hard surface ornaments in the way of sculpture and what was a neo-classical house cried out for handsome pieces in the classical manner. Around Vicenza they are still manufacturing life-size stone statues in the baroque idiom and, as I wrote to him on 29 September: 'A few of these would give the garden a terrific lift in visual terms.' And so they did. Four splendid statues of the Seasons, sculpted to the best quality, were imported from Italy and sited symmetrically along the aerial hornbeam hedge. What the Prince didn't know is that I ordered two of one of them and that a lorry bearing the one I had paid for continued on from Gloucestershire to here, where it was eventually lowered by crane into position in the glade opposite the front door to the house. We call her Flora, for she clutches with her right hand a basket of stone blossoms. There she nestles beneath the great cedar of Lebanon against a background of evergreens and amidst a springtime planting of hamamelis and small rhododendrons. Everyone who comes to the house through the front door sees her in a perspective across the knot garden framed by the tall columns of *Juniper communis* 'Hibernica' and Victorian gothic gate piers painted blue and gilded. When I take parties around the garden I refer to Flora as my name-dropping statue.

But I am happy to have embraced Highgrove into the

garden, for both gardens were started not so far apart in time and both share many of the same impulses, among other things a taste for formality, one for fantasy and a commitment to the organic. The last came fully with the arrival of Robin Stephens, a sworn enemy to the use of all chemicals in the garden. When the Highgrove gardeners came here once they brought plants, one of which, a penstemon, I am particularly fond of. Its flowers are an incandescent pinkish-purple which is almost luminous in the border. From time to time the Prince crosses my path and the talk is always of the garden, with me goading him on to some new excess. Nowadays down the line he comes on royal occasions at Westminster Abbey, where I hold the honorary post of High Bailiff and Searcher of the Sanctuary. I recall our last exchange was about him being biffed in the eye while pruning. Such are the travails of the active gardener. All those things remind me of what was a happy chance in my life, the opportunity to design hedging and topiary on the grand scale. I am told that when the Prince lectures on his garden he always remembers to toss me a bouquet. For that I am grateful.

On 3 July 1995 I wrote in my diary an entry that records the lifting of our spirits by a visit of gardeners from the Netherlands:

We opened the garden to a group of Dutch garden owners. They came in two batches of fourteen. I had worked like blazes tweaking the garden so that it would be *à point* and that included spending £48 on two standard white roses, 'Kent', in full flower to fill in the ghastly gaps in the Flower Garden. As a result it looked pretty good. I'd been asked what I charged and I said, 'Oh, forget it. I love the Dutch' [that was a cherished memory of Jan van Dorsten who had died young in 1986]. Could we bring you a plant? was the reply. 'Well,' I said, 'I love box.' So along Laskett Lane came this bevy of upper-class Dutch, each clasping a pot with a three-foot-high box tree in it. These were laid like tribute at my feet and I declared that I would make a new garden in remembrance of their visit. We both had a tremendous time showing them the garden and we didn't regret the decision to visit. It was such a pleasure to show it to those that know and I learnt so much about box, how to cut it properly, take cuttings, prune it and how to encourage its bushiness. Both groups stayed about two hours and we were left in a happy haze.

That entry captures something which should not go unrecorded, for its impact can be traced at The Laskett, that is, the influence of post-war Dutch garden-making. I first became aware of that soon after embarking on my career as a writer of books on small garden design. Such books are inevitably dependent on the visual sources available. Indeed I regard such publications as offering the average reader a repertory of ideas which they can copy, picking and mixing. Quite early on I was struck again and again by the fact that the most exquisite tiny formal gardens, so much to my own taste, were always Dutch. But it was only in the late eighties and through the nineties that we began to visit the Netherlands and actually see these gardens. They haunt my imagination – there is a heroism attached to some of the finest, for they were made from nothing immediately after the Second World War, when everything had been levelled flat. One garden-maker I recall telling us how she began after 1945 by planting a shelter belt of trees which she then had to wait for a decade to grow before she could embark on her garden. Land is scarce in Holland so even to have a garden is a privilege, one which is fully responded to. Inevitably such gardens are small, calling for a high degree of style and plantsmanship to cram a lot into a tiny space. I have never seen their equal.

Shortly after that visit by the Dutch garden owners I took a group on a tour of Dutch gardens, insisting that the tour operator not only include the grand gardens of the likes of

Het Loo but also some of the tiny ones. At the time I wrote an account trying to pinpoint what was their essence:

On the tour I noticed the sameness of the gardens, all beautiful, but very much clones of each other. They had very little if any built structure, rarely any sculpture and, if there was, often minute and kitsch. Architectural structure came from box edging to beds and low yew hedges backing flower borders, these charmingly delineating areas which contained planting whose context was colour rather than seasonal effect; blue and lilac and yellow and white being favourite combinations. All the gardens had a very strong sense of the importance of greens, in fact the best gardens were virtually nothing but shades of green using a great variety of clipped greens as a framing device or planted in the borders as formal accents. In fact, in some instances it was a case of too many box balls which seemed to almost breed overnight. There was no use of very strong colour at all and therefore it was all very much 1980s good taste gardening, so that in the end I longed for a bold, vulgar gesture. But, alas, no luck.

The Dutch make much use of small standard trees, especially acacias, as mopheads to form miniature avenues and there is also great inventiveness with modest materials. Four bricks and a plank and *voilà* a seat which, through imaginative planting, is lifted into forming a picture. Above all these Dutch gardens have a huge charm of scale, being always domestic and never assertive or grand. There are always narrow paths of soft-coloured brick or setts with a great use of pattern. There is always too an area with a table and comfortable chairs dressed with cushions and a cloth. The borders in the main, however, were overplanted, stuffed in fact, which meant that one failed to see the plant forms. But these small gardens really gave me ideas for the Folly garden where the scale must shrink dramatically compared with the main garden, so that people will be taken by surprise when they come across it.

The Folly Garden (the cottage was purchased in 1995 and absorbed into our domain) was laid out during the winter of that year, a simple chequerboard of narrow paths with small beds around the existing old apple tree up which John Vere Brown's 'Gardener's Rose' climbs. This is a tiny formal garden in the Dutch manner held in by a low yew hedge about a metre high with finials trained to accentuate the corners and the entrances. In its initial phase the gift of so many box bushes enabled me to clip some into balls and others into cones, planting them to emphasize the symmetry of the composition. There is a central vista from a stone bench beneath a *treillage* arbour festooned with honeysuckle, the beds I filled with cottage-garden plants and I began to train a holly cake-stand as a bold decorative vertical in the midst of one of them. In two others I planted suckers from the Frewin quince, which I then proceeded to prune and keep as a bush, inspired by the use of quince trees with their golden fruit in the late autumn in the flower borders of Holland.

The Netherlands continues to remain my second gardening home and I count it a privilege that we met the most famous of all late-twentieth-century Dutch gardeners, Mien Ruys. The occasion was 16 September 1998 during another tour of Dutch gardens. This is what I wrote:

British people are wholly ignorant of Mien Ruys. So was I until I noticed looking through pictures of late-twentieth-century Dutch gardens how her name kept cropping up. She cropped up in the way that I would find myself in a garden in which I would yell out 'Isn't that marvellous?' and then discover that it was her again. Then four years ago we visited her garden at Dedemsvaart and I began to understand why. She was ninety-two then and all I glimpsed was a black bundle in the distance as someone mumbled with awe, 'That's Mien Ruys.' The gardens are extraordinary, twenty-five or so of them laid out over a period of seventy years from 1925 onwards. They are quite unique in giving in one place the whole history of this country's gardens running from the tail-end of the Arts and Crafts Jekyllesque style down to the uncompromisingly modern decking of today. The gardens all have dates and they must be grasped because only then can one understand their full significance, ones like the Reed Pond Garden, 1960, with its innovatory plastic container, or the Sunken Garden, 1960s again, with its totally original use of railway sleepers. Everywhere we wandered we were aware that in creating this series of small gardens here was a woman who had met the late twentieth century head on, uncompromising, modern and with no looking back, no nostalgia, unashamedly using today's materials, concrete in every form down to re-cycled plastic in the Marsh Garden. Here were roof gardens for flat dwellers, gardens for children and for every circum-stance relating to how ordinary people live now. This was gardening in post-1945 democratic Europe. Her planting was masterly and simple, masses of ground cover and simple herbaceous plants, but always done with a twist, like mean-dering blocks of asters beneath roses.

Suddenly one of our group ran up and said it was Mien Ruys looking for us. We gathered ourselves together in haste for this epiphany and rushed hither and thither to find her. There she was, ninety-six, propelled in a bath chair like some icon around her gardens, shrouded up like a parcel, her feet in sensible shoes, her hat an old 'tea cosy' on her head. Her impact was electric, a presence was felt. Every one of us instinctively bowed to this venerable figure. Julia said that we had come to offer her homage, which I echoed. Her hands were puffed with arthritis, her eyes slightly falling from sock-ets full of rheum, her face weather-beaten. But the intelligence was there in the features and the dart of the eyes. Then she spoke: 'I have been gardening for seventy years. Do you like my garden?' Her bowed face peered upwards smiling. We did, indeed we did. A voice behind her reminded her that she had met Gertrude Jekyll. 'Yes, I had tea with her. I am the last person living who spoke to her.' 'At Munstead?' I asked. 'Yes, at Munstead.' [Later I learnt that wasn't quite true. Both Christopher Lloyd and Graham Thomas, both happily still with us, were 'blessed' by her when young!] We had encountered a legend, a link in gardening terms to Edwin Lutyens and to William Morris. Again and again she said that what we looked at had taken seventy years. 'Young,' I said, 'for a garden.' She smiled and understood. Little by little we made our adieus and the queen as it were resumed her progress. This was a woman, tough, resilient, modest, yet exuding humanity with a still compelling interest in the garden: what grew well, what flowers prospered, how was this or that doing, did it work, if not how could she make it better. Surely she will go down as one of the great figures in the story of the garden. I stood there after transfixed, stunned and silenced. So this was what it was like to be a true gardener.

Such encounters are landmarks in a gardening life. Mien Ruys had come too late in a sense to influence The Laskett garden, other than through her followers, but Dr Ian Hamilton Finlay did not. It was on 28 June 1995 that I at last saw Little Sparta. This was a garden I had long known about from reading and from endless pictures. It had already impressed itself on my mind so powerfully that long before this visit I had concluded that it was the most important garden to be made in the British Isles in the second half of the twentieth century. I still stand by that judgement.

Ian Hamilton Finlay is a Scottish poet, sculptor and gardener who has chosen the garden as the principal vehicle for his poetic expression, above all in his own at Dunsyre in the Scottish Lowlands. And it is that decision which has lifted his garden away from anything else, apart, that is, from the vast landscape terrain created by Charles Jencks and Maggie Keswick not far distant from Little Sparta, which I went to on the same day. But for me to see Little Sparta was the fulfilment of a dream and I was not to be disappointed.

Here is how I recorded what still remains in my memory as one of the most influential and overwhelming garden experiences of my life. That I got there I owe to a radio series I took part in called *Growing Spaces*:

I had always wanted to visit this garden, believing it to be the most original of all post-war gardens. Annie [the producer] and I were given the time of 1.30 p.m. for the interview, but we wandered in the garden first. I was quite unprepared for its scale, which is modest, a mosaic of small contained areas and meandering paths with trees, shrubs and much low-maintenance planting. The garden comes as such a surprise, for the approach is up an ascent through three farmyard gates and along a rough track. There it sits at the end, on the hillside, like some symbolic aberration. Ian Hamilton Finlay suffers from agoraphobia and never leaves his domain, learning about the world around him through books and photographs. Perhaps this accounts for the scale of the myriad sculptures and inscriptions peppered across the landscape. Everywhere one walks there are tiny columns or plaques or strange gate piers, like the ones bearing hand grenades. There is such a plenitude as one wanders up and down through what is an extraordinary fantasy world surrounding a small lake. It is like a contemporary Bomarzo: a huge gilded head of Apollo stares up from the ground, trees are planted into the sculpted bases of columns, dedications here and there commemorate the painters Albrecht Dürer and Caspar David Friedrich and the heroes and villains of the French Revolution. There are many buildings and monuments, but all quite small, among them a pyramid and a grotto celebrating Dido and Aeneas. The imagination roams around the classical world with inscriptions from Ovid and others and swoops down the centuries to embrace the French Revolutionary period and then on to the condition of our own time as Hamilton Finlay sees it with strange tableaux like that on the topos *Et in Arcadia Ego* [And Death even in Arcady], which depicts shepherds discovering a tank with a skull and crossbones on it. Great use is made of columns of all kinds, both complete and broken and also capitals. A crofter's cottage looking across a pond has incised into its facade classical columns and an inscription identifying it as the Temple of the Muses.

As we skirted the pond a small elderly man appeared waving a sheet of paper. It was Ian Hamilton Finlay, a kindly, avuncular figure who spoke with a soft, almost lilting, Scottish accent. The paper was a plan of the garden and off we set again and then, on the dot of 1.30 p.m., we went to the house, a mere cottage, and carried our chairs onto the terrace to do the interview about the garden he had designed at Luton [and which I had opened], but the principles of it were also those of Little Sparta. Here is a man who left school at fourteen and who has surrounded himself with an imaginary landscape peopled with allusions which could only ever come from a deep knowledge of classical literature, the German Romantics and French Revolutionaries. He was tremendously fluent, lamenting the impoverishment of the garden in our own age, one whose basis was the colour supplement and television. In the past the garden was a point of departure and a setting for profound ideas, esoteric ones, and he cursed those who had let education slide so that even allusions so elementary as those to Apollo and Daphne could no longer be understood. But his was an extraordinarily benevolent view of things, for all he wanted of his visitors was for them to enjoy the garden. I asked him whether it mattered to him that they did not understand it. No, he replied, there are many levels of understanding and none was to be despised. I found it difficult to reconcile this gentle man with the image so often projected of him outside as a crypto-Nazi sympathizer who depicted Apollo holding a machine gun and not a lyre.

The garden made an enormous impression on me. There are lessons to be drawn for The Laskett. I admired the modesty of it. There was little money here and yet he has created something more significant in its way than either Sissinghurst or Hidcote, a recovery of the great tradition stretching back through William Kent to Alberti.

I, of course, wrote afterwards thanking him for what for me had been a seminal experience. As he could not travel I sent a copy of an article I had written on The Laskett garden in *Hortus*, along with a set of photographs. A letter came back soon after:

The wee booklet on your garden is charming. It makes you and your wife sound like Adam and Eve:

Verdure
and blossoms
boughs heavy
with fruit
bend down, above. . .

(translations of part of a poem by Paul Klee). This impression is all the nicer for being obviously inadvertent. You and your wife also make me imagine a kind of magic weatherhouse, in which the Man and the Lady both appear outside together, at once. . . I still don't understand how you (together) can maintain such a vast and intricate garden. I mean that kind of not understanding which contains amazement and approval in equal proportions.

Well, the amazement and approval was on my side, for the Little Sparta garden was for me an act of revelation of an almost Pauline intensity. Here was a man who had put back meaning into the garden on a scale and with a complexity we could not aspire to. But his inspiration was huge. How much I admired his unashamed elitism. In the same letter he wrote: 'It never seems to occur to certain people that what seems elitist to them, can seem quite ORDINARY and NATURAL to others. Of course it is only educated people who accuse other people of being elitist (alas); the word is unknown to ordinary people, some of whom in spite of everything still think it a good idea to make an effort.' In pin-pointing the garden's appeal to me I cannot escape the fact that its riddling allusions took me back to where I began my intellectual life proper, at the Warburg Institute during the years 1956 to 1959 when I sat at the feet of one of their greatest polymathic scholars, the late Dame Frances Yates. The Warburg's remit is the history of the classical tradition in the West, with an emphasis on the migration of symbols and ideas. The greatest works of art, and that includes gardens, were multi-layered compositions which called for an exercise of the intellect to unravel them on a variety of levels. The ability to read such things called for a shared mental vocabulary, absent in the fragmented civilization of our own age. But it made me realize that we must etch more forcefully meaning into our garden, even though it was meaning only for us.

This was a turning point. In 1995 I was sixty and Julia sixty-five. By then people had begun to write about The Laskett garden as ranking among those of any importance made during the second half of the last century in Britain. It was Rosemary Verey who said that it was the largest formal garden to be created in the country since 1945. If that was so, and she had said that her comment had gone unchallenged, then we needed to get a move on and instead of talking about this, that or the other project, actually carry them out as far as our limited means permitted us.

And this is what we did.

Seven

TRIUMPHS AND TRIBULATIONS

THE MIDDLE OF THE 1990S WAS, AS I HAVE INDICATED, A dramatic turning point in the garden's history, one marked by feverish activity and dramatic changes, so much so that the reader could easily lose his bearings. A series of entries from my diary captures the ferment, referring to various of the projects either achieved or in hand or contemplated. It also pinpoints so much that animated this decade, the drive to complete the hard landscaping, to etch in meaning and an intense interest in introducing colour, other than that of flowers, into the garden's composition. The first entry is from September 1996:

This has been a year of huge activity in the garden, pressured only by the realization that we are no longer young. The Yew Garden was paved and the redundant box trees from Monaughty [given us by Douglas and Sophie Blain] were planted. Julia's design, choosing ochre, reddish and grey slabs, worked enormously well. It will call for much re-cutting of the hedges and a wait for them to grow again. The new box I intend to cut abstract, so that the old-fashioned parterres in the middle of the garden will have a modernist frame. Reg Boulton produced for me the slate inscription, 'Green Thoughts', based on the poem by Andrew Marvell, linking the garden back in time.

In front of the house everything is in chaos and at a stand-still in the making of our nineties garden [later called the Howdah Court]. The mount of turf from the Yew Garden still stands. Julia has bought two iron spiral staircases for it [she called the mount the elephant and what straddled it the howdah, hence the garden's name] and I gave her a large

177

cast-iron 'eighteenth-century' window frame which will free-stand. We are going to investigate water, two fountains. There is a huge amount to do here when the builders return in October. It is so unlike anything we've done elsewhere.

Disaster struck the Rose Garden. The roses began to die and so had to go. I purchased four Italianate baroque statues of the Seasons to replace them. They look marvellous . . . Then the already failing amelanchier [it was on rock within a foot or so] had its death warrant sealed by a woodpecker. We've bucked this decision for years, but now we have to do it, cut down and uproot all four. This is a huge blow. We've consulted and they will be replaced by four ten- to twelve-foot-high beech trees, whose roots go lateral, which will be clipped into standards and underplanted with box. This means that they will keep their leaves in winter and link with the beech hedging opposite [along Tatiana's Walk]. But it is quite a dramatic thing to have to do.

Meanwhile at the Temple Reg Boulton has carved 'Memory, Mother of the Muses' in Greek, the key to the garden's iconography, across the lintel. It looks splendid. But there's more to do . . . It's age and the purchase of The Folly which has brought on such a ferment. The Folly with its bright colour [pink] and sense of fantasy has triggered us. We got the 'Professor' [our nickname for Reg Boulton] to paint the ground of the column at the head of Elizabeth Tudor blue and, later, applied the same treatment to the Shakespeare Monument. The garden begins more and more to look unique.

The narrative continues on 3 December:

We had great plans for the garden but they all seemed doomed to frustration. A 1990s fantasy garden [the Howdah Court] was to be created in front of the house with a mount, found objects, the knot gravelled and a couple of fountains. The builder started and then, in June, moved off leaving a bomb-site. He said that he would come back but hasn't, in spite of endless promises running through the whole of the autumn. He was also supposed to have paved Elizabeth Tudor and put up a pair of gate piers framing the vista into the Orchard.

In the end I got things moving again. The great decision was that the amelanchiers in the Rose Garden had to go . . . A team headed by an engaging young tree man, Chris Mason, came on a brilliant winter's Saturday in November and achieved moving three. A fourth, too large to be got out whole, had to be sawn up. Two were planted near The Folly and, with luck, they'll survive, if well watered in May and June. Four eight- to nine-foot-high beech were planted in their place and clipped into standards. The following week some lovely glossy green *Buxus sempervirens* arrived from Elizabeth Braimbridge [of Langley Boxwood Nursery] to go around the bases.

So that was a triumph. Meanwhile Sharon Powell of Crowther's rang and said that she had seen two pieces of the fourteenth-century Palace of Westminster at a place in Stow-on-the-Wold. They seemed to be 'me', she said. They were. What a wonderful way in which to mark *The Story of Britain* [published that autumn]. One is seventy-three inches high, a huge coat of arms of Edward I, quite magnificent. The other, a huge rose with a crown over it. They had come from the Bishop of Lincoln's palace, where they had formed part of the gate piers. Originally they had made up part of the decorative parapet between the second and third floors of the Palace on the waterfront.

Through Sharon we got on to Steve Tomlin of Reclamation Services at Catbrain Quarry, Painswick. For once everything went like clockwork. On a sun-dappled day, two excellent masons, who had been trained at Gloucester Cathedral, came and the gate piers and their finials went up in the Orchard in a morning. Alleluia! They look stunning. Suddenly that part of the garden's compositions came together and the 'proscenium' framing the vista to the Stag [called Franco for some weird reason after my Italian publisher, Franco Maria Ricci] looked a knock-out.

Today, December 11th, I am writing this, for tomorrow they deliver the armorials. The Gothick Arbour, riddled with wet rot and disintegrating, has been moved to another alcove in the Orchard hedge and a huge ironwork support has been cemented into the ground to take the grandest armorial. I wonder how it will look? Splendid certainly, but there will be knock-ons as I don't know whether the planting there and the blue wire obelisks will look right with it. However, we shall see.

At the moment the 'Rose and Crown' armorial will go at the head of the Serpentine, where there was the old exit from the Rose Garden. Meanwhile I've pressed on with Reg Boulton for the plaques for the column at the head of Elizabeth Tudor. The column was one of Elizabeth I's emblems and I want plaques linking her and Elizabeth II. So I'm hoping for two crowns and two ERs representing each sovereign.

After Christmas, on January 6th, Steve Tomlin and his men return and promise to pave Elizabeth Tudor. I don't care any longer what it costs! I want it done and I won't be killed off by what I've labelled 'Hereford syndrome' any more.

From this the reader will have gathered that the Yew Garden was paved in 1996, that a totally new garden, the Howdah Court, was in the making in front of the house, that a pair of gate piers was erected along the Serpentine framing a vista into the Orchard, that the paving of the great avenue of pleached limes we call Elizabeth Tudor was adumbrated, that I had purchased some important sculptural pieces, and that Reg Boulton, who has been referred to earlier, was busy carving inscriptions for various parts of the garden. The armorials, I might add at this juncture, came from what was a new Bishop's Palace at Riseholme into which the then bishop, John Kaye, moved in the year of Queen Victoria's accession, 1837, three years on from the famous fire which had destroyed Westminster Palace and brought these fragments onto the market.

The diaries continue with the story in March of the following year. I was again cursing the Hereford builder who had let us down:

> . . .a well-meaning, hopeless Hereford man, who couldn't read a plan, never came when he said he would, and drove us raving. Depression set in, but yet the will to get on and do things, born of the realization of advancing age, was there. At sixty-one and sixty-six we must press on. But how? Steve Tomlin fell into our lap via Crowther's . . . Ex London School of Economics and the Foreign Office, this is an engaging Mr Fixit of a person who runs an architectural salvage yard near Painswick and also has an energy and an excitement about our garden. So it is that he came to site both those armorials and through him came Richard who put up the gate piers in the Orchard . . . And so Jon and Philip followed, and the great Elizabeth Tudor walk was laid to Julia's design. The change is extraordinary, like a renaissance palazzo floor stretching into the distance. And then there was much fudging, because the Shakespeare Monument was a bit 'off', but, by vanishing into asymmetry, few would spot that it was so now. Steve produced piles of broken tiles and other bits for the paving of this area. The great path is lined with a low yew hedge and hollies which I intend to train.

I continue the story on 8 July:

> Everyone who sees the garden is amazed, but Julia and I still feel that there is so much more to do . . . Steve Tomlin and his gang are at last getting on with the front of the house garden. The knot is done, infilled with gravel and lapis and amethyst

glass cullets. The fountains have begun to be lowered into place and the 'howdah' [the viewing platform designed by Julia utilizing the two spiral staircases, Victorian radiator panels and scaffolding poles] is being mocked up at Painswick next week. It begins to look extraordinary and everyone visiting the garden was much excited about the project and also admiring the house painted blue and yellow. Suddenly, for the first time, one 'sees' the house and, colour-wise, it is now at one with the garden, like some pavilion of fantasy in its midst. Also we've kept Reg Boulton going. He's doing the plaque for the Oman pinnacle.

These two years saw the greatest transformation of the garden since its inception. There were more works to come, for we later introduced crossed paths in the Orchard and re-landscaped the drive to the house, tearing out the old thuja hedge, replacing it with a wall incorporating sections from the sides of a Victorian gothic bridge across the Thames. The bridge or its double can be seen in Stanley Spencer's painting *Swan Upping* in the Tate Gallery. That was done in 2001. But neither of these changes eclipsed the massive works which had gone before. It is, however, one thing to list off the changes and record them happening, but it is quite another setting them into the context of what was a new phase in the garden's development, one which was affected by several other converging factors which must be taken into consideration.

I have already discussed the impact of the visit to Dutch gardens and to Little Sparta. That catches the fact that the experience of other gardens still impinged on our vision twenty years on, providing fresh stimulus to alter and develop The Laskett. Two other garden experiences in the 1990s left an impact and led me to put pen to paper. One was Mark and Arabella Lennox-Boyd's garden up in Lancashire at Gresgarth, where we stayed in May 1993:

This garden had a terrific impact on me. I felt that ours lacked blossom and roses. I decided to change the Small Orchard, place tulips ['Prinses Irene', bright orange and a present from Arabella] round the topiary, edge the path with box, enlarge beds, etc. We drove back after lunch and sat in the Temple with a glass and mused on our creation which was so very different. Gradually we got a balance. After all we hadn't got an open chequebook and four gardeners.

For a designer who was one of the apostles of formality in the eighties, Arabella's garden was surprisingly sinuous and asymmetrical, focusing on a lake in whose waters the handsome Victorian Gothick house was reflected. There were formal areas, but what stuck in my mind was the floriferous richness and plenitude of the planting. That we only began to rectify on any scale later when Shaun Cadman arrived as our gardener, whose fortunate obsession was plants. Then, really for the first time, The Laskett also became a garden with flowers in any quantity.

The second inspiration was Portmeirion, the creation of Sir Clough Williams-Ellis, where we spent my birthday in August 1994. Once again I was entranced:

Portmeirion was lit by an enchanted light, its thirties pinks, blues, terracottas and whites make this garden rich in ideas, wit and fantasy. Hydrangeas flourish here, the steep site displaying them to advantage garlanded down the hillside in pink and blue. Clough Williams-Ellis must have been an early pioneer of architectural salvage, for Portmeirion consists of bits and pieces of old buildings and sculpture, a melange of countries and styles put together in the spirit of thirties romanticism.

I did actually meet him at a Royal Academy Dinner, a dandified figure then in his nineties, elegant in knee breeches.

Portmeirion was inspired by Italy, a fairy-tale village scattered around a bay in north Wales. To be there is like finding oneself suddenly walking through a capriccio by Rex Whistler. But there's an originality to it which is emancipating, and certainly with its uninhibited use of recycled elements and brilliant colour it contributed to my release from the eighties revival of the world of Jekyll and Lutyens.

That captures something else. In the nineties garden style suddenly moved on. The heritage decades of the seventies and eighties were over and new impulses manifested themselves. Already the garden we had planted had become a representative of a period which had passed. But there was to be no question of radically altering it, rather it was to be left as a memorial to those decades. The nineties saw what was billed as the new planting coming in from Germany with its abundant use of grasses, known in this country, in the main, through the work of the Dutch gardener Piet Oudolf. It has never held great appeal for me, but Oudolf's own garden, with its firm formal structure of clipped yew in the Dutch tradition, has a fresh brilliance. Only he could have sculpted the field hedge holding in one side of it into clouds, thus echoing those scudding through the sky above.

There was also Derek Jarman's garden at Prospect Cottage in the shadow of Dungeness, which was light years away from the ilk of Barnsley. This was a composition whose basis was stones, shingle, driftwood and scrap metal, from which spring weeds and wildflowers and into which he planted a cornucopia of other blooms. But its essence resides in the use of found objects and their placing and the arrangement of stones in abstract patterns. This in a sense was the private garden catching up with where the visual arts had gone during the preceding decades. It also had meaning, for Jarman made it as he was dying of Aids. This was not a designer-packaged plot, but one charged with powerful and moving resonances which had been achieved with very little.

To that we might add the work of Ivan Hicks, at one time gardener to Edward James, the patron of the Surrealists. His gardens too make an abundant use of found objects. I recall his work at Groombridge Place in Kent where, in a small area of woodland, he had created a vast spider's web of twigs several metres high and suspended it between the trees. Old rotted tree stumps were spiked onto rusty iron bars and plunged into a pond, giving haunting reflections. What must have been a section of sewer pipe was rammed into a bank and within its mysterious, darkened interior he had suspended a tiny piece of mirror-glass which revolved and glinted.

Such new garden experiences were liberating and indirectly fuelled the changes at The Laskett. What also fuelled those changes was the different pattern of our own lives. Virtually up until 1990 we had been London-based, opening up the house for a short period and closing it up again quickly. After I left the Victoria & Albert Museum we began to live here the whole time, with only periodic darts into the metropolis for essential meetings and the supply of books. But the old round of London life vanished, which again was such a release. No longer were we on parade, although we both continued to work hard. I had to carve out for myself a second career, for after thirty years of public service and directing two of our greatest national institutions I was left with precisely £12,000 p.a. on which to live. I had to start on the workshop floor again, learning how to do radio, television and, above all, how to write. The earlier years of the decade were eased by the consultancy for the public spaces within the Canary Wharf Development under the aegis of Olimpia & York, which threw me together with the likes of Laurie Olin, the brilliant Philadelphia landscape architect. That was hugely stimulating. In the second half of the decade I became a successful author. And that meant that from time to time there was an injection of income which permitted significant garden projects to become a reality.

The developments in the nineties were also aided by a change in Julia's pattern of existence, for work as a theatre designer is a young person's profession, being cripplingly demanding in every sense, physical as well as mental. As she increasingly confined herself to supervising her own productions back on stage at the Royal Opera House, she was released and, therefore, able to design some of the most important and original additions to the garden. Julia had strong views about, for example, paving, where she saw opportunities for ground-level pattern which were rarely exploited. The result has been combinations of old and new paving materials in a manner I have not seen in any other garden. It was her decision to pave Elizabeth Tudor, the most daring and spectacular *coup de théâtre* perhaps in the entire garden. I vividly recall taking a group around and explaining that soon the long green walk would vanish beneath paving. The reaction was one of horror, all except for Lesley Jenkins of Wolterton Old Hall, another brilliant gardener, who sidled up to me and whispered: 'Don't take any notice of them. It's going to be fantastic.' And it is. The Howdah Court, undoubtedly our most startling lurch into a new direction, is almost wholly Julia's.

To all this must be added the significant arrival of a gardener, first in the form of Robin Stephens, untrained, but a willing pair of hands. No longer was each year a battle against the impinging tide of brambles and areas gradually came under control. His successor, Shaun Cadman, trained at Pershore, was our first qualified gardener. Once again we were able to move the garden forward, thanks to his genuine enthusiasm and love of plants and, I might add, of this garden. Both of them in their own way entered into what I can only describe as the spirit of the place, the *genius loci* as Alexander Pope would describe it.

What I have delineated so far throws up a number of things that call for explanation. Where did the ideas about colour come from and what do they mean? What about all these plaques with their inscriptions and images, what too do they mean? And even that is not the end of it, for there is so much more to be told. There are the disasters – drought, disease, the ruination of a garden – as well the triumphs, not yet mentioned. Nor have I told the tale of that much-loved creature, the Rev. Wenceslas Muff. All these are interwoven into the garden's story, but where to begin? That is almost arbitrary, but, working from the premise that a cat may look at a king, I shall begin with Muff.

MUFF CAME OVER THE FIELDS IN THE LATE SUMMER OF 1981. There are some cats you look after and there are others who look after you. Muff was one of the latter. I suppose he had been a Christmas present to some Birmingham child and, when the family went on holiday, was tossed out of a car window somewhere along the A49. Whatever his past, this pathetic, black, starved bundle arrived and followed me around the garden wherever I went, throwing himself upside down in front of me. A cat cannot send out a more potent message. I was enslaved, although aware that the Lady Torte de Shell would not warm to competition, nor did she. It wasn't easy taking on a second creature as we were still on the London run, but we argued that the alternative of abandoning this loving animal was much worse. So it was that he took up residence.

I had always wanted a large long-haired cat and he was to be both. Why was he called Muff? As he reclined before us I said to my wife, 'What shall we call him?' She looked down on this beautiful rectangle of black fur tinged beneath with red and said, 'He looks like Wenceslas Hollar's engraving of a lady's muff.' Working from T.S. Eliot's principle that you must never give a cat a dull name, he was therefore christened Muff and then Wenceslas after the seventeenth-century engraver and Reverend because he was black. We always used to hold that he was a dissenting cleric.

Muff belongs to the story of the garden for, even in excess of Torte, he was the greatest rabbiter. One winter he culled over thirty out of the sixty or so which we managed to put down that year. He had an absolutely set route around the garden. We would catch him on it, a systematic inspection of rabbit holes, at each one of which he would pause, check and then move on. He too brought his catch into the house for us to admire and then, like Torte, he would consume them, working from the ears down. We didn't warm, however, to finding the odd joint of rabbit tucked away around the house for eating later.

Muff was part of our existence for just over a decade. By saying that he looked after us I mean precisely that. I would be working in my writing room on one side of the house and Julia would be on the other at her drawing board. Up the stairs I would hear the thud of this mega-cat arriving, for he grew large. A pitter-patter followed, and then a face with a pair of green eyes and a handsome reddish beard would peer around the door, checking that I was all right. The routine would be repeated as he made his way over to my wife's studio block, after which he would make his exit, via the cat flap, out into the garden to resume his duties as pest-control officer.

I am glad that he knew five years of us living at The Laskett. Animals find a way of telling you what they think. Both Torte and Muff resented us leaving for London. Torte would deliberately flatten herself under a bed and refuse to come out; Muff pulled the hairs of his coat off his back. As soon as we came to live at The Laskett, Muff stopped his coat depilation. Those were happy years until, in the autumn of 1992, he was bitten by a feral cat who transmitted to him feline Aids, FIV. At that time I wasn't keeping anything beyond my Garden Diary but even then the staccato entry under the last week in November speaks for itself:

All this week one long tragedy, in and out of the vet every day. He went downhill from Wednesday. On Friday the blood test told us that nothing could be done. The decision was reached Saturday a.m. at the vet's. Nothing but grief and trauma. Dot [Simpkins, our daily] came and helped us clear up. Robin dug the grave. A great light went out of our lives.

Those brief sentences hide a torrent of emotion and tears and a deep sense of bereavement, as one by one the evidence of his existence was tidied up and put into the loft. It was typical that George Clive, a deeply shy and sensitive man, wrote to us a letter of condolence, for the loss of a beloved creature can, in its way, be as heart-rending as any other.

There's an emptiness to a house once such a creature has departed. But in the end a leap has to be made and, on 11 December, I wrote: 'Started investigating cats.' Some years before we had read an article about American Maine Coons, monsters with long fur, tails like ostrich plumes and eyes like luminous saucers which stared up at you. This time we determined that we would have two, so that there would not be a recurrence of being left creature-less. Eight days later we collected two tiny Maine Coon kittens, one a silver tabby and the other a tabby and white. The former was called William Larkin, Esquire of The Laskett, after an obscure Jacobean portrait painter, the latter Herzog Friedrich von Sans Souci, as we had just visited Potsdam. But, in fact, in short Larkin and Souci. They too have a tale to tell, but it is one which does not involve the garden, for to avoid a recurrence of Muff's fate, his successors have become house cats with a capacious pen in which to savour the country air. And, to emphasize the change, they were cats we looked after rather than the other way round.

But to return to Muff. He was buried behind the sugar-loaf yew from Sutton Place in a quiet, restful spot bordered with clipped laurel and from which an arch leads on to the surprise of the great sweep of Elizabeth Tudor. We chose this because it was at the close of a favourite walk of his, which for some eccentric reason is called Sir Muff's Parade, for up and down it he would go on patrol. I was determined that such a major figure in our domestic life should not go uncelebrated. That decision was to bring Reg Boulton into our lives and precipitate a whole stream of commissions to him through the garden. Our introduction we owe to Elizabeth Organ who runs the Kilvert Gallery at Clyro. I had known her years before when she was married to Bryan Organ, who painted the portrait of me as a young man now in the National Portrait Gallery. What we needed was an artist craftsman who would be able to execute panels to be inserted onto a monument that was basically a reconstituted-stone pedestal atop which I had sited a large ball which was eventually gilded.

On 18 January 1993 I wrote: 'Reg Boulton came at 10 a.m. about Muff's Monument, inscriptions on slate set onto the pedestal. He wants to include a relief of Muff based on the Leman painting.' The latter referred to a portrait I had had painted of Muff by Martin Leman as a birthday present for Julia, in which Muff appeared like an apparition beneath a starry sky. But, in fact, the image on the plaque was to owe much more to a second portrait, a drawing by a friend, the painter Michael Leonard, in which Muff was depicted with his clerical bands. Above this cameo relief hovers the letter M, designed as a tribute to this great cat by another friend and cat-lover, the sculptor Angela Conner. That was one panel. Two flanking ones bore his two greatest attributes, 'BRAVE' and 'LOVING', while the last recorded his name and the dates, that of his birth being only approximate, c.1980.

On any tour of the garden this celebration of a cat comes as a surprise, for it is tucked away behind the yew in a hidden spot. Always people smile when they see it and that is as we would wish it, for Muff always brought us happiness and joy.

Little did we know that our deep desire to commemorate him would lead us on to so much else in the garden.

THE PLAQUES ON THE MUFF MONUMENT WERE SET IN PLACE ON 30 January 1993. Four days later I was to write:

> Thoughts on inscriptions in the garden: Ashton Arbour: each side 'Month' 1976; 'Enigma' 1968; Column – Elizabeth I – ER and emblems and crown on the top. All Souls pinnacle – 'Homo sum' – arms; Shakespeare Monument – FVS 1980; Shakespeare medal.

As far as the reader is concerned this cryptic *aide memoire* signals that I had moved on to outlining a programme of inscriptions through the garden. That programme is still ongoing.

What the entry reveals is that so many of the ornaments in the garden have a meaning and that that meaning needed highlighting with an appropriate inscription. For over a decade we have worked with Reg Boulton, piecemeal adding to this or that tableau. His contribution in terms of his elegant plaques carved with a sure hand in the best calligraphic tradition cannot be underestimated. By staying with the same artist craftsman we have also ensured an aesthetic unity of style. Without the financial resources for major sculpture commissions, we have also personalized and changed the character of what are ornaments available to anyone out of a catalogue. To which I must add at this juncture that, when it comes to ornament in the garden, I have no snobbery whatsoever. To me whether it is real or phoney is irrelevant, ornament in the garden is what you can successfully get away with.

The inscription on the Temple and the plaques on the Shakespeare Monument we have already encountered, but what about the rest? What resonances do they have? Perhaps

I can begin with the column at the entrance to Elizabeth Tudor. That I purchased in a sale of reconstituted-stone ornaments in 1992. The column was an emblem of Elizabeth I, symbolizing her constancy and reflective of her motto, *Semper Eadem*, 'Always the same'. It can be spotted in the background of several of her portraits (the subject of my first book in 1963). For me it also brings to mind the man who figures substantially in another of my works, *The Cult of Elizabeth*, Sir Henry Lee. He worshipped the Virgin Queen, organizing annually those great festivals of chivalry, her Accession-day Tilts, each 17 November. At his retirement tilt in 1590 he laid down his arms at the foot of a crowned pillar and two years later welcomed his sovereign to his country house at Ditchley in Oxfordshire with, among other things, a song with the lines:

> *Constant Piller, constant Crowne,*
> *Is the aged Knightes renowne.*

In this way Gloriana is firmly drawn into the garden, and what could be more appropriate than that the pillar looks towards a monument to Shakespeare, the greatest Elizabethan of them all? But the plaques on the pedestal also link the reigns of the two Elizabeths, for ER II appears with the imperial crown of Great Britain on two of them. In the year of Elizabeth II's Golden Jubilee a gilded crown was added to the golden sphere on the column's summit, bringing to fruition a scheme I had first envisaged a decade before.

In the Yew Garden, which was paved and largely replanted in 1996, is the slab bearing the words: 'Green Thoughts'. That is a garden of greens, or it still was in that year, nothing but clipped box in patterns in one huge parterre held in by walls of dark green yew pierced with arches. The inscription's origin is a verse in perhaps the most famous garden poem in English literature, Andrew Marvell's *The Garden*. It reads as follows:

Meanwhile the Mind, from Pleasure less,
Withdraws into its happiness:
The Mind, that Ocean where each kind
Does straight its own resemblance find;
Yet it creates, transcending these,
Far other Worlds, and other Seas;
Annihilating all that's made
To a Green thought in a green Shade.

Whether I should have multiplied the thoughts I know not, but my own are certainly multiple when looking at this garden with its allusions back to the formality of the seventeenth century as well as its revival in the late Victorian period and in our own era. What it asks the visitor to do is pause and think, perhaps catch the allusion to Marvell, but above all bring his own thoughts to a garden picture. Without such a dimension what we look at is a mere design solution, something sadly to which most gardens have been reduced in the twentieth century.

In the Christmas Orchard there is a quote from another famous seventeenth-century poem, which again is meant to stir the mind of the visitor to contemplate wider horizons. It comes from Book IV of Milton's *Paradise Lost*, at that moment when Satan first glimpses the Garden of Eden, a vision which included:

> *. . . a circling row*
> *Of goodliest Trees loaden with fairest Fruit,*
> *Blossoms and Fruits at once of golden hue*
> *Appeerd, with gay enameld colours mixt . . .*

I alighted upon these lines while I was writing an introductory cultural history of the island, *The Spirit of Britain*. Not only did they seem apposite for the Orchard with its flowers and fruit, but they were part of a passage of poetry which became almost a sacred text for all gardenists, and one of the founts inspiring the landscape movement of the eighteenth century. What more could one want?

From this you will have gathered that I have a profound belief that any garden should also exercise the mind. A simple quote in the Fountain Court is a prime instance of this, for without catching the allusion its meaning remains opaque. Let me start by saying that the Court, as the garden developed, became the entrance proper to the main garden and therefore the inscription was designed to act as a kind of invocation to the visitor. Around our initials JR and the date, 1973, when we began the garden, there is inscribed the Latin word *Circumspice*, 'Look around'. Increasingly only those who belong to the older generation know the context, although the reference is not that obscure. St Paul's Cathedral has no monument to the great architect Sir Christopher Wren, only this inscription: *Si monumentum requiris circumspice*, 'If you wish to see his monument, look around'. And that indeed is what we bid those who make the journey through our garden to do, for they are looking at our monument.

Two of the inscriptions particularly relate to Julia. The first, which I have already described, is on the pedestal supporting the pinnacle from All Souls which is a mnemonic for the Oman dynasty. The two others relate to the Ashton Arbour. In my preliminary listing of inscriptions in February 1993 that had figured, but nothing was done about it. Two years later, in May 1995, I was bemoaning that fact: 'There is, however, still much to do in the garden to complete the programme: the plaques for "Enigma" and "Month" for the Ashton Arbour . . . We must press on, but where's the money coming from?' That was an oft-heard lament, but eventually, in 2002, the commission was set in hand. On one side it read 'ENIGMA', with the initials E, A and O for Elgar, Ashton and Oman. On the other it read 'MONTH', with C, T, A and O for Chopin, Turgenev, Ashton and Oman.

Both *Enigma Variations* and *A Month in the Country* have appeared earlier in this story, but the full circumstances of both these masterpieces by Sir Frederick Ashton have yet to be told. *Enigma* goes back to the 1950s when Julia was a student at the Royal College of Art. At that time she had the misfortune to contract typhoid fever, from which she almost died, but, as she was coming to, the strains of Elgar's immortal music filled her mind and she went on to outline a scenario for a ballet and design both the sets and the costumes. Her professor, Sir Hugh Casson, was so impressed that he arranged for her to leave her portfolio at the door of the Royal Opera House, Covent Garden, for Ninette de Valois to see. Six months later she collected it, thinking that probably no one had even bothered to look at its contents. In that she was proved to be wrong, for if any story is one of hope, it is this one. Eleven years pass, by which time Julia had left her post as a BBC television designer and gained fame for her work on stage and screen. One day the telephone rang at her parents' house in Putney. It was Sir Frederick Ashton: 'Are you the Julia Trevelyan Oman who left a portfolio of drawings at the stage door of the Royal Opera House eleven years ago?' She answered in the affirmative. Ashton went on: 'The time was not right for that ballet then, but it is now.' The moment, in 1968, that the curtain arose revealing a misty gauze of elm trees and, behind, the house and garden of Elgar, the audience burst into applause. The reception of the ballet was rapturous.

Month is another story, for at one of the rehearsals of *Enigma* Ashton had turned to her and said, 'You are going to design my next ballet, which will be based on Turgenev's *A Month in the Country*.' Once again there was a passage of time until, at a dinner party early in June 1975 given by the pianist Moura Lympany, I saw Fred pushing the salt cellar and other objects on the table around and talking intently to Julia. What he was describing were the elements he needed on stage for the ballet, which had its premiere in February of the following year with Lynn Seymour as Natalia Petrovna and Anthony Dowell as the handsome young tutor she falls for. Both ballets still hold the stage, in the case of *Enigma* over thirty years on and in that of *Month* twenty-five. Both are recognized as central to the Ashton choreographic inheritance. The two plaques recording their collaboration rightly look towards what we call Covent Garden. *Month* is important for something else, for the set made use of a certain shade of blue which Julia had seen on the Smolny convent in St Petersburg. It was the genesis for what were to become the garden's livery colours of blue and yellow.

THE INSCRIPTION WHICH, ALONG WITH 'MEMORY, MOTHER OF the muses' on the Temple, best encapsulates the garden was on a feature which I have not as yet described, the Triumphal Arch. That came in 1997 and is a testament that triumph can indeed follow tribulation. Let the entry in my diary for 17 August take up the story:

> The quiet of a hotel lobby in a ghost town [Bologna, as it happened] as it was Ferragosto, enables me to put down the full horror of our garden 'massacre' which took place on 8th August. Robin was doing a splendid job cutting the Rose Garden hedge. The last section to be cut was the culmination of the vista, which was to be trained into an arch through which one descended into the Scandinavian Grove. Something radical must have gone wrong with my powers of communication, for I had described to him what had to be done. Later, by chance, I walked into the garden to check something for an article I was writing. I turned the corner to the great vista and then was as one stricken, a great chunk of the hedge, which I had waited twenty-three years to grow, had gone. The vista was wrecked. It was as though I had been confronted with a corpse. I was transfixed, horrified, stunned. I couldn't get over

what had happened. It haunted me all day and all night. It was the most appalling blow. Five years at least would be needed for it to grow back.

Robin came in on Saturday and we both tried to put it right. We equalled the damage both sides, so that it at least looked symmetrical, but the damage remained. I racked my brains as to how to solve the problem, the wiping out in twenty minutes of one of the garden's great set-pieces. The one effect which we had never done was to build a garden gate, mainly because we couldn't afford to. Afford it we now have to. In order to deflect the eye from the horror that had happened, we would have to build it. I recalled ages ago a 'baroque' doorway which Chilstone [the suppliers of reconstituted-stone ornaments] had and rang them. It would, I said, have to be free standing. No one had ever thought of that, so at least it'll be original. Mercifully Steve Tomlin is virtually in residence. What was generally used as a 'front door' would be given not the usual pilasters but solid pillars. The architrave would have to be more solid and steel rods would need to run up through the pillars into the architrave. So be it. It'll cost me Robin's pay for the year to put this disaster right. This is the biggest reversal yet, but I have been pledged that everything will be delivered by the end of September and the arch go up as from 1st October. But I could have done without any of this happening.

I confess that the desire for a garden gate of this kind went back to my work on Inigo Jones, who designed classical garden gates in this manner for updating gardens in Jacobean England. A beautiful surviving example is now at Chiswick House. I had always thought the idea entrancing.

On 5 October I wrote:

The weather has been thrice-blessed, golden sunshine and the warmth of summer. Steve Tomlin saw that we had his best man, Dave Russell, to put up the great arch. Steve had found in Bristol a stunning set of stones for the pavement on which it would stand. On the Wednesday they went down. On Thursday the two great pillars went up. They were left to consolidate on Friday and stood there like the famous device of the Emperor Charles V [the twin pillars of Hercules and the motto *Plus ultra*, 'Even further']. Already the eye was taken from the disaster behind. But Saturday was the day it went up. It looked terrific, huge, but, from a distance, taking up the lines of perspective as though we had always planned it. Reg Boulton came and is going to carve the great Latin inscription provided by Joe Trapp's son: 'They who plant a garden, plant happiness.' At the time I was writing the chapter on the 1640s and 1650s [in *The Spirit of Britain*] and looking at photographs of the doors in the Double Cube Room at Wilton. There the great door has a huge armorial cartouche as part of the pediment. I said, could he do the Oman arms like that? Yes, he could. It would look terrific. Perhaps I can now afford to adopt those arms and round off the story. When I was knighted I couldn't afford to.

The cartouche and the adoption of the arms have yet to come, but the rest is there. To say that we were thrilled with the result would be an understatement. Today the Triumphal Arch forms one of the garden's most splendid surprises. But what of the source for this particular inscription? At the time a great friend, Julie Nightingale, had given me as a present a tiny terracotta plaque which bore an old Chinese proverb, 'They who plant a garden, plant happiness.' How true that had been for us over the decades. But I wanted it in Latin. So Joe Trapp, the former director of the Warburg Institute, was called upon and his classicist son and daughter-in-law came up with alternative Latin versions. The one we chose was '*Conditor Horti, Felicitatis Auctor*'. I cannot think of a more fitting culmination to our garden's grandest vista.

*

AS I HAVE SAID, COLOUR IN THE GARDEN BECAME AN INCREASING preoccupation during the 1990s and by it we meant not that from plants but that which could be applied to the garden's artifacts. The volition towards experimenting with colour sprang from visits abroad, seeing gardens in Italy and, later, in Bohemia, Moravia and Germany. There, the use of colour wash was ubiquitous and there was no overt cult of ageing. Even marble statues were given a coat of paint. It also came from a knowledge of garden history and visits to restored period gardens, such as William III's Palace of Het Loo at Apeldoorn where even the plant supports were painted dark blue with golden crowns on their summit.

It was John Vere Brown who prompted us to explore these possibilities when, on a visit, he had looked at the drear back wall of the Temple saying why on earth didn't we colour-wash it. I record action to this end on 15 April 1993 when I wrote:

A glorious spring day with blue sky, sun and warmth. Mike Jones, the painter, came and we at last embarked on what we had been planning. The pedestals on either side of the Ashton Arbour, the panels of the pedestals in the Flower Garden and the pedestal of the Stag in the Orchard were painted. All of it looked quite marvellous. Thus excited, we went on to paint the pedestals of the obelisks in Covent Garden and let Mike paint the balls on their top gold.

The colour Julia chose was one which we had seen used in Italy, a warm pale cinnamon, for at that stage we were quite tentative. In later repaintings we have intensified the depth of the colour to far greater effect. The yellow indeed now glows with a sunny warmth even on the darkest and dreariest winter day.

That initial foray was furthered as a result of a tour to Bohemia and Moravia later that year which took in a series of baroque towns, then undergoing restoration, where the houses were being painted pink, pistachio, ochre and terracotta. I recall our arrival back at The Laskett, stepping out of the car and looking at our house painted a safe magnolia and thinking how dull and colourless it looked. It was then that we decided to paint it blue and yellow. Those colours were then gradually taken out across the garden, for example with various plant supports being painted blue along with our trellis work and also any wooden garden arches. This use of colour wash was to be confirmed by a visit to German gardens in 1995. As The Laskett garden developed through the nineties that colour theme became more and more pronounced as the artifacts increased. The Howdah Court Garden in front of the house is a composition in blue and yellow which is even emphasized in the spring through planting 'Golden Apeldoorn' tulips in profusion.

When we began to do this it was certainly novel, for Rosemary Verey was much taken with it, later ringing me up from Elton John's house at Windsor asking me what colour to paint the seats in his summerhouse. We took our commitment to stronger colour further in 1995 with The Folly, which Julia decided should be bright pink, a suitable colour for what was a folly in every sense of the word. Its effect on the locality was somewhat electrifying. I recall opening an exhibition in Hereford and two *grandes dames* approaching me and saying, 'You must be horrified at the colour those people have painted the cottage at the bottom of your drive.' To which I had to reply, 'Oddly enough, it was us.'

The English seem notoriously nervous of colour, something which does not afflict either the Welsh or the Irish. The English are also nervous of gold. Nothing as far as I'm concerned enlivens a winter's day more in a garden than a flash of gold glinting as the sun catches it. Unfortunately gold does not come cheap, so that the splashes here are relatively restrained, but I confess to my love for the gilded fountains of

Versailles and Peterhof. However, with the aid of a gold-leaf-fixated student from Herefordshire College of Art we gilded the balls on Muff's Monument and on the column to Elizabeth, both to sensational effect. Since then the antlers of the recumbent Stag at the close of the great Orchard vista have been gilded. Every form of gold paint has been tried on them, but with no real success. Nothing, but nothing, can replace real 22-carat gold leaf.

SO MUCH FOR THE BUILDING, STRUCTURE AND ORNAMENTATION, but what other major changes came in the garden during these years? One was the gradual transformation of what had been a dull turn-around for cars at the top of the drive into what we now call the Fountain Court. Up until 1988 all that had been done was to plant some handsome conifers on either side of the decaying Judas tree, which Julia would never permit me to fell. It was, I admit, seen directly from the break-fast-room window and in spring its bluish-pink flowers were a pretty sight, but all I could see, as the years progressed, were the tree's branches lurching more and more apart. And then, all of a sudden, it happened. Julia said that I could take the tree down, but on one condition, that I gave her a fountain.

On 28 August 1988 I wrote: 'Discussed fountain on mound.' This telegraphic abbreviation of intent was to be the preface to a five-year saga, one of the kind which drove me in the end to swear that I would never again employ this or that 'little man' to do something. The fountain basin was dug out in January 1989, but it was not until the same month two years later that I was to write 'work on the fountain'. Eventually, on 31 August 1992, comes the note: 'Mike Powell got the fountain going.' That we got it going at all was thanks to George Clive, who put us on to Mike Powell, for the odd labour we had used to erect the fountain had no clue as to how to make it function. The same year we banished the turn-around, paving and planting it, thus forming an entrance to the garden proper which fully warranted Reg Boulton's plaque inscribed '*Circumspice*'.

This was the happy end of a more than tortuous saga involving small builders who came and went, one that reached its climax in the frustration which marked the initial phases of the Howdah Court and was only resolved by the arrival of Steve Tomlin. I cannot recount our elation at seeing that fountain throw up its first jet of water. Water is such a gift to any garden, and when it moves, plashes, shimmers and sparkles it is pure poetry. For us the fountain is ideally sited, for we look at it both at breakfast and lunch. In winter it is, of course, bagged against damage by frost, along with much of the other statuary. But, when we deem spring to have finally arrived, it is unveiled, serviced and then the switch controlling the pump is put on in the kitchen. Whoosh, up it goes. If any single event in The Laskett garden year signals that spring has come, this is it.

I have mentioned our visit to Gresgarth in 1993 and my lament about our lack of flowers. That lack had become something of a fixation already four years earlier. It was prompted as much as anything by a burgeoning career as a writer of books on garden design. In the case of these I had a rule never to write about anything that I had not done myself. I may not, of course, have done whatever it was successfully, but at least I had tried. Every garden book I read, for instance, seemed to contain a diagram as to how to fan-train a peach tree. Any attempt by me to apply the directions of such a diagram to one of our own trees was generally the harbinger of plant death.

But to return to flowers. In October 1989 there appears the entry: 'Began to dig Flower Garden'. That was in response not only to a keen awareness of my own ignorance, but also to the fact that now we actually lived more or less permanently in the country we could embark on such a feature, with the knowledge that we would be there not only to tend it but to enjoy the result. I recall saying to Rosemary Verey, 'I'm making a Flower Garden,' to which came the reply, 'And about time too.' I began to plant it in March and, even as early as May, I was able to record that the 'Flower Garden looked wonderful for a first year'. It was in 1990 that we visited Giverny, where I was overcome by its abundant deployment of yellows, purchasing, on our return, rudbeckias, ligularias, helianthemums and heleniums. The effect of this on the Flower Garden is caught in August of the following year, when I wrote: 'Yellow transforming Flower Garden.'

I would never count myself a master planter of borders, for my focus has always been on the broader scenic effects. Julia has always been the better plants person. Nonetheless the nineties witnessed a far greater concern with developing variety in the planting, the control of palette range, a concern with leaf and plant shape and above all with securing year-round seasonal interest. In the case of the Orchard, for example, a whole cycle emerged starting with snowdrops and white hyacinths, 'L'Innocence', beneath the Stag at the close of the vista from the Serpentine, moving on to an explosion of avenues of several varieties of narcissi defining walks or accenting particular features. This sequence began with two six-foot-wide ribbons of 'Sempre Avanti' leading to the Stag, followed by walks or bouquets of 'Pomona' and 'Flower Record'. Then came the blossom on the fruit trees lasting into May followed, in June, by standard wisterias and roses, clumps of the purplish-crimson Rugosa 'Roseraie de l'Haÿ' and the pink into white specie *Rosa roxburghii* and then a group of single specimen roses like the bright crimson Rugosa 'F.J. Grootendorst' and the semi-double pink rose 'Céleste'. Add to them 'Phyllis Bide', which is trained over the blue *treillage* arches, a quite marvellous rose with plentiful foliage and flowers of a mixed colouring which includes pink, cream and yellow, but whose greatest virtue is that it flowers prolifically throughout the season. In the autumn comes the fruit, each tree bearing fruit of a kind different in size, shape and coloration, along with the hips of the roses. Any fruit we don't harvest can stay on the trees until December, retained just for its decorative qualities.

That kind of elaboration is equally mirrored in the gradual extension of borders along the Serpentine, so that in the end they extended its entire length and accommodated such features as a swathe devoted to hostas and another to Michaelmas daisies (the latter thanks to a generous gift of several varieties from another great local gardener, Charis Ward of Abbey Dore Court). This enthusiasm for taking more interest in planting I rarely recorded, but, at the close of 1990, I did suddenly write down what I had been up to in the Silver Jubilee Garden:

> Everything bar the roses was had up, the large potentillas discarded. I feel that I am, at last, beginning to know how to plant a border. This time the change was triggered by wishing to have an autumn finale of Michaelmas daisies. They have been ordered from Picton Nursery and gaps left for them. I have tried to plant everything in large drifts moving from white to purple, trying to think in sizes and in what flowered and when, those that flowered on and off for a long period and those that kept good green leaves through until the autumn.

That must have worked, at least for a time, because I noted in the October of the following year: 'Michaelmas daisies in the Jubilee a really lovely effect, shades of mauve and purple and cascades of second bloom from the "Iceberg" roses.'

Gardening is a perpetual process of learning to look. As everything grows the composition eternally changes. It is so easy to become blind to things changing, which is why I always value the visit of a good critical eye. Rosemary Verey, Arabella Lennox-Boyd and Mary Keen are three who have made perceptive criticisms upon which I have acted. But changes can also come about through self-realization that something is wrong, an admission that a particular longed-for effect was in fact a mistake. What we call Covent Garden is a small essay on precisely this.

That had begun its life in the eighties as four yew topiary peacocks sitting on cubes flanking a yew arch in the hedge encompassing the Orchard. In the foreground I had planted two *Sorbus cashmiriana*, lovely trees with spherical white berries in autumn, but which never seemed to quite take off. The tableau was framed by *Elaeagnus pungens* 'Maculata' and laurels, from which arose two by now large walnut trees, and had, as its backdrop, in the distance, the old trees which stood before the house, including the magnificent cedar of Lebanon. It all ought to have composed beautifully, but somehow it never did. That fact always nagged me, which explains why never-ending alterations to Covent Garden recur in my Garden Diary. In October 1988 I wrote: 'remodelled Covent Garden: *Sorbus cashmiriana* felled; paving taken back; laurels cut to make a formal hedge; elaeagnus pruned.' The year after, in an attempt to solve the problem, two obelisks were deposited there and, in 1990 in July, I altered the Orchard hedge 'to reveal the peacocks'. This endless fiddling, none of which had solved it, reached a culmination on 29 May 1995:

The great decision was to demolish two of the topiary peacocks on Covent Garden. I was like a chainsaw murderer. But when I had done it, I knew that I had been right. The area had never worked, being topiary on topiary. It lacked planting interest, so Robin dug a pair of borders. First I toyed with thyme, then Julia suggested heather, and then I realized that the answer was silver and grey. Most of it was garnered from around the garden: *Phlomis*, *Santolina*, *Helichrysum*, *Stachys byzantina*, *Dianthus*, a silver rosemary, *Lychnis flos-jovis*, *Cerastium*. It looks minimal, but, if it flourishes, it will look right against the purple *Prunus* X *cistena* hedge we have planted there. . .

It has since developed into a silver, grey and purple border; the *Prunus cistena* failed and was replaced by purple beech. After years, it is a success, but it took some bravery to murder those two peacocks.

There were, of course, many other developments in the nineties, ones such as the steady expansion of my wife's *Malus* collection to almost a hundred varieties, but two things only I will mention. One was Julia's conversion to the importance of compost-making, the result of a visit to Princess Sturdza's garden, near Dieppe. This amazing woman, who wallops your foot with a crook if it impinges by as much as an inch on one of her beds, transforms beech leaves into soot-black compost in just six weeks, or that is what she says. Julia was bowled over, and ever since that visit The Laskett has become a monument to such mounds, which stand in serried ranks each at a different stage of ripeness. Onto these every form of kitchen waste and garden foliage is piled and left to rot. The regular annual dressing of every tree, shrub and border with compost, along with well-rotted farmyard manure from a local stables, has needless to say transformed the garden.

And what of the climate during the nineties, for all gardeners study the weather avidly? It was very hot and dry in 1989 with drought in July. January 1990 brought a hurricane that blew the Charlie Tree over, which fell across the Knot Garden in front of the house. On 3 August of that year it was 94 degrees, the hottest day since 1911, and I wrote in September: 'many plants and trees ill, unhappy or dead.' June 1991 was the wettest since 1727, while the summer of 1995 was the worst in terms of drought since 1976:

This summer we have begun to re-live the drought of 1976. Week in and week out the sun has gone up like a golden disc into a bright blue sky. At first we were delighted, but then, as the weeks passed, thoughts took another direction. Each day began at 6.45 a.m. when I stepped into the garden in my pyjamas to water the Flower Garden, the Michaelmas Daisy Border and the new grey border. That was before breakfast. Robin would then arrive and we would move on to the Rose Garden, the Jubilee Garden, the Fountain Court and the Knots. And then there were cans and buckets to the clematis and roses in the Spring Garden and to the box cuttings. Gradually we became more and more manic, dreading the dawn of each day. The poplars have withdrawn, the silver birch tree leaves are yellow and the fruit trees in the Orchard have begun to drop their fruit. If we don't get rain within ten days, I fear frightening casualties.

But any gardener expects to cope with extremes of weather, just as, sooner or later, the hand of disease can be extended across a domain. In that case we were to be the victims of a quite disastrous visitation.

THE YEAR WAS 1999 AND THE SAGA BEGAN IN JUNE. ON 5 JULY I wrote an account of what occurred:

Gardening is always the same. Everything goes along smoothly as long as you keep up with the traffic, weeding, feeding, clipping, pruning, mowing or whatever and then, suddenly, wham, something happens. Almost a fortnight ago a mysterious fungus hit the Knot Garden in front of the house. I showed it to Rosemary Verey who said rip out the plants and burn them. One was sent to Elizabeth Braimbridge, box 'queen' of the UK. We spoke: 'Hit it hard,' she said. Apparently it has cropped up all over the place on the 'Suffruticosa' as in our case. No one knows why. Our plant was sent off by her to a laboratory. We await the result. Meanwhile we were to put on spray. Needless to say it rained, spreading the fungus and not allowing us to dowse the Knot. Eventually, last Friday, we did. But it rained after. I looked this morning and it is still spreading. We'll hit it again with spray on Thursday and pray. I dread it spreading, for it could wipe out half the garden. One's left with a gnawing sense of anxiety. Mercifully there's no sign yet of it having spread beyond the 'Suffruticosa' in the Knot.

A second account follows, written in November, ominously headed 'The Great Box Disaster':

This year has been marked by the greatest disaster since the major frosts of the early eighties, box blight [*Cylindrocladium buxicola*]. It seems to have arrived here via some new box to surround the fountains at the front of the house. I began to notice something affecting the Knot Garden dwarf 'Suffruticosa' about May or June. Leaves turned brown and fell off leaving black twigs. I tore the plants up and burnt them. Langley Boxwood Nursery sent their expert. We then hit it with spray. No luck. It turned up on the other side of the garden. By late summer it had invaded the parterre in the Yew Garden. Then our new friends, John Glenn and Mary Anderson [who run a garden design and restoration consultancy in Lincolnshire], came. The advice: rip it all up and burn it. Suddenly I realized that we would have to destroy some of the garden's great set pieces, for by now it had invaded the JR parterre on the far side of the field. What we did learn from John Glenn and his laboratory inquiry is that it is not airborne. The disease is transmitted by contact with infected plants by secateurs, shears and gloves in contact with them. At the moment a great deal of the box still remains uncontaminated and I think much of the disease must have been spread by myself via the shears. All of this has been devastating and complicated because of thinking what we could do. John and Mary were for us wiping out everything, but my instinct has been to create nursery beds and plant the infected box in them and watch. Also we intend to leave in place the uninfected set pieces which will only be nipped out on sight of infection. I suspect that we may be in for a long saga on this one. Julia has already begun to think about a new parterre using green and golden yew and the new standard golden yews given us by John Glenn. But 2000 will be a tricky year. What is certain is that the shears, etc. must be constantly sterilized. . .

A disaster like this reinforces the fragile and mutant nature of the garden as a work of art. Drought, wind, frost and disease can all, at a stroke, wipe out years, even decades, of work. In most cases it means replanting what has been lost and waiting for it to grow. In the case of box blight the scenario was far worse for box could not be replanted in the same place since the spores linger in the soil for years. A single spore on the sole of a boot could transmit the disease across the garden. As I write it has raged now four years, in spite of every precaution being taken. At the moment it appears, apart from occasional outbreaks, to be in a state of remission, and indeed in areas where box has not previously been planted new box has been added.

At moments like this it is amazing how gardeners similarly afflicted come together. The Laskett was not the only garden in which box blight wreaked havoc. John Glenn also had his box decimated. He, like me, is a keen advocate of formality and was instrumental in converting me to the potential of golden yew, wooing me in particular with gifts of clones of those from the most famous of all Victorian topiary gardens, Elvaston. During the whole box crisis we were in constant contact, but he was adamant that there was no cure and that the longer we left the diseased plants in the soil the more it would spread. And he was right. So it was one day that, broken-hearted, I asked Shaun to destroy the parterres in the Yew Garden. One set piece after another followed – the Knot Garden, the hedging in the Rose Garden, the JR parterre in the Hilliard Garden, the topiary in our Fiftieth Birthday Garden and then all the box in The Folly Garden, that given by those Dutch visitors on that happy summer day. I can't describe the sense of desolation each of these acts of destruction wrought on me. Suddenly we were back to blank expanses of bare earth in gardens which demanded formal clipped elements. Substitutes somehow had to be found in order to achieve a similar effect but with different planting material.

In gardening you win some, you lose some. Once the decision had been made to uproot and destroy the diseased plants, we were able to move forwards and we owe much to John Glenn's suggestion that we use, for example, heathers, and clip them as they did for parterres in the Victorian period. This we have done with both the JR parterre and for the Knot Garden. Both have been a huge success. In the case of the Yew Garden a completely new scheme has been planted with low green yew hedges infilled with gravel and with verticals of golden yew standards. In the bordering beds, beneath the containing hedge, we planted masses of *Rosmarinus officinalis*, a plant that always flourishes here. And indeed it did, providing billowing spikes of purplish blue in sharp contrast to the clipped formality either side of it. For other parts of the garden we have used *Lonicera nitida* 'Bagessen's Gold' and golden privet, an inspiration remembering Rosemary Verey's use of it in her potager. Overall the devastating wound has been salved, if not as yet completely healed.

HOW CAN I END THIS SAGA OF THE GARDEN? I CAN'T, FOR A garden is always in the process of making or, at least, it is in our case. Two diary entries for 2001 capture what is still a continuing story. One is from February:

> The year as always enters somewhat dully, not helped by a winter of horrendous wet and, now, bitter cold and frost. Poor garden. Rosemarys and euonymus killed off by the cold, the turf churned to mud. The box disease reached the Rose Garden, a tragedy. Out it came and, as usual, John Glenn to the rescue with a dwarf form of golden yew which arrives on

8th March. Then I shall be able to bear to look on the garden again. Julia agreed to the thuja hedge up the drive being rooted out, a great transformation. The clipped golden thuja 'soldiers' either side were rearranged as pairs of sentinels and a large space cleared in the shrubbery near the front gate for the new garage. But the exciting thing is to see for the first time the Howdah Court and the view to the house. I had no idea that the hedge was ten to twelve feet wide in parts. On the side we planted two mature beech plus yew bastions in the making and two silver hollies 'Elegantissima' sent by the holly lady, Louise Bendall, as a comfort, hearing of the fate of the Rose Garden box. Aren't gardeners nice?

And on 17 April comes this:

This has been an endless and drear winter. Fifty-nine inches of rain have fallen onto the garden. It is sodden. The skies are overcast and it is so cold. It has been so long like this, now into the seventh month, dull and depressing and not helped by the awfulness of the foot and mouth epidemic which encircles us . . . Outside spring has come so late. It is now the second half of April and freezing cold. Sun a rare phenomenon. But the spring flowers are beautiful and the builders are busy. A new garage has gone up at the bottom of the drive and the gothic ironwork, sides of an old bridge across the Thames, are being put in place to hold in the Howdah Court. Gravel has gone down from Muff's Monument to the ER walk and paving is to be laid at the top of the new crinkle-crankle borders [Sir Muff's Parade]. At least one leylandii is to be felled to open up a vista between the two halves of the garden and a gravel walk is to be put on top of the mound. That will take the garden to virtual completion in terms of lay-out.

And, for the time being at least, it has.

Epilogue

PORTRAIT OF A MARRIAGE

I T IS MARCH OUTSIDE IN THE GARDEN AS I LAY DOWN MY PEN. It has been a dull grey day with bitter winds from the north-east, but still there is much joy to be had. As I step out of the back porch there is Julia's 'treasury', a still-life of plants in pots which changes with the seasons, but always with something in flower to greet us as we pass into the garden. Today there were deep purple, white and pinky-orange hyacinths, 'Woodstock', 'L'Innocence' and 'Gipsy Queen' if I remember rightly, along with tiny narcissi and bergenia to greet me. In addition there was a *Ribes laurifolium* in a pot waiting to be planted, a trophy picked up by Julia in the marketplace at Ross-on-Wye. Its greenish-yellow flowers are welcome in late winter and early spring, but it awaits its home in the garden. So also do a group of pulmonarias, more to add to her collection of some fifty plants which had been purchased at one of the Royal Horticultural Society's spring shows in Vincent Square.

Strolling around the garden there is no lack of flower, masses of the common cheerful pink of *Bergenia cordifolia*, but also 'Bressingham White', 'Silberlicht' and 'Baby Doll'. In the Folly Garden the *Chaenomeles*, which flower so early, defy the greyness of the day with the intensity of their scarlet reds and vibrant deep pinks, the dark blood-red C. *speciosa* 'Simonii', the deep pink of C. x *superba* 'Pink Lady', the scarlet of C. x *s.* 'Rowallane' and the bright red of C. x *s.* 'Fire Dance'. Julia's Scandinavian Grove is a miracle resembling Botticelli's *Primavera* with its dappled scatterings beneath the silver birch trees of pale lemon primroses, tiny 'Tête-à-tête' daffodils, violets, primulas, chionodoxas and white, cream and magenta hellebores. Not far away Elizabeth Tudor has unrolled her carpet of daffodils along her entire length. The mahonias and viburnums are in flower and, along the Serpentine, the *Cornus mas*, which I planted twenty-five years ago, has reached an astonishing size and is spangled all over with tiny yellow blooms. The palest of green shoots are already on the quince trees and the roses are also tentatively pushing forth shoots. Everywhere too the herbaceous plants are thrusting up through the earth.

What all of this spells is spring and the renewal of the garden's annual cycle of life into death followed by resurrection. For those that ponder the garden this holds a great mystery. The Laskett garden is so many things, inseparably intertwined. It is nature tamed by art, a *jardin d'amour*, a memory system, a manipulation of space, an illusion, but over and above everything else, it is a private sacred space in which the true circle of a marriage has been tenderly inscribed. It has always been an emotional struggle as to whether to open or not, even to the smallest number. It is not that one doesn't wish to share its joys as well as its sorrows, it is the fact that the garden is so intensely personal, so enmeshed into the fabric of our very being, our actions and our thoughts, that, for the perceptive, to be allowed even a glimpse of it is to peer into the mirror of one's soul. For its creators The Laskett garden is charged with an atmosphere which is almost, at times, overwhelming in the depth and complexity of its meaning. But I wouldn't have it any other way.

What is life after all but a flower that throws up its leaves from the dark earth into the light, unfurls ever larger until, at its zenith, its petals open in response to the warmth of the sun? But such a blossom also fades and falls, to return once more to the earth from whence it sprang. And so do we. Can anything in life be more beautiful than making such a mirror of the human condition? Let Andrew Marvell speak once more for me:

Fair quiet, have I found thee here,
And Innocence thy Sister dear!
Mistaken long, I sought you then
In busie Companies of Men.
Your sacred Plants, if here below,
Only among the Plants will grow.
Society is all but rude,
To this delicious Solitude.

The garden to me is a mirror of the three greatest virtues, faith, hope and love, for to cultivate one calls for the exercise of all three. But, we are told, the greatest of them all is love and indeed how well I know the truth of that. So when the end comes all I ask for is that someone, be it Julia or a dear friend, will step out into that garden once more and break off a fair branch of rosemary to lay on my coffin, and that my ashes be scattered on the patch of God's earth which in this transitory life I have loved most.

2005

REMEMBER ME

THIS BOOK WAS PUBLISHED THE WEEK JULIA DIED OF TERMINAL cancer, here at The Laskett on 10th October 2003. I leave to the readers imagination the effect of that event on the author. I'm glad that I wrote this book, just in time it now seems, for I couldn't write it now.

Her funeral took place in Llanwarne Church, where we worshipped, on a golden autumn day a week later, on 17th October. It was, as she requested, like a harvest festival, a celebration of a joyful homecoming. Carol Wells, the wife of David who had found us The Laskett all those years ago, decorated the church with flowers and fruits from the garden. Shaun Cadman, our gardener, paid his tribute in decking the pathway to the porch with fruit and produce again from the garden, not hesitating to add comfortable seats and the odd clipped box, bidding everyone as they left to help themselves to a medlar, quince, apple or pumpkin.

The day before, again as she wished, Julia's coffin was brought to The Laskett. David Hutt, now Subdean of Westminster Abbey and my best man, went before it reading the psalms and I followed in tears. Along the pleached-lime avenue we walked up and round to Julia's Christmas Orchard where it was laid on trestles, her head turned towards the stag with the golden antlers. Around it gathered our small 'family', Dot, our beloved daily, her husband, Mick, and Shaun. Prayers were said, a branch of yew was used to sprinkle the coffin with holy water (I have it still) and a candle lit and placed at the foot, for there the coffin would rest overnight. Suddenly I whispered to Shaun, 'Fetch me a branch of rosemary'. How could I have forgotten! Reverently I laid it on the coffin.

This book opened with the story of the Oman rosemary and so it unexpectedly closes with this deeply symbolic plant. At the funeral a huge sheaf of it tied with blue and yellow ribbon, The Laskett colours, lay on Julia's coffin just below the chancel steps. The service opened with me reading the opening paragraphs of this book. Up into the pulpit I went, looked at the packed congregation head on, smiled and read. God gave me the strength, I know, for this was a thanksgiving for a great life and marriage. Few of us are as lucky. At the close I stepped down and took the great sheaf of rosemary in my arms. The pall bearers lifted the coffin and slowly bore it down the nave, David ahead and me behind, my head bowed. At the crematorium my last act was to lay that sheaf on the coffin and then, suddenly, it was all over.

I now move on to October 2004. It was Julia's wish that her ashes should be laid to rest in the orchard. Once again the day was magical, but this time for a deeply private rite. David came down from London. He asked me to hold the ashes. I was tremulous about that simple act but suddenly, as soon as I held them, I knew that all I bore were her mortal remains and that her spirit had never left either this house or garden. I was filled with an inexpressible sense of joy. Once again we moved through the garden pausing to remember. Beneath an Oman quince I read part of the article she had written on quinces. We had, of course, to take in Muff's grave, for cats had been part of our existence. We went along the lime avenue too, for it was that little book on Elizabeth Tudor which had led to my proposal. We stopped at the Ashton Arbour and recalled Julia's great artistry in the theatre. And then, at last, to the orchard.

I had had made a white marble urn and sited it discreetly beneath the pendulous branches of an Oman quince tree. Close to it Shaun had already planted a border of Oman rosemary and later he was to add snowdrops. Julia had come home. A gospel reading and some prayers. David lifted the lid and I placed the ashes within. The lid was replaced only to be lifted again when my ashes join hers. I knelt down and David placed both hands on my head and gave me a blessing for what years lay ahead for me without her.

The Laskett garden remained and remains a great solace, for it swiftly spoke to me as she would have wished. It spoke, as every garden does, not of mummification but of growth and change and moving on. That process is a kind of rebirth. It calls for an exertion of the human will and also the knowledge that the greatest tribute you can pay to one who has gone is to make a new life. That I have done, but never forgetting. Around the urn I had inscribed these words from the Christina Rossetti poem, 'Remember me', which was read at the funeral: '. . .if you should forget me for a while And afterwards remember, do not grieve.'

GARDEN TOUR

THERE IS A SET ROUTE AROUND THE LASKETT GARDEN. In that sense it is within the tradition of the great landscape creations of the eighteenth century, like Stowe in Buckinghamshire, which was meant to be toured in a particular way so that the visitor should see a succession of garden pictures, each of which had meaning. The Laskett garden is by no means as precise as that, in that there is not a thought sequence but, rather, a pictorial one which moves from large to small, from wide to narrow, from light to dark, from formal to informal, from loose to tight. More important even than that, to journey around it in a particular way preserves the element of surprise so crucial to any really exciting garden experience, for the planning of the four-acre site is such that the visitor is given the illusion that the space is much larger than it really is. What follows is such a tour, moving area by area through the garden and giving details of the history of each space and of its planting. Although this is essentially 'our' garden, there are areas which are more specifically under supervision of one rather than the other of us. The more formal elements are my domain, areas like the Yew Garden, the Jubilee and Rose Gardens, Elizabeth Tudor, the Folly Garden and Covent Garden. Others I think of as more specifically Julia's: the Howdah Court, the Scandinavian Grove, Hearne's Oak Garden, the Christmas Orchard and the Kitchen Garden. Contributions are endlessly made to each other's sections, and there are parts which just seem neutral.

Although a great deal of the planting detail is

included, this is not a definitive description of every single plant in the garden, bearing in mind that much thrives and withers, comes and goes and also moves, added to which, as every gardener knows, all too often the label has vanished or you've forgotten what you'd planted. By the time this appears in print plants will have been added or have migrated or, sadly, died. My wife is the plant collector. In her case through the garden are scattered almost a hundred *Malus* varieties as well as collections of historic apples (about sixty), quinces (about a dozen), snowdrops (about sixty), *Pulmonaria* (about fifty) and *Chaenomeles* (about twenty). I should add, too, that this Garden Tour does not enlarge on every memory and person who comes to mind through associations with every part and plant.

The reader is asked to follow the tour by referring to the numbered plan on the following pages.

Any tour begins with the YEW GARDEN [1] which stretches to the east and, when we came, was an expanse of lawn with, to one side, a shrubbery, in which a small summerhouse nestled, and, to the other, a gravel path bordered with rose beds. In the centre of the lawn, near the house, was a wellhead, a remnant of an earlier garden scheme, and the lawn stretched towards a large rectangular pond at the far end. This area was to be the site of our first garden room, the beds for the hedging being dug in August 1974 and the yew planted in December. This was to be a room with openings, the two from the house affording vistas to finials which are today atop pedestals in the Flower Garden. Within the room there was a central vista out towards an obelisk sited in what was an antechamber now known as TORTE'S GARDEN [2], because the first of our cats, the Lady Torte de Shell, lies buried there. The obelisk has also moved elsewhere and in its place there is a small container filled with sempervivums. This small area is virtually unchanged from when it was planted in September 1974: four Irish yew flanked by conifers – *Chamaecyparis lawsoniana* 'Somerset', *C.l.* 'Wisseli', *C.l.* 'Erecta Viridis' and *C.l.* 'Wyevale Silver', *Cupressus arizonica* var. *glabra* 'Conica', and *Juniperus virginiana* 'Burkii'. A thuja hedge was planted to screen out the dilapidated pond in which, at a later date, I cut a window. The shrubs here are *Mahonia* x *media* 'Charity' and *M. pinnata* and in spring there is an underplanting of daffodils. Behind the hedge is a working area but it is also where the catalpa tree called the Second Lord Plunket grows.

Initially the interior of the Yew Garden consisted of a series of symmetrical beds cut into the turf and planted with box infilled with thyme and santolina, virtually all of which died in the drought of 1976. The following year I planted my first serious small parterre of *Buxus sempervirens* 'Suffruticosa' and two others with our initials in box, R and J. The latter the gardeners almost immediately destroyed with weedkiller and were replaced by two hawthorn standards. Nothing much happened to this garden until 1980, when a large room was added to the house necessitating its replanning. The inherited artificial well was demolished and the concealing hedge of the yew room facing the house was swept away, the sides being extended towards the house. The finials were re-sited and underplanted with rosemary and standard roses were planted in perspective, although all of them were killed in the frost of 1981. It was then that the present *Amelanchier lamarckii* were planted, each inset into a clipped 'Versailles tub' of *Crataegus*. In 1982, on the demise of my father-in-law, the Lion from Barry's Houses of Parliament [a] arrived and was sited in its present position (see above, pages

130–1). After we came to live here the existing parterre was enlarged and a second one of equal size was created in 1990, both to designs by Julia. It was then that they were planted in spring in patterns with orange and white tulips and orange crown imperials. In 1992 the conservatory was built and the existing stone terrace made with its pierced screening, the finials being moved to the Flower Garden. The screening is engulfed with honeysuckle, rosemary and a *Clematis tangutica* and the terrace area and walls around the house planted with *Bergenia cordifolia*, thyme, primroses, a 'Brown Turkey' fig, *Jasminum humile* and *Chaenomeles speciosa* 'Simonii' and *C.* x *superba* 'Jet Trail' and *C.* x *s.* 'Crimson and Gold'. A *Hydrangea anomala* subsp. *petiolaris* clambers up the north-facing wall and across the conservatory. In summer the agapanthus, which overwinter in the conservatory, are arranged across the terrace area.

In 1996, the Yew Garden was paved, turning it into one huge box parterre, and the inscription 'Green Thoughts' placed at the entry from the terrace (see above, pages 192–3). The periphery beds were planted with dwarf rooting stock *Malus* 'Evereste', *M.* x *zumi* 'Golden Hornet' and *M.* x *atrosanguinea* 'Gorgeous'. Disaster struck in 1999 when box blight wiped out the entire planting of box, bar two golden box standards, and we had to start again. The new scheme, designed by Julia, was of two parterres of green yew infilled with golden pea gravel and golden erica with golden yew standards as vertical accents and, at the centre, an inverted corinthian capital through which a golden yew grows to be clipped into a ball (all the golden yew a gift from John Glenn). The surrounding beds beneath the yew hedging have been planted with *Rosmarinus officinalis*.

In some of the compartments *Lonicera nitida* 'Bagessen's Gold' has been planted. As it is now this is a garden of contrasting greens and golds, the only colour being when the rosemary blooms.

To the north of this garden runs a strip of land which, working from the house end, includes the Cat's Pen, GLYNDEBOURNE [3] and the CANAL. The first is engulfed by a *Rosa banksiae*, *Rosa* 'Gloire de Dijon' and a golden hop. The second is a small paved area, held in by box hedging, with box topiary in which the inherited summerhouse has been incorporated. In this space there is a changing display of plants in containers including, in summer, agapanthus, and the trellis screening is engulfed by a jasmine and *Rosa* 'Phyllis Bide'. The Canal is a narrow paved walk terminating in a *Cornus mas* with a low box hedge holding in what is largely an inherited shrubbery which includes *Mahonia* x *media* 'Charity', a guelder rose and a cotoneaster, to which we have added a mulberry, a *Chaenomeles speciosa* 'Moerloosei' and a large *Buxus sempervirens* which goes back to a cutting my wife took from some on Box Hill when she was young. The Canal's main display is of spring flowers including *Narcissus* 'Pipit', 'Tête-à-tête' daffodils, *Hyacinthus orientalis* 'L'Innocence', *Iris reticulata* and primulas.

Along the south side of the Yew Garden runs the DIE FLEDERMAUS WALK culminating in the pinnacle from All Souls [b], the tribute to the Oman family (see above, pages 131–2). On one side it is held in by a yew hedge, on the other by one of beech which has windows cut into it, giving the ability to have views both into and out of the Spring Garden into the Yew Garden. The Walk began as one of grass but was paved in 1996, at the same time that the pinnacle was lifted onto its pedestal and the commemorative slate plaque added.

Crossing from Torte's Garden across the Oman Pinnacle, access is gained to the SPRING GARDEN [4], a small triangular piece of land to the south. This is planted with a group of the blue-grey *Cupressus arizonica* var. *glabra* up which attempts have been made to train both roses and clematis, including *Rosa* 'Albertine', 'Climbing Souvenir de la Malmaison', 'Adélaïde d'Orléans', 'Mme Alfred Carrière', and 'Kathleen Harrop'; *Clematis montana* var. *rubens* and *C. m.* 'Tetrarose'. In addition there is a single eucalyptus and a group of the *Malus* collection: M. x *purpurea* 'Lemoine', M. x *atrosanguinea*, M. *hupehensis* (syn. M. *theifera*), M. *pumila* 'Cowichan', M. x *gloriosa* 'Oekonomierat Echtermeyer', M. 'Red Glow', M. x *adstringens* 'Almey', M. x *moerlandsii* 'Profusion', M. x *purpurea* 'Aldenhamensis' and M. *domestica* 'Merton Knave'. There is a bay clipped into a large cone, the one presented to me by the National Portrait Gallery (see above, page 124). In spring the garden is carpeted with white 'Mount Hood' daffodils and the containers filled with wallflowers and hyacinths.

The Spring Garden leads on to the area in front of the house which includes the Glade and the Howdah Court gardens. THE GLADE is a swathe of greensward beneath the cedar of Lebanon which from the moment we arrived we determined to populate with spring blossom that we could look down upon from our bedroom window. Over the decades the planting has developed as a frame around the statue of Flora [c], a duplicate of one I obtained for Highgrove in 1990 (see above, page 166). The shrubs include a rose purchased in Brighton in 1972, just after we married, several *Hamamelis*: H. x *intermedia* 'Pallida', H. x *i*. 'Jelena', H. x *i*. 'Diane' and H. *mollis*; *Chaenomeles* x *superba* 'Boule de Feu', C. x *s*. 'Hollandia'; *azalea* 'Silver Slipper', *Berberis thunbergii*

'Helmond Pillar'; *Pyracantha angustifolia, P.* 'Golden Charmer', *P.* 'Soleil d'Or'; *Rhododendron* 'Pink Pearl', 'Gomer Waterer', 'Jacksonii' and 'Madame Masson'.

The naturalized bulbs include snowdrops, both double and single, aconites, cyclamens, *Narcissus* 'Tête-à-tête', *N.* 'Peeping Tom', *N.* 'Little Witch', *N.* 'Thalia', *N.* 'Hawera', *N. jonquilla, Iris* 'White Wedgwood', *I.* 'White Excelsior', *Lilium martagon, Narcissus bulbocodium* (hoop petticoat daffodil), winter-flowering *Crocus tommasinianus* 'Barr's Purple', *Crocus sieberi* 'Violet Queen', *Scilla mischtschenkoana* (syn. *S. tubergeniana*), *Scilla siberica* 'Spring Beauty', *Tulipa sylvestris, Puschkinia scilloides* var. *libanotica, Allium moly, Muscari armeniacum* 'Blue Spike' and *Muscari comosum* 'Plumosum'.

The house itself has vines and a *Rosa* 'Albertine' clambering up it. The paving and the yew hedging in front of the house arrived in 1982. Otherwise the area which was to become what we call the HOWDAH COURT [5] was an expanse of lawn punctuated only by a Judas tree (the gift of Michael and Gillian Borrie) to one side, and six *Juniper communis* 'Hibernica', planted in 1975, which formed a mini-avenue stretching from the front door to the glade. Towards the latter we planted a *Crataegus crus-galli* and a *Malus toringo* subsp. *sargentii*. The first sign of any development occurred in 1989 with the planting of the Knot Garden in green and golden box based on a design in John Marriott's *Knots for Gardens* (1618). This was infilled for a number of years with lavender and thyme until, in 1996, the decision was taken to create a new garden in this area, utilizing found elements such as old windows, Victorian radiator panels, spiral staircases and heating grilles, a mixture of old and new paving in several colours, infills of glass cullets into the knot and carpentry work painted blue. Two fountains were made from the capitals of old gate piers, and old industrial brick and metal grilles formed pedestals to display three sculptures of bears which had begun their life as part of a tableau designed in 1980 by Julia for the conservatory at Warwick Castle on the theme of the bear seeking the ragged staff (the cognizance of the earls). These were the work of Astrid Zydower and rescued on the installation's demolition. In the paving was incorporated our initials and L for The Laskett. The hard landscaping was completed in 2001, when the old thuja hedge up the drive was demolished and sections from a bridge over the Thames were used to form a decorative screen and painted yellow and blue. When that was done two of the *Juniper communis* 'Hibernica' were removed to afford a vista from the drive over to the howdah itself.

The name Howdah Court came from the viewing point which straddles a small mount made of the turf excavated in order to pave the Yew Garden. The garden today incorporates topiary in yew, holly, box and *Ilex crenata*. Box, killed by blight, has been replaced by erica which is clipped to form the knot and a low hedge around the fountains. There is much rosemary and thyme and golden touches are introduced with *Berberis thunbergii* 'Aurea' and the two *Cotinus coggygria* 'Golden Spirit' which frame the vista to Flora. There is also low yew hedging around the knot garden and elsewhere two conifers clipped into topiary corkscrews. The garden's apogee is spring, when the beds are filled with 'Golden Apeldoorn' tulips bringing the blue and yellow of both house and garden into unity. Raised beds on the drive side include *Skimmia* x *confusa* 'Kew Green' and *Osmanthus heterophyllus* 'Goshiki', a *Rosa* 'Albertine' trailing through the 'window', hellebores and *Cotoneaster horizontalis*. Beneath the drive wall there is a long bed filled with part of a collection of bergenia which also stretches through and around the Fountain Court. As well as the common *Bergenia cordifolia* there are 'Ballawley', 'Bressingham White', 'Schneekissen', 'Silberlicht', 'Wintermärchen', 'Eric Smith', *B. ciliata*, 'Bressingham Ruby', 'Bressingham Bountiful', 'Baby Doll', 'Morgenrote', *B. purpurascens*, 'Rosi Klose', 'Abendglocken', X *schmidtii*, 'Bizet', 'Bartók', 'Margery Fish'.

The DRIVE borders are still in the making. The one to the east runs beneath the screening wall of gothic ironwork, the other to the west is pierced by a gravelled walk flanked with blue trellis. Both have been superimposed upon what was foundation planting through the years, two *Nothofagus nervosa* and a number of golden conifers clipped into large balls, between two of which is a *Liriodendron tulipifera* 'Aureomarginatum', the gift of Andrew Lyndon Skeggs. The eastern border has two common beech trees being shaped into tiers, two roses, David Austin's 'William Shakespeare 2000' and a gallica, 'Tuscany', and a planting of what will be shaped yew and green and golden box. Towards the garage there is a *Cornus kousa* var. *chinensis*. In spring the border is planted with wallflowers and tulips. The western border to the left of the blue trellis passage is planted with *Hamamelis* X *intermedia* 'Arnold Promise' and *Cornus sanguinea* 'Winter Beauty' and further up a mixed planting including *Anemone* X *hybrida* varieties and perovskia, *Rosa* 'Reine des Violettes', *Rosa gallica* var. *officinalis* and *Cydonia oblonga* 'Isfahan' flanks the trellis. The trellis has growing up it *Ficus carica* 'Kadota', 'Celeste' (also known as 'Celestine', 'Grise de la Saint-Jean' and 'Cotignane', among others) and 'Goutte d'Or' and *Clematis chiisanensis* and Tangutica clematis 'Anita'.

The western border to the right of the trellis forms part of FOUNTAIN COURT [6] which is, in effect, the entrance to the main garden in what we refer to as the Field. This began as an island of turf with a Judas tree, a turn-around for cars, backed by a larchwood screen with climbing roses leading on to the old kitchen garden. In September 1975 the island was planted with conifers to protect the house from the strong winds from the Black Mountains: *Chamaecyparis lawsoniana* 'Pottenii', *C.l.* 'Alumii', *C.l.* 'Fletcheri', *C.l.* 'Columnaris Glauca' and *C.l.* 'Erecta Viridis'. In 1988 the Judas tree was cut down and work began on the fountain, necessitating the felling of a number of the conifers. By then the larchwood screen had long gone and the backing was a beech hedge which, in July 1989, I cut into a large curve, opening up a vista from the Fountain Court into the Small, or Arabella, Orchard. Before the hedge on either side were pairs of Irish yew flanking small statues and, immediately flanking the entrance to the orchard, a pair of large box cones which had begun their life in containers in my Brighton house. Finally, in 1992, the decision was taken to do away with the turn-around and pave it, inset with flowerbeds.

The fountain is surrounded with hedges of *Berberis thunbergii* 'Atropurpurea Nana' from which arise two medlar trees. The main planting is of species and Rugosa roses including, facing the fountain to the left: *Rosa* 'Céleste', 'Great Maiden's Blush', 'Alba Maxima' (the Jacobite Rose), *R. forrestiana*, 'Geranium', *R. macrophylla*, *R. rubiginosa* (syn. *R. eglanteria*) and *R. soulieana*; and to the right: 'Roseraie de l'Haÿ', *Rosa rugosa* 'Alba', *R. rugosa* 'Rubra', 'Frau Dagmar Hastrup' and 'Schneezwerg'. To these have been added rosemary, *Brachyglottis* (Dunedin Group) 'Sunshine' and clipped accents in *Buxus sempervirens*, *Lonicera nitida* 'Bagessen's Gold' and *Crataegus*. Underplanting includes hardy geraniums, euphorbia and bergenia. There is a spring planting of tulips, principally 'Queen of Night', and more are added in containers as well as random groups of narcissi and hyacinths. On one side there is quince: *Cydonia oblonga* 'Le Bourgeaut'. In the midst of the paved area, just before the entrance to the path through the Small Orchard, there is the slate plaque with the inscription *'Circumspice'* and the date 1973 (see above, page 194).

The area between the Fountain Court and the old garage was formerly the old kitchen garden. In the mid-1970s this was laid out as two rooms divided by what was called TATIANA'S WALK (from *Eugene Onegin* which Julia designed for the Royal Opera), leading to the Silver Jubilee Garden, all delineated by beech hedging. The first, known as the SMALL ORCHARD or the ARABELLA ORCHARD [7] (Julia designed Strauss's opera for Glyndebourne), was given its brick path in 1992. That is flanked by a low box hedge and beds containing box balls and David Austin roses in white and yellow, 'Molineux', 'Glamis Castle', 'Winchester Cathedral' and 'Graham Thomas', which in springtime are underplanted with 'White Dream' tulips. The area either side is a mixture of topiary specimens around which, in spring, 'Prinses Irene' orange tulips are planted, interspersed with fruit trees, including a quince, 'Leskovac', from Frewin Hall (see above, pages 31–2), underplanted with aconites and snowdrops. 'Devonshire Quarrenden', 'Margil' and 'Golden Spire' apples, a Portugal quince (*Cydonia oblonga* 'Lusitanica') and another, 'Seibosa', complete the planting. The large walnut tree, beneath which there is a stone bench, has striking foliage which goes pale buttery yellow in late autumn, *Juglans regia* 'Laciniata'. The other small orchard, called SCHÖNBRUNN [8], is given over to quince varieties: 'Meech's Prolific', 'Sobu', 'Ekmek', 'Champion', 'Vranja' and 'Lusitanica'.

Tatiana's Walk leads the visitor to the grand vista across the Silver Jubilee Garden on through the Pierpont Morgan Rose Garden to the Triumphal Arch. Both gardens occupy the site of what was an old lawn tennis court. On the north-western side this quickly runs down onto rock with flooding as an occasional hazard. The SILVER JUBILEE GARDEN [9] was laid out in 1977 in commemoration of that event. Three years earlier, in 1974, what was an expanse of grass had been given a frame of evergreens including *Thuja plicata* 'Rheingold'; *Chamaecyparis lawsoniana* 'Erecta Viridis', *C.l.* 'Ellwoodii', *C.l.* 'Fletcheri', *C.l.* 'Pottenii', *C. pisifera* 'Squarrosa' and *Cryptomeria japonica* Elegans Group, interplanted with clipped shrubs, in the main laurel. The garden consists of a single brick path with a circle of stone at the centre on which stands a sundial [e] from Cecil Beaton's garden at Reddish House (see above, pages 89–90). This began as a white garden but rapidly moved on to being one of white with shades of lilac, violet, lavender and purple to which, in recent years, there have been added touches of pale yellow. The planting is mixed but the beds are given structure by clipped box balls. Planting fluctuates but there are firm points of reference, such as the circle of *Rosa* 'White Pet' around the sundial and, in the spandrel beds, the *Rosa* 'Iceberg' and the David Austin rose 'Charlotte'. The central path is flanked with *Geranium macrorrhizum*. The plants in the beds include *Geranium phaeum*, *Cephalaria gigantea*, *Lunaria rediviva*, *Galega officinalis*, *Geranium phaeum* 'Album', *Anemone* x *hybrida* 'Elegans', *Geranium* 'Johnson's Blue', *Papaver orientale* 'Perry's White', *Eupatorium purpureum*, *Tradescantia*

(Andersoniana Group), 'Concord Grape', *Salvia* x *sylvestris*, *Campanula persicifolia* var. *alba*, *Phlox paniculata* 'White Admiral', *Bergenia* 'Bressingham White', *Centaurea montana* and *Lilium candidum*.

The path leads to the PIERPONT MORGAN ROSE GARDEN [10], so called as it was planted from part of the proceeds of delivering the Walls Lectures at that institution in the autumn of 1974. For many years this was our only floriferous garden and over the decades has undergone many changes. When the Silver Jubilee Garden was created the Rose Garden took on a contrasting role, being formal and symmetrical in its planting as against the Silver Jubilee's pell-mell. Originally the vista was closed by a seat at the centre and the exit to the Serpentine was in the north-west corner. In January 1988 that was changed and the exit became central, leading to a flight of steps down into the Scandinavian Grove.

In the centre of the garden stands the urn from Bride Hall (see above, pages 128–9), known as JOHN TAYLOR'S MONUMENT [f]. Four composition statues of the Seasons stand in the corners of the spandrel beds. These came in 1996 to replace large but ailing roses. One leaves the garden through the TRIUMPHAL ARCH [g] with the inscription '*Conditor Horti, Felicitatis Auctor*' (see above, page 198). This is flanked by two obelisks topped by golden balls underplanted with rosemary. Although some box topiary and hedging remains, the majority was destroyed by box blight in 1999. Around the central bed there are four standard beech clipped into mopheads as vertical accents and the beds are edged with a hedge of a dwarf form of *Taxus baccata* Aurea Group. The planting is simple and symmetrical. At the end of each spandrel two old roses face each other: *Rosa* 'Königin von Dänemark', 'Fantin-Latour', 'Louise

Odier' and 'Souvenir de la Malmaison'. A froth of pale purple *Nepeta* surrounds all the statuary in the garden, the beds otherwise being planted with the David Austin rose 'Geoff Hamilton' and underplanted with *Alchemilla mollis* and *Astrantia major* 'Hadspen Blood'. There is a random spot planting of hyacinths in the spandrel beds and, from time to time, a rich planting of tulips in the central one. Reconstituted-stone pineapples flank an exit into the Christmas Orchard. The Rose Garden is really at its height in late June into July, taking over from the Jubilee.

From there the visitor descends to the SCANDINAVIAN GROVE [11], so called after the silver birch trees. These determine the garden's life, for this is a springtime garden which bursts into bloom from early January and is over when the leaves come onto the trees in April. It consists of a small rectangle of land held in, on one side, by the yew hedging of the Rose Garden and, on the other, by clipped laurels. The paths, little more than tracks, lead to Elizabeth Tudor, Sir Muff's Parade and the Serpentine. In the middle is a *Prunus* x *subhirtella* 'Autumnalis Rosea'. The planting is wholly informal, resembling a verdure tapestry of flowers which include: *Helleborus hybridus*, *Helleborus foetidus* varieties, wild garlic, yellow crown imperials, *Pulmonaria* varieties, white and purple violets, primroses, snakeshead fritillaries, a violet *Vinca*, Doronicum, Lamium, *Primula* varieties, *Corydalis flexuosa* 'China Blue', *C. f.* 'Purple Leaf', *C. f.* 'Nightshade' and *C. f.* 'Père David', cowslips, *Viola* 'Coeur d'Alsace', *Asarum europaeum, Galanthus* 'Brenda Troyle', *Ajuga reptans* 'Atropurpurea', *Narcissus assoanus*, *Hepatica* x *media* 'Ballardii', *Tellima* and *Narcissus* 'Tête-à-tête'.

Turning left the visitor comes to SIR MUFF'S PARADE, a walk bounded on one side by the yew hedge of the

Rose Garden and on the other by a bank running parallel with the drive with a gravel walk along its summit. At the top end is a small PARNASSUS [12], a seat amidst a shrub planting of evergreens including Portugal laurel, common laurel, *Aucuba*, *Osmanthus delavayi*, *Pyracantha* 'Teton'. The seat is encompassed by a blue *treillage* arbour up which climbs *Lonicera periclymenum* 'Graham Thomas' and *Fremontodendron* 'California Glory'. This area incorporates early plantings of conifers, *Thuja occidentalis*, *Chamaecyparis pisifera* 'Plumosa Aurea', *Calocedrus decurrens* and also a *Ginkgo biloba*. There is box hedging and underplanting which includes *Helleborus* varieties, dicentras and ferns. Opposite the Parnassus a short flight of steps leads to the gravel walk along the mount. The walk is punctuated with blue treillage arches up which grow yellow *Rosa* 'Laura Ford' and white *Rosa* 'Félicité Perpétue'. To the eastern side of that mount there is a planting of trees and shrubs: pollarded *Robinia pseudoacacia*, silver birch, *Acer platanoides* 'Drummondii', *Aronia arbutifolia* 'Erecta' and *Cornus kousa* var. *chinensis*. Beneath there is wild planting into the field grass of primroses, cowslips and snowdrops.

From the Parnassus there is a paved area followed by the grass walk called Sir Muff's Parade, which is flanked by crinkle-crankle borders at the foot of a short avenue of pollarded *Robinia pseudoacacia* interplanted on the eastern side with *Malus* 'Butterball', M. 'White Star', 'Stellata' and *M. spectabilis*, and on the western with *Malus* x *purpurea*, M. 'Golden Nugget' and *M. orthocarpa*. On either side the borders are filled with a mixed planting including *Sidalcea* 'Sussex Beauty', *Ribes sanguineum* 'White Icicle', *Lysimachia punctata*, *Helleborus* varieties, *Pulmonaria* 'Mawson's Blue' and *P. rubra* 'Bowles Red', *Astilbe* x *arendsii* 'Brautschleier',

Campanula glomerata var. *alba, Anthemis tinctoria* 'E.
C. Buxton', *Actaea* (syn. *Cimicifuga*) *matsumurae*
'White Pearl', *Aucuba japonica* 'Crotonifolia', *Buxus
sempervirens, Tellima, Ligularia dentata* 'Desdemona',
Tiarella 'Mint Chocolate', *Skimmia* x *confusa* 'Kew
Green', *Pieris japonica* 'Debutante', *Ilex aquifolium*
'Silver Lining' and 'Elegantissima', *Thalictrum delavayi*
(syn. *T. dipterocarpum*), martagon lilies, *Leucanthemum*
x *superbum* 'Sonnenschein', *Physostegia virginiana*
'Rosea', *Astilbe chinensis* var. *pumila, Chamaecyparis
lawsoniana* 'Golden Wonder', *Campanula punctata f.
rubriflora* and geranium varieties.

At the far end of Sir Muff's Parade stands the solitary
yew from Sutton Place with its topiary crown (see
above, page 163) with an underplanting in spring of
hyacinths. Behind the yew stands the monument to the
Rev. Wenceslas Muff [h] (see above, page 190), from
which a gravel path leads through to the avenue
ELIZABETH TUDOR. What is seen at present is the third
successive avenue, the first being of poplars, the second
of *Nothofagus nervosa*, the third and final of pleached
Tilia platyphyllos 'Rubra'. The limes are trained to
form three tiers and underplanted with a swagged beech
hedge. Within that is a strip of grass filled in spring with
daffodils. The central path is bordered by a low yew
hedge punctuated with holly standards and a row of
large staggered Irish yew. On the northern side the
avenue is backed by a leylandii hedge while, on the
southern, the backing is part of the Serpentine shrubbery, a mixture of conifers (including *Thuja plicata,
Chamaecyparis lawsoniana* 'Lanei Aurea', x
Cupressocyparis leylandii 'Castlewellan'), silver birch
trees, *Taxus baccata*, common laurel, *Pyracantha,
Viburnum tinus* (laurustinus), *Elaeagnus, Viburnum* x
bodnantense and purple berberis.

At the eastern end there is the CROWNED COLUMN [i] celebrating Elizabeths I and II, with both their crowns and initials on slate plaques on the base pedestal (see above, page 192). This is backed by an exedra of clipped laurel. To the south is a *Malus* x *magdeburgensis*. At the opposite end of the avenue stands the SHAKESPEARE MONUMENT [j] (see above, pages 132–3), framed by two large topiary yews together with clipped Portugal laurels and backed by an exedra of x *Cupressocyparis leylandii* 'Castlewellan' and other evergreen shrubs. In the vicinity there are Malus varieties: *M.* x *robusta* 'Red Siberian', *M.* 'Golden Gem', *M.* x *adstringens* 'Hopa', *M.* x *zumi* 'Golden Hornet' and *M.* x *moerlandsii* 'Liset'.

Turning left from the Shakespeare Monument there is a path leading past the leylandii hedge to the FOLLY GARDEN. This is a substantial area and the only part of the garden which is not inward-looking but from which a panorama of the surrounding landscape towards Gloucestershire can be enjoyed. The land here falls away quite sharply to the south forming an upper and lower level. On arrival there is an upper gravel walk, edged with a low yew hedge. Within this there are Dawyck beeches, the boles of old poplar trees up which roses, honeysuckle and clematis have been trained, in particular *Clematis* x *jouiniana* 'Praecox' and *C. montana* 'Tetrarose', a *Tilia* x *euchlora*, yew and holly topiary, pine and quince, and, proceeding along the walk, handsome trees, a *Quercus rubra*, a *Fraxinus excelsior* 'Pendula' (the gift of Jules Prown) and a *Sassafras albidum* (the gift of George Clive), Rugosa roses and other shrubs including *Hamamelis* x *intermedia* 'Ruby Glow', *Lonicera* x *purpusii* 'Winter Beauty', two *Chaenomeles*, and, towards the close of the walk, a group of *Malus* including 'Sun Rival', *M. toringo* (syn.

M. sieboldii), 'Royal Beauty' and 'Adirondack'. All of this is underplanted with snowdrops and narcissi. From that end the approach to The Folly is down a MEDLAR TUNNEL [k], within which there is a low box hedge, to an open space flanked by beds with a mixed planting of lupins, hardy geraniums and the rose 'Silver Anniversary'. On the banks there is a *Prunus mume* 'Beni-chidori', a *Stewartia pseudocamellia*, a *Hydrangea quercifolia* 'Snow Queen' as well as buddleias and *Hydrangea macrophylla* varieties.

There is a walkway around the cottage which is festooned with climbers, among them a *Wisteria sinensis*, an *Actinidia deliciosa* and *Parthenocissus quinquefolia*. Along the bank wall there are figs, 'Brunswick' and 'Brown Turkey', *Rosa* 'Léontine Gervais' and 'Albertine', *Lonicera periclymenum* 'Graham Thomas', rosemary and clipped box. On the eastern side is a small cottage garden held in by a low yew hedge. This is divided into rectangular beds edged with brick and tile with a small central walk to a wooden arbour up which honeysuckle and a clematis climb. The existing handsome old apple tree has been incorporated into the garden, up which now scrambles 'The Gardener's Rose' and a second rose, 'Perpetually Yours', which was bred for the appeal for the Hereford Cathedral Perpetual Trust. Once this garden was planted with the box donated by Dutch visitors (see above, page 167), but this perished of box blight. Two beds have quinces pruned into shrubs underplanted with variegated ivy, two more have bay topiary centrepieces surrounded by dwarf 'Munstead' lavender, while the other beds have a mixed herbaceous planting, including a tree peony, mahonia, salvia, phlox, *Papaver*, martagon lilies, *Stachys byzantina*, asters, *Dicentra*, hardy geraniums, *Teucrium*, *Echinacea* and *Euphorbia characias*. A holly cake-stand provides a strong ever-green vertical.

Leaving this garden the visitor enters the Lower Garden, consisting of an Upper and a Lower Walk. The LOWER WALK is the grass one straight ahead. The bed parallel to the yew hedge holding in the Folly Garden is filled with *Rosa* 'The Fairy', hardy geraniums, a golden-leafed shrub and, to one end, *Malus prunifolia* 'Fructu Coccineo'.

The shrubbery walk is flanked by two *Amelanchier lamarckii*, ones transplanted from the Rose Garden. The shrubbery itself is a mixture of evergreen clipped accents in holly and yew interplanted with mahonias, *Chaenomeles* and *Malus*. The *Malus* include 'Strathmore', *M.* x *zumi* var. *calocarpa, M.* x *purpurea, M.* 'Purple Wave', *M. coronaria* 'Elk River', *M. c.* var. *platycarpa, M. c.* var. *p.* 'Hoopesii', 'Noakes', 'Laura', *M. floribunda* 'Excellenz Thiel', 'Goldfinch', *M. prunifolia* 'Fructu Coccineo', *M. sikkimensis* and *M.* 'Coralburst'. The *Chaenomeles* include *C. speciosa* 'Simonii', *C.* x *superba* 'Pink Lady', *C. speciosa* 'Rubra Grandiflora', *C. speciosa* 'Geisha Girl', *C.* x *superba* 'Rowallane', *C.* x *s.* 'Ohio Red', *C.* x *s.* 'Fire Dance', *C. speciosa* 'Nivalis' and *C. s.* 'Moerloosei' (syn. *C. s.* 'Apple Blossom'). The area also includes plantings of silver birch, *Betula utilis* var. *jacquemontä* 'Snowqueen', *Hamamelis* x *intermedia* 'Arnold Promise', forsythia, quince, Rugosa roses, a *Hydrangea aspera* Villosa Group, *Mahonia pinnata, Syringa laciniata* and a smoke tree, *Cotinus coggygria*. In spring the area is car-peted in daffodils, narcissi, primroses and anemones.

The UPPER WALK begins with a *Quercus rubra* under-planted with *Buxus sempervirens* cut into clouds surrounded by small beds planted with hardy gera-niums and rosemary interspersed with box and yew topiary. A low yew hedge and two holly standards lead to an arch in the long hedge. The long walk is lined in the main by inherited, self-seeded trees but to that we have added quince and a pine from La Mortella (see above, pages 161–3), all underplanted with spring flowers. Opposite there are beds and shrubbery held in by a tapestry hedge of beech, field maple and golden privet. Within these enclosures there are further *Malus*: 'Montreal Beauty', *M. domestica* 'King of the Pippins', *M. sikkimensis*, 'Rudolph', 'Mahonia' and 'Ruffiensis'. There are roses: 'Honorine de Brabant', *R. xanthina* 'Canarybird', 'Variegata di Bologna', 'Sally Holmes', *R. macrophylla* and *R. gymnocarpa* var. *willmottiae*. Shrubs include *Syringa vulgaris* 'Vestale' and *S.v.* 'Charles Joly', *Elaeagnus* x *ebbingei* 'Gilt Edge', *Aucuba japonica* 'Crotonifolia', *Ilex* x *attenuata* 'Charles Notcutt' and golden fastigiate yew. Other trees include *Prunus* 'Royal Burgundy', *Sorbus cashmiriana* and *Cornus kousa* var. *chinensis*. The first large border contains a mixed planting with many varieties of hardy geranium and a collection of over fifty varieties of pulmonaria.

The gravel path leads to a seat and past that to the bottom of the drive. At this end again there are banks planted with flowers and evergreens and yew topiary in the making, but before this is reached the visitor turns left through an arch of carpenter's work, crosses Elizabeth Tudor, goes up a flight of metal steps and winds his way leftwards in the Scandinavian Grove and emerges in the SERPENTINE. This winding walk was painted on the field grass by me in 1975 and has gone through many changes over the decades until it reached its present form. Basically, to the right lies the Christmas Orchard contained within a yew hedge, while to the left there is a large shrubbery which includes trees (silver birch and a Swedish whitebeam) and, in particular, a large planting of evergreens (*Thuja plicata*, *Chamaecyparis lawsoniana* 'Lanei Aurea' and 'Triomf van Boskoop' as well as *Prunus lusitanica*). Through this shrubbery runs a tiny walk thick planted with snowdrops and aconites in springtime. The Serpentine now opens on the right with an armorial with a crowned rose encircled with the Garter from the medieval Palace of Westminster [l] (see above, pages 179–80), surrounded by a mixed planting including *Rosa* 'Bourbon Queen' and *R. x centifolia* 'Cristata' (Chapeau de Napoléon) surrounded by sidalcea, rue, rosemary, hemerocallis and salvia. On the left follows a long narrow border which includes an *Acer griseum* and is backed by a low yew hedge and planted with a collection of hostas: *H. undulata* var. *albomarginata*, *H. montana* 'Devon Desire', 'Honeybells', 'Christmas Tree', Wheaton Blue', 'Ginko Craig', *H. undulata* var. *undulata*, *H. sieboldiana* var. *elegans*, 'Blue Boy', *H. fortunei*, *H. fortunei* var. *albopicta* and 'Golden Tiara'. Opposite is a wide border beneath a planting of fruit trees including *Malus x zumi* 'Golden Hornet', apples *Malus domestica* 'Jupiter', *M. d.* 'Lord Grosvenor' and 'Arthur Tanner', and a 'Black Worcester' pear. Beneath there is a mixed planting with ever-green box and golden yew accents and including *Persicaria*, hardy geraniums, saxifrage, *Crocosmia* varieties, *Euphorbia*, hellebores, *Anemone x hybrida* 'Elegans', golden privet, bergenia, pulmonaria and a ribes. In spring there are 'Mount Hood' daffodils.

At the close of this first part of the Serpentine there is a pause where gate piers flank a vista through the Christmas Orchard to the reclining stag who looks towards, at the Serpentine end, the figure of BRITANNIA [m], set amidst four columnar evergreens:

Chamaecyparis lawsoniana 'Columnaris Glauca' and *Cupressus arizonica* var. *glabra* 'Conica' surrounded by shrubs: *Buxus sempervirens*, *Viburnum rhytidophyllum* and *Mahonia* x *media* 'Charity'. The gate pier vista is flanked by two large clumps of *Eupatorium purpureum*. After that the meandering borders resume until they come to a pause with two yew drums. The borders include two maples, an *Acer pensylvanicum* and an *Acer griseum*, a *Malus* 'Street Parade', a mulberry and the apples 'Coeur de Boeuf', 'Scotch Bridget' and 'Lemon Pippin'. Running behind the borders on both sides there are shrubs such as snowberry, *Exochorda* x *macrantha* 'The Bride', *Chaenomeles*, golden privet, a huge *Cornus mas*, skimmias, mahonias, escallonia and pyracanthas. Before them, apart from a Michaelmas daisy border, which incorporates three roses trained as pillars ('Ferdinand Pichard', 'Variegata di Bologna' and *Rosa gallica* 'Versicolor'), there is a mixed and varied planting including dicentras, ligularia, penstemon, hemerocallis, nepeta, pulmonaria and an *Acer palmatum*. A stone bench backed by clipped golden box affords a view in both directions on the southern side.

Past the yew drums comes the FLOWER GARDEN [13]. This had been a rose garden with a pergola astride the walk and was relaid-out as a flower garden in 1986. On either side it is backed by the evergreens, both conifers and shrubs, all of differing textural and colour attributes, which together form a verdure tapestry background setting off the foreground flowers. In the foreground on one side there is a *Pyrus salicifolia* and, on the other, a *Malus* x *purpurea* 'Neville Copeman', beneath which a full-length terracotta statue of a vaguely *art nouveau* figure nestles. Within the beds there are two dwarf trees, an *Acer pseudoplatanus* 'Brilliantissimum' and an *Acer negundo* 'Flamingo', and topiary in box, yew, *Ilex aquifolium* 'Golden King' (given by Rosemary Verey), as well as standard *Euonymus fortunei* 'Emerald Gaiety' and *Syringa meyeri* 'Palibin'. The planting is a mixed and shifting one with a stress on the yellows reflected in rudbeckia, heleniums, helianthemums, ligularia and helianthus. Other plants include *Potentilla fruticosa* 'Princess', *Astrantia, Phlomis fruticosa, Sedum spectabile, Acanthus mollis* and *A. spinosus, Crambe cordifolia, Hemerocallis, Euphorbia* and *Inula magnifica* (a gift of Christopher Lloyd).

The visitor leaves the Flower Garden through a yew arch flanked by urns on pedestals and enters the HILLIARD GARDEN [14]. This is the centre of the north–south axis of the garden looking down through the Birthday Garden and the Beaton Bridge to the Shakespeare Monument and, in the other direction, up to the Victoria & Albert Museum Temple. The Hilliard Garden began as a circle of yew breaking the avenue, initially planted in November 1973. To that was added, two years later, a *Rosa* 'Cantabrigiensis' at the centre. In 1976 the garden was gravelled and further beds made planted with herbs. It remained like that until 1985, when the creation of the Birthday Garden led to it being paved. Then, in 1988, with the construction of the V & A Temple, the rose was removed to open up the vista along the whole length of the north–south axis. Then the entire area was paved which, it was immediately recognized, was not a success. The solution (which I owe to Alan Titchmarsh) was to lay out a parterre, one based on a large baroque example in the garden of the Palace of Het Loo, but having our initials J and R at its midst. This remained until destroyed by box blight a decade later when an alternative had to be found. That was heather with a containing outer hedge of *Lonicera nitida* 'Bagessen's Gold'.

Off the Hilliard Garden there is a small enclosure called HEARNE'S OAK GARDEN [15] after the oak boundary tree within it. This is a simple paved area with an obelisk in its midst and beds which contain Julia's collection of snowdrops. Returning to the main garden and descending south we come to the BIRTHDAY GARDEN [16] which was laid out in 1985–6 when I was fifty, but which celebrates both our half-centuries. Designed by Julia, it is octagonal and has four small statues of the Seasons in the guise of putti in the spandrels. The garden is enclosed by a low yew hedge except for four niches which contain the statues and its planting is simple. Beneath the statues there are bouquets of *Bergenia cordifolia* while the rest of the garden was originally of clipped box. That too was lost in the blight visitation and conifers and golden privet are being trained as replacements. Outside the yew hedge there is the David Austin rose 'Compassion' and, on the west side, *Rosa* 'Wickwar' (given by Sally Westminster).

From here the visitor steps down onto the BEATON BRIDGE [17], built in 1988 on the occasion of the publication of *Cecil Beaton: The Royal Portraits*. The site had always been a difficult one in planting terms with odd dead areas of earth which continually frustrated any attempt to create an Italianate avenue of columnar evergreens. The planting outside these attempts was, however, successful and the specimens of *Viburnum opulus* 'Fructu Luteo' and 'Notcutt's Variety', planted in 1978, still arch over the bridge. Clipped yew has been used as topiary architecture linking the sections of the balustrading, and there is shrub planting behind which also includes a *Quercus rubra* planted very early on. Over the balustrading an attempt has been made to train roses, among them 'Mme Alfred Carrière', but, again, lack of light has impeded their progress. At the bottom of the steps there are two fastigiate golden yews and a planting of box, rosemary and hardy geraniums.

Turning back and reascending we pass through the Hilliard Garden to the final vista, called MARY QUEEN OF SCOTS [18], to the V & A Temple. This area is held in on the eastern side with a shrub-planting of laurels and *Prunus lusitanica*. On the eastern side the laurels are clipped to form a hedge. Leaving the Hilliard Garden there are two statues of lions supporting shields, their bases hidden by clipped purple berberis, and an avenue to the Temple of golden yew domes, clones from the famous Victorian topiary garden at Elvaston and gifts of John Glenn. This area began as one of briar roses but is now a dazzling display of *Malus*: *M. floribunda*, 'Oakes', *M. x zumi* 'Golden Hornet', *M. coronaria* var. *dasycalyx* 'Charlottae', *M. x schiedeckeri* 'Hillieri', 'John Downie', 'Golden Gem', *M. x adstringens* 'Hopa', 'Snowcloud', *M. pumila* 'Dartmouth', 'Geneva', *M. baccata* 'Dolgo', 'Winter Gold', 'Royalty', 'Wisley Crab', *M. tschonoskii*, *M.* 'Evereste', *M. x schiedeckeri* 'Red Jade', *M. x adstringens* 'Simcoe', *M. bhutanica* (syn. *M. toringoides*), 'Van Eseltine', *M. domestica* 'French Crab' and *M. x atrosanguinea* 'Gorgeous'.

Halfway along Mary Queen of Scots there is a cross axis which now stretches from the Ashton Arbour, through Covent Garden and the Christmas Orchard to the Rose Garden. The ASHTON ARBOUR [19] was planted in 1976 while Julia was working on the sets and costumes for Sir Frederick Ashton's ballet *A Month in the Country*. This was never more than a rectangular enclosure, initially with a seat from which to contemplate the vista. In 1986 the flanking urns came, reproductions of ones in Kew Gardens, and in 1998 the seat was replaced by a statue of an unidentified medieval king [o], one of two (the second of Henry III is in the Orchard) which were part of an early nineteenth-century restoration of the Palace of Westminster, possibly that of Sir John Soane in the 1820s. In 2002, the inscriptions commemorating the association of Julia and Ashton were added (see above, pages 194–6). Around them are beds filled with blue and pink hydrangeas, hardy geraniums and bergenia.

Through the Ashton Arbour access is had to a narrow strip of land, generally referred to as the WINTER ROSE ALLEY in reference to Emily Winter Rose, the wife of James Anderson Rose, the solicitor for the Pre-Raphaelites and an Oman connection, with, on one side, an avenue of *Chamaecyparis lawsoniana* 'Erecta Viridis' leading to the Hearne's Oak Garden, interplanted with *Viburnum* x *bodnantense*, and, on the other, an area planted with medlars against a background of tall *Chamaecyparis lawsoniana* 'Emerald Spire'. This is a naturalized area with a frieze next to the field hedge of *Acer platanoides* 'Crimson King' and *A. p.* 'Drummondii'. It is important to point out that purple is taken through much of the planting in every part of the area leading up to the Temple, from some of the leaves and fruits of the various *Malus*, to the use of purple beech and berberis hedging as well as trees whose leaves turn crimson and burgundy in the autumn.

Opposite the Ashton Arbour are two beds replicating those under the Kew Gardens urns and then a low purple beech hedge holding in COVENT GARDEN [20]. This is a small rectangular area, whose history is recorded above (pages 205–6), flanked by hedges of laurel and with two walnut trees arising at the far end. The yew arch leading to the Orchard is flanked by a pair of busts of satyrs. Within this area are two beds planted with grey-silver and purple-bronze plants around four topiary yews, two of which have topiary peacocks atop them. The planting includes *Brachyglottis greyi* and *lax-ifolia*, nepeta, rue, bronze lysimachia, *Phlomis fruticosa* and *Stachys byzantina*. In spring there are hyacinths, 'Woodstock' and 'Splendid Cornelia', followed by *Allium albopilosum* and *A.* 'Purple Sensation'.

The VICTORIA & ALBERT MUSEUM TEMPLE [n] is really the climax of any garden tour with its inscription in Greek, the key to the garden, 'Memory, Mother of the Muses'. Its erection in 1988 I have described above (pages 144–7), but it was built into an existing planting of Dawyck beech and a *Betula pendula* 'Tristis', a present from Angela Conner and John Bulmer, planted in the autumn of 1977. The Temple is flanked by busts of Victoria and Albert silhouetted against blue trellis which is planted with, among other things, *Rosa* 'Paul's Himalayan Musk', *Clematis montana* 'Elizabeth', *Rosa* 'Veilchenblau' and *Vitis coignetiae*.

From the Temple the visitor moves into the NUTCRACKER GARDEN [21], named after the production Julia did for the Royal Opera House. This is an informal area around a *Liquidambar* and a *Cedrus atlantica* as well as a large *Prunus lusitanica*. There are more *Malus: M. pumila* 'Cowichan', *M.* x *atrosanguinea, M. hupe-hensis* (syn. *M. theifera*), *M.* x *robusta* 'Yellow Siberian', *M.* x *purpurea* 'Eleyi', *M.* x *micromalus* (syn. *M.* 'Kaido'), *M. kansuensis, M. baccata* 'Lady Northcliffe', *M.* x *moerlandsii, M. pumila* 'Niedzwetzkyana', *M.* x *robusta, M. sylvestris, M. transitoria* and 'Veitch's Scarlet'. There are roses, *Rosa* 'Frühlingsgold' and 'Frühlingsmorgen' and *Rosa* 'Wickwar'. In spring there are naturalized bulbs, aconites, snowdrops, *Anemone blanda* and narcissi. Raised beds surrounded by clipped box cones are filled with hellebores, violets, tulips, iris and *Anemone* x *hybrida* 'Elegans'.

From here or via Covent Garden we enter the

CHRISTMAS ORCHARD. This is now quartered by paths bordered east–west by a low beech hedge and north–south by a low yew hedge flanked by two pairs of fastigiate golden yew to emphasize the perspective to the recumbent stag we call FRANCO [r] and on which there is the quotation from Milton's *Paradise Lost* (see above, pages 193–4). The Orchard is encompassed by a yew hedge cut into swags, pompoms and cake-stands with bays accommodating sculpture, a bust of Diana in reconstituted stone and two original pieces, both from the pre-1834 Palace of Westminster, one medieval, the arms of Edward I [p] (see above, pages 179–80), part of the Thames Embankment facade, and the other early nineteenth century, Henry III holding in one hand a model of the Shrine of St Edward the Confessor in Westminster Abbey [q] (appropriate, for after its acquisition in 1998, I was to become two years later High Bailiff and Searcher of the Sanctuary there). Over the east–west path straddle two arches of carpentry work supporting the rose 'Phyllis Bide' leading to the Rose Garden, which is prefaced by two small statues of Boy Warriors. The Orchard itself has a floral sequence, beginning in spring with a bouquet of snowdrops beneath the Stag followed by white hyacinths. Then avenues of several varieties of narcissi criss-cross the Orchard, the most important being the flanging planting of 'Sempre Avanti' on either side of the north–south path. Around the arms of Edward I there are blue, white and red (pink, really) hyacinths representing the colours of the Union Jack in reference to the armorial which commemorates the publication of *The Story of Britain*. The spring flowers lead on to the blossom on the fruit trees and then come roses and standard *Wisteria sinensis*. The roses include a number of the Rugosa 'Roseraie de l'Haÿ', *Rosa* 'F. J. Grootendorst', 'Céleste', 'Noisette

Carnée', *Rosa roxburghii* and *Rosa rubiginosa* (syn. *R. eglanteria*). In the autumn the roses provide hips, and the fruit follows on the trees.

The fruit trees are all dwarf rooting stock and include the following apples: 'Bramley's Seedling', 'Egremont Russet', 'Kidd's Orange Red', 'Lord Lambourne', 'Sunset', 'Tydeman's Late Orange', 'Warner's King', 'Worcester Pearmain', 'Beauty of Bath', 'Reverend W. Wilks', 'Pitmaston Duchess', 'Rosemary Russet', 'Braddick's Nonpareil', 'Ingrid Marie', 'Mabbott's Pearmain', 'King's Acre Pippin', 'Doctor Harvey', 'Api Rose', 'Keswick Codling', 'Norfolk Beefing', 'Catshead', 'Costard', 'Herefordshire Beefing', 'Yellow Ingestre', 'Calville Blanc d'Hiver', 'King's Acre Bountiful', 'Brabant Bellefleur', 'Scotch Bridget', 'Bess Pool', 'Kentish Fillbasket', 'Lady Sudeley' and 'Lord Hindlip'. Pears include 'Joséphine de Malines', 'Doyenné du Comice', 'Vicar of Winkfield', 'Pitmaston Duchess', 'Winter Nelis', 'Packham's Triumph', 'Beurré Superfin' and 'Beurré Hardy'. There is also a 'Prune Damson' (syn. 'Shropshire Prune') and a quince.

Leaving the Orchard the path leads to the KITCHEN GARDEN. Within this practical working area there is a small greenhouse, compost heaps, a space for a bonfire, sheds for storing tools and equipment, beds for cuttings and dumps. The Kitchen Garden is a practical space the size of one and a half tennis courts with one decorative element, a series of wooden arches which form a central vertical feature, up which climbs the 'Gardener's Rose' and honeysuckle. The beds are all raised and accommodate a rotation of crops designed to keep the house in vegetables and salad greens for as much of the year as possible. Herbs are also accommodated here. Around the enclosure are fruit bushes and also more fruit trees, including plums: 'Pershore' (syn. 'Yellow Egg'),

'Marjorie's Seedling', 'Aylesbury Prune' damson, 'Laxton Cropper', 'Victoria' and 'Warwickshire Drooper'; apples: 'Lane's Prince Albert', 'Charles Ross', 'Annie Elizabeth', 'Cox's Orange Pippin', 'Queen Cox', 'Peasgood's Nonsuch', 'Newton Wonder', 'Howgate Wonder', 'Blenheim Orange', 'Orleans Reinette' and 'Laxton's Superb', and pears: 'Louise Bonne of Jersey' and 'Glou Morceau'.

The path out of the Kitchen Garden leads down to the house past a group of medlars and the exedra framing an OBELISK [d] which forms the close of the great vista from the Rose Garden. The visitor finds himself back in the Fountain Court having covered the whole garden.

PHOTOGRAPH CREDITS

Copyright to the black and white photograph section is held by the following:

Page 1 top and bottom: Oman Productions Ltd
Pages 2–5: Oman Productions Ltd
Page 6 top, middle left and bottom: Oman Productions Ltd
Page 7: Oman Productions Ltd
Page 8 top: Cecil Beaton by courtesy of Sotheby's London

The right of Oman Productions Ltd to be identified as the author of the photographs has been asserted in accordance with ss. 77 and 78 of the Copyright, Designs and Patents Act 1988.

Copyright to the colour photograph section is held by the following:

Pages 1, 2, 3, 4–5: Andrew Lawson
Page 8: Gary Rogers, Hamburg
The endpapers are by Jonathan Myles-Lea.

The remaining images are from the author's collection. Every effort has been made to trace copyright holders and any who have not been contacted are invited to get in touch with the publishers.

ACKNOWLEDGEMENTS

INSPIRED EDITORS ARE RARE IN AN AUTHOR'S CAREER. FRANCESCA Liversidge is one such, and her commitment to this book, and also that of her colleagues at Bantam, has been total. I can't thank them enough for sharing a vision. In particular I'd like to mention Sheila Lee, who worked tirelessly on the illustrations, and Mari Roberts, who not only copyedited the book but also orchestrated its smooth way through the press. Kenneth Carroll had the design ideas, which were beautifully brought to fruition by Julia Lloyd. I'm grateful to Tony Lord for his horticultural expertise, exercised in these pages, and I'd also like to thank Neil Gower for his thrilling new aerial view of The Laskett garden. To these I must add my literary agent, Felicity Bryan, whose encouragement during the initial stages was crucial. Lastly I must mention my wife, whose book it is as much as mine, and whose passion for snapping the transient moment has enriched these pages so signally.

ROY STRONG